CW00530499

A HISTORY OF THE
THE TOWN AND COUNTY
OF
HAVERFORDWEST

A HISTORY OF THE
THE TOWN AND COUNTY
OF
HAVERFORDWEST

edited by
DILLWYN MILES

First Impression—1999

ISBN 1 85902 738 5

Printed in Wales at
Gomer Press, Llandysul, Ceredigion

CONTENTS

Aerial view of Haverfordwest.

(*Crown copyright: Royal Commission on the Ancient and Historical Monuments of Wales*).

FOREWORD

Tradition has attributed to Haverfordwest an ancient origin. It was a Romano-British town built by the would-be Emperor Magnus Maximus.[1] It was a fort erected to the glory of Alun, the legendary king of Dyfed,[2] as indicated by the seventeenth century equation *'Kaer Alun = Hwlffordd'*.[3] It was a settlement of the Saxons of Wessex who had sailed up the waters of 'Deepmowe' and established a town called 'Gladmuth – that is, Cleddau mouth'.[4] And then the Vikings had supplanted these names with their own *Havrafiord,*[5] the *fiorðr* of Havra whose kinsman Hogni had endowed the town with its colloquial name 'Honey Harfat'[6]

This mythology was invented by frustrated historians who could not believe that a town like Haverfordwest did not have an early, even a prehistoric, origin. There was no chambered tomb or tumulus, nor was a stone axe or bronze halberd or encrusted urn ever found. It is difficult, however, to accept that the strategic site upon which the castle stands was not occupied as a promontory fort when the area all around was peppered with raths, or that there was no primitive settlement at this lowest crossing-point of the river, but there is no evidence of any habitation and only time and the excavator's spade will tell. Haverfordwest has no recorded history pre-dating the Anglo-Norman period.

The need for an updated account of the town has long been expressed to me, often with a request that I should produce one, to which I could only reply that I had neither the time nor the expertise to do so. I therefore turned to people who are skilled and knowledgeable in their fields and they all responded splendidly to produce a symposium that covers the main features of the town's history.

Terrence James, Head of Information Management of the Royal Commission on the Ancient and Historical Monuments of Wales, writes with the authority of one who has researched the Haverfordwest Deeds deposited at the County Record Office. The late D J Cathcart King, author of *Castellum Anglicum,* was regarded as one of the country's leading castle historians. Michael Freeman worked at the county museum at Haverfordwest Castle before he became curator of the Ceredigion Museum. Dr Siân Rees, Inspector of Ancient Monuments and Historic Buildings, has excavated at the Priory for fifteen years. Richard Suggett is the Investigator at the Royal Commission on the Ancient and Historical Monuments of Wales, and Robert Scourfield is Buildings Conservation Officer for the Pembrokeshire Coast National Park Authority. Dr Roger Turvey obtained his doctorate for his research into the history of the Perrot family. John Howells is head of the Department of Archaeology at Trinity College, Carmarthen. Roland Thorne was the deputy editor of *The History of Parliament* and has made a close study of the political scene in Pembrokeshire. I want to thank them all for their authoritative contributions and the readiness with which they gave them.

For the loan of photographs that enliven the book I wish to thank the Royal Commission on the Ancient and Historical Monuments of Wales, Cadw: Welsh Historic Monuments, the National Museum of Wales, Robert Scourfield, Sam Nicolson, the Pembrokeshire Record Office and the County Archivist, John Owen, the Cultural Services Manager, Pembrokeshire County Council, Mary John, and Diane Turner and Susan Jenkins, of the Pembrokeshire County Library, the Town Council and the Town Clerk, Pat Lewis, the Gild of Freemen of Haverfordwest and its clerk, Paul Lucas, and Gerald Oliver, chairman of the Haverfordwest Civic Society. For their assistance in a variety of ways I am indebted to Terrence James and Richard Suggett, Sister Bosco, Terence O'Brien, Thomas Lloyd, Tony Insell, and to Mairwen Prys Jones, of Gomer Press, for the care she has taken in the production of the book. A special tribute goes to my son, Anthony, for his invaluable help in arranging the contributions for publication, and to Judith for her constant help and encouragement.

Haverfordwest, 1999.   DILLWYN MILES

THE ORIGINS AND TOPOGRAPHY
OF MEDIEVAL HAVERFORD

Like many of our towns, Haverfordwest owes its origins to the foundation of a castle outside which a small community of traders and artisans settled. Its lord granted privileges to his burgesses which encouraged settlement and growth, with the laying out of streets and buildings where none had stood before. By the end of the thirteenth century Haverford (as it was known in the Middle Ages) had grown into one of the largest towns in medieval Wales. The reason for this apparently phenomenal growth is undoubtedly the result of a number of complex, interrelated, factors. Our evidence for the earliest period is inevitably unsatisfactory, but Haverfordwest is fortunate in having a large number of surviving deeds of properties within the town dating from the later thirteenth century onwards.[1] Such a collection is almost unique in Wales. In addition to these are other private and public records dating from the later Middle Ages, but there are unfortunately no good surviving surveys, or extents, which describe the size of the town during the early years. For this, the historian and archaeologist must use other documents like valuations of burghal income to calculate the number of burgages. In addition to evidence in the form of written records, there is also the layout and topography of the town itself. Quite often it is possible to deduce phases or periods of growth by studying the town plan as it survives today and in nineteenth- or twentieth-century maps. The present-day layout of Haverfordwest is an inheritance from those early medieval 'planners' and as such can be used as a document to demonstrate how and why the town developed in the way it has. This 'document' is a unique record of Haverfordwest's past and its preservation is as important as that of any of its medieval buildings. Any conservation policy must be soundly based on a thorough understanding of how and why the town developed in the unique way it has. In a sense, then, the study of the past provides information that helps us understand more fully the environment in which we live, and how better to preserve it.

EARLY DEVELOPMENT – THE FIRST 100 YEARS

From a military standpoint, the site of Haverfordwest is eminently suitable for the establishment of a strong fortification. The castle stands on a rocky knoll of Cething Sandstone of the Silurian System, rising some 28 metres above sea level. It also overlooks the tidal reaches of the navigable Western Cleddau which flows 140 metres to the east. To the north and south the land falls less steeply to small stream valleys and it is only to the west, where the land drops more gently, that defence is weak.

Although it has been stated by antiquarians, and repeated more recently[2] that the first castle was founded by Gilbert de Clare, Earl of Pembroke, there is no authority for this. The first castle is recorded about 1110[3] and was founded by a certain Tancred (or Tancard), a Fleming, whose son Richard is described as lord and governor of the place by Giraldus Cambrensis when he visited the castle in the year 1188. A large settlement of Flemings in south Pembrokeshire is recorded during Henry I's reign. As *Brut y Tywysogion* uncompromisingly puts it, the Flemings 'occupied the whole cantref of Rhos, near the estuary of the river called Cleddyf, and drove away all the inhabitants from the land.'[4] The establishment of a large community of Flemish farmers throughout the rural hinterland around Haverford, not only dominated but totally replaced the native populace thus ensuring favourable conditions for trade and commerce in this period. Indeed the early twelfth-century settlement of Flemings was so entire that this corner of Wales completely lost its Welsh character, the language was obliterated and Flemish gradually gave way to English as the dominant language. Giraldus records a Fleming addressing his brother in Flemish at Haverford in the early thirteenth century. George Owen's statement that no Flemish was spoken in his day has to be balanced against what another sixteenth-century writer reported, namely that some Pembrokeshire families were still capable of conversing in Flemish as late as 1567-77.[5]

It has been suggested that the second element in the place-name Haverford might be derived from the Norse word for fjord (*fiorðr*),[6] but

Charles[7] dismissed this, noting the obvious point that 'it is still possible to ford the Cleddau here at low tide'. Thus he proposed *hæfer* (a buck or he-goat) + ford – a ford used by bucks. 'West', he notes, was used from 1409 to distinguish it from Hereford. There is no evidence, historical or archaeological, for any pre-Norman activity at Haverford.[8]

There is little documentation to reconstruct the embryonic years of the town's history. Undoubtedly, a small trading community soon developed around the early castle. The existence of Flemish settlements in the surrounding territory of Rhos provided not only a stable military environment, but the prerequisites for trading activity to ensure economic success. Discussion on Flemish settlement by Lauran Toorians has shed interesting light on the context within which such places as Haverfordwest were founded. Flemish settlement in Britain was fairly widespread in the twelfth century, and the Flemings became renowned as hard-working, hard-fighting and capable tradesmen, well suited to the foundation of towns in newly conquered areas. The 'capitals' of Flemish settlement in Rhos and Daugleddau appear to have become Haverford and Wiston – although place-name elements give ample testimony to other settlements bearing Flemish personal names, like Letterston, Tancredston and Reynaldston, to name a few. The ebb and flow of warfare throughout the century is marked by attacks by the Welsh recorded in 1115, 1136, 1147, 1189 and 1193. To facilitate their survival the Flemings were offered immunity from (?certain) tithes.[9] With Flemish settlement secure, by the thirteenth century the planted boroughs of southern Pembrokeshire were more favourably placed than many other contemporary castle-based towns in the rest of Wales, situated as some were within hostile Welsh territory.

Giraldus is our main source for the early history of the town. He relates how Tancred's castle was sited near the abode of Caradog Fynach at St Ishmael *(Sancti Hysmaelum Rosensi Provincia)*. Lloyd suggests that this is Haroldston St Issells (rather than St Ishmaels near the mouth of the Haven) whose church is dedicated to Ishmael.[10] But there are other Ismael dedications close to Haverford, at Camrose, Uzmaston and Rosemarket, and they too are all sited within Rhos. In his *Speculum Duorum*,[11] Giraldus relates a story about a knight called Ernaldus who compared the character of a man with the cloth usually made at Haverford, 'too much grey wool, and too little native black wool'. This is evidence for cloth manufacture and wool trade in the town's early history, a trade at which the Flemings were adept.[12] Little is known of Tancred himself, but one of his daughters married Giraldus's brother Philip, lord of Manorbier and another married Odo of Carew; Tancred was married to Giraldus's aunt.[13] Giraldus described Richard fitzTancred as the son of the man who attempted to detain the body of the saintly Caradog from being carried to St David's in 1124;[14] Richard fitzTancred was 'a great and mighty man in his own day and in his own land' and was referred to by Ernaldus as 'my lord'.[15] Giraldus clearly admired Richard, 'a man of virile temper . . . who was tall and stately' and who made two pilgrimages to Jerusalem. But for Richard's sons he reserved his unconstrained invective: one son (?William) 'if indeed he is his son . . . was either sired by someone else, or perhaps inherited the devilish side of his mother'; the next brother was 'his junior in age, but his wickedness was greater'.[16] Richard made a grant of, *inter alia*, six burgages in Haverford to the Commandery of Slebech and his son Robert also granted two carucates of land in 'Coferun'[17], which Rees placed between Haverford and St David's (?Cuffern).[18]

Richard fitzTancred's son Robert is mentioned in 1204 and, in 1207, he was confirmed in his rights by King John. Robert had inherited a powerful lordship from his father, and appears to have been favoured by John for the king entrusted him with the keeping of Cardigan Castle for a short period. By the beginning of the thirteenth century Haverford must have grown to a comparatively large size, and Robert was undoubtedly mindful of encouraging further growth, for in 1207 he was granted the right to hold a Sunday market and an annual fair in the town – clear indications of the lord's positive approach to commerce. Before 1210 an Augustinian priory was founded, probably at the instigation of Robert, about half a mile downstream on the banks of the Western Cleddau. In a patent of Edward III in 1331 which confirms an earlier, undated grant for certain properties to the priory, it is recited that Robert gave the priory three churches – St Mary's, St Thomas's and St Martin's in Haverford.[19] This grant of what became the three parish churches, has been taken to form part of the original endowments to the priory when it was founded.[20] Giraldus does not mention the existence of the priory during his visit in 1188, so it is possible that it was founded after this date, but before Robert's removal as lord in 1210.

Fig. 1 St Martin's Church and Queen's Square 1998. This open area is arguably the site of the earliest market in Haverfordwest, when Castleton formed the core of the early foundation.

(*Crown copyright, Royal Commission on the Ancient and Historical Monuments of Wales*).

The existence of three churches by this date is an indication of the rapid growth the town had undergone. The earliest of these three must be St Martin's, as it is located close to the castle in what became known as Castleton (Fig. 2). This early foundation is supported by the dedication to Martin, which is common to the early-Norman period. The date of the other two churches is more problematical. St Mary's is sited away from the early nucleus in an area that by the mid-thirteenth century had become a new focal point within what is arguably a *resited* market place. The third church, dedicated to St Thomas à Becket was located even further from the castle and remained on the fringes of the borough well into the later Middle Ages. Becket was not canonized until 1173, which at least gives a *terminus post quem* for the dedication, if not the church itself. It is possible that Giraldus may have had some hand in the dedication of the church, for he was an avowed admirer of the martyr,[21] and fashioned himself on Becket, in his attempt to reinstate St Davids' metropolitan authority and the independence of the Welsh Church. Whatever Giraldus' role, we are on safe ground in assuming that St Thomas' church was founded in the last quarter of the twelfth century, and it is probable that St Mary's was also founded about that time.

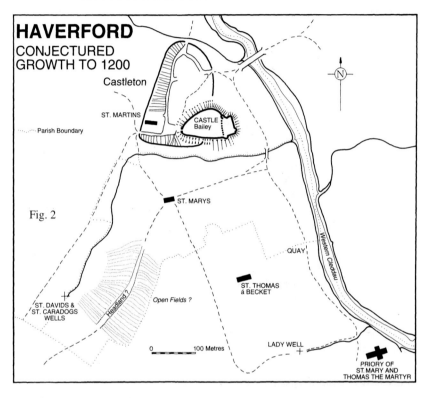

Fig. 2

The presence of three churches and the priory, along with the castle, gives us a minimum amount of information for conjecturing the growth of the town up to the beginning of the thirteenth century (Fig. 2). Using surviving evidence for the street plan and the known line of the defences of Castleton, it is suggested that population growth forced an expansion beyond the 'castle borough' of Castleton resulting in growth in new areas and the building of St Mary's and St Thomas's churches. No doubt settlement around these churches was contemporaneous, or soon followed. The routes from the castle lead north to the town mills, east to the bridging point (or ford – Bridge Street is mentioned in 1312), west to St David's, and south to the churches of St Mary and St Thomas. Further routes linked the bridge, quay and the priory along the river's west bank and also the quay to Castleton via St Martin's. The small open area between St Martin's and the castle gateway (Queen's Square) must have functioned as the main market place in the twelfth century.

The later medieval borough has a puzzling preponderance of streets running towards the south-west i.e. Barn, Dew and Hill Streets (Fig. 2). In an attempt to explain why so many routes were required to run south-west, it is suggested here that at an earlier date, open fields were located between the brook running east of Barn Street and the rear of properties to the west of Hill Street. The modern property boundaries either side of the upper part of Dew Street appear to follow the lines of medieval burgage plots, but in addition their slightly curving, s-shaped alignment is reminiscent of open-field strips. It is therefore possible that these burgage plots were laid out over former open field furlongs; such a practice is recorded in towns and villages elsewhere, including the thirteenth century extra-mural development along Lammas Street, Carmarthen.[22]

The rows of cultivation strips would have been bisected by a headland, and this may explain the origin of Dew Street itself. If such an open field system did exist in this period, it would explain not only the emergence of Dew Street with its fossilized strips changing into burgage plots in the thirteenth century, but would have dictated the layout of adjacent streets. This would have prevented a planned gridded layout and enforced the adoption of parallel development along Hill and Barn Streets. We might speculate upon the land use of other areas of the early town prior to their development. The whole area between the brook south of the castle and the hill up to St Thomas' (High and Goat Streets) could well have been common pasture or open fields.

THE THIRTEENTH CENTURY

Haverfordwest was already a thriving borough by the beginning of the thirteenth century, a century that was to see a massive population increase throughout Europe. By the 1280s, under Edward I, Wales became totally subjugated and many new towns were founded in hitherto unconquered territory. Haverford was fortunate in that it was not the focus for much Welsh hostility, undergoing only one recorded attack, in 1220; this factor alone would have ensured sufficient stability for continual growth. By comparison, Marcher boroughs in other areas were often besieged by the Welsh. For example, Carmarthen a royal borough, was constantly the focus of Welsh hostility, and was attacked on no less than ten occasions in the century.

But there were other factors at play to explain Haverford's success. As we have seen already, King John granted Robert fitzRichard the right to hold a Sunday market and an annual fair in the town in 1207.[23] Haverford was very well placed to gain a monopoly of trading over a wide surrounding area of rich farmland. The only competition in this period north of the Haven came from Wiston, Narberth, Newport and St Davids (Rosemarket's status in this period is uncertain). Clearly Haverford was centrally placed, which in part explains its continuing success as a market town to the present day.

For some unknown reason, Robert fitzRichard fell out of favour with the king: when John returned from Ireland in 1210 he was deprived of all he had, and in 1211 he died in exile[24]. In October 1213 Haverford was granted to the great William Marshal for a fine of 1000 marks[25] and now became part of the demesne lands of the Earl of Pembroke. William Marshal was fabulously wealthy and a large part of his most valuable estates were across the Irish Sea in the vast fief of Leinster held by the service of 100 knights. As a result of William's important holdings across St George's Channel Pembroke had become of prime importance as a staging post for the sea crossing of the Marshal and his officers.[26] Haverford now became associated with this traffic and undoubtedly benefited from it. At the same time Marshal was granted the custody of Carmarthen, Cardigan and Gower, restoring him to dominance in south Wales.[27]

In addition, Haverford was to receive from William Marshal a charter giving some of the most favourable privileges to its burgesses for any town in the realm.[28] As one of Marshal's biographers has noted, he had always shown himself a friend of commerce – 'or at least a believer in the prosperity it brought'; he had founded the port of New Ross in Ireland and a number of chartered towns, and his English lands were well endowed with fairs and markets.[29] So good were the privileges of his charter, that it must explain in part the apparently phenomenal growth of Haverford throughout the thirteenth century. Unfortunately, we do not know the actual date it was issued, but it must have been between 1213, when Haverford was granted to the Marshal and 1219, the year of his death. Subsequent charters were issued by his sons, William Marshal II, in September 1219 and between 1219-29, and by Gilbert about 1234-41.[30] The first charter granted personal freedom in the form of franchise by residence, when it stated that 'a man, whatever his status . . . who dwells there for a year and a day without being challenged shall be free'.[31]

The ability to sell or mortgage his burgage without the lord's permission (and perhaps without payment) was another right more akin to *laissez-faire* than feudalism, when the same charter stated that it should be 'lawful for the burgesses to give, sell or mortgage their lands, houses, burgages, saving the right of the lord excepting to religious houses'[32]. In addition heirs of burgesses could inherit the property of their fathers whatever their age on the payment of 12d. The combined effect of these privileges alone would create an environment that could enable some burgesses to accumulate a number of holdings and without partible inheritance or the forfeiture of property during wardship of minors and subsequent payments of heavy 'reliefs' to enter on inheritance, a class of property owning burgess families soon emerged. The ability to invest in property in a society where investment opportunities were limited was a considerable advantage and explains why, when the first runs of Haverfordwest deeds appear in the 1280s, many half- and quarter-burgages are already mentioned. As the population of the borough expanded a land market was created, burgages were sub-divided or sold off for money or rented out. The fact that so many medieval deeds for the borough survive at all may reflect the large number of conveyances transacted by this date – and this is perhaps a reflection of the favourable property clauses in the charter.[33]

A monopoly of trading was also ensured by William Marshal II's charter, which excluded trading by merchants from outside Haverford or Pembroke; Haverford's burgesses were given freedom from paying toll, pontage and passage 'where ever our power extends, excepting our demesnes, where ever they are wont to pay custom'. This charter also gave them the right to 'have a merchant guild for the advantage of themselves and of their town'.[34] Many of the remaining clauses were for privileges enjoyed by other boroughs, but the right to dispose of property made Haverford's burgesses particularly favoured *vis-à-vis* their contemporaries in many other towns. Combined with the fact that Haverford had managed to escape the hostile attentions of the Welsh, even during Llywelyn the Great's rampage through west Wales in 1215, the borough's charters had given the town an important early boost, ensuring not only continued, but greatly accelerated, growth.

The only hiccup in this otherwise uninterrupted success story came in the year 1220 when Llywelyn returned to ravage the towns of the west. After destroying the two castles at Narberth and Wiston, he turned his attentions on Haverford 'and mercilessly ravaged the cantref of Rhos'.[35] Llywelyn was by this time an avowed enemy of the new earl of Pembroke, William Marshal II, and the latter's losses were alleged to have been colossal. In the event, the castle at Haverford appears to have been strong enough to withstand the attack, but Llywelyn 'burned all the town up to the gate of the castle'.[36] Unfortunately, the chronicles tell no more about this event. We can only speculate about the real nature and extent of damage. The houses in and around Castleton and its adjoining suburb, whose presumed earth and timber town defences could not have been very extensive by this date, were destroyed. William Marshal II's charter of 1219[29] may thus have been an attempt to redress the damage and speed up rebuilding of the town.

All William Marshal the First's sons died without male heirs. In consequence, the ownership of the huge Marshal estates was partitioned between his five daughters and their heirs (Fig. 3). Haverford fell to Eva de Braose, but since she was already dead, the lordship was split again, this time three ways between her surviving daughters and their respective husbands: Maud and Roger Mortimer, Eva and William de Cantiloupe, and Eleanor and Humphrey de Bohun.[37] It would appear that not long after the partition of 1246 Eva and William de Cantilupe assigned their share of the lordship to Humphrey de Bohun, and in 1248 Humphrey de Bohun 'junior', Humphrey's heir, received seisin of Haverford. Roger Mortimer's share of the lordship remained the same, as an inquisition post mortem of his estates in 1282 shows that he still held a third, and this passed to his heir, Matilda.[38]

Fig. 3 Descent of the Lordship of Haverford to the middle of the 14th century.

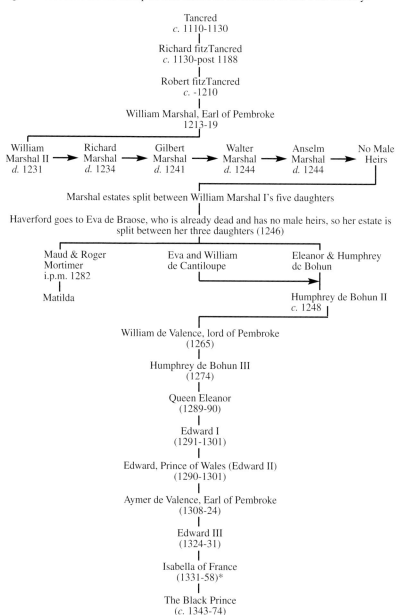

*Probably in the custody of the Black Prince from *c.* 1343

From 1263 Humphrey de Bohun and Roger Mortimer took opposing sides in the Barons' War, the latter siding with the Crown. Both men were evidently deadly enemies: Roger's castle and town at Radnor were destroyed by the Montfortian side in 1264, and Humphrey's castles at Huntingdon and Hay were captured and then bestowed on Roger Mortimer.[39] In such circumstances it is unlikely that Roger would have received his share of the revenues of the lordship. With Haverford held by Humphrey de Bohun, the town and castle were besieged and captured by the King's brother, William de Valence, lord of Pembroke. Haverford was subsequently held by William during the minority of Humphrey's heirs.[40]

Before this, however, Humphrey had taken steps to fortify the town, for in 1263 the bailiffs and burgesses of the town were granted the right to levy murage for seven years.[41] This is the only grant of murage the town was to receive, which in itself may indicate how little troubled Haverford was by warfare. It must be remembered, however, that wall-building may not have been solely dependent on murage grants: Pembroke does not appear to have ever received them, and Tenby received only one, yet both towns still possess substantial walls[42]. The fact that very little remains to be seen of Haverfordwest's walls could reflect their original slight nature; it is possible that a defensive circuit was never completed. There are good surviving stretches of stone wall along the western flank of Castleton (to the east of Perrot's Road) and a cross-section was observed by the author in 1981 between 34 and 35 Church Street adjacent to the site of St Martin's Gate. It may be then that only Castleton was enclosed with stone defences and the rest of the town, in the expanding areas around St Mary's and St Thomas's remained either undefended or perhaps only enclosed by earth and timber. There is however ample documentary evidence for the existence of gates in the latter areas. South Gate stood at the upper end of Market Street, and West Gate in Dew Street is depicted in Peter Lea's plan of the town in an edition of Saxton's map of 1690 (Fig. 4). So Leland's reference to the 'wallid towne', and the fact that one of its churches was 'without the toune in [the] suburbe' supports the picture of a town defined by gates and walls.[43] The revenues from murage could have been devoted largely to the construction of Castleton's walls and the gates of the enlarged town. Wall building was an extremely expensive undertaking, and the

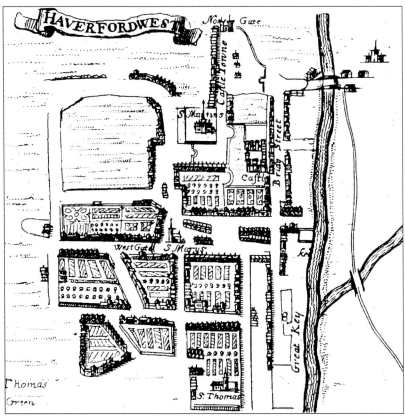

Fig. 4 Peter Lea's stylized map of Haverfordwest in 1690. This is the earliest surviving map of the town and, despite its shortcomings, it provides useful information. Two town gates are named (North and West) and two others are possibly depicted in conventionalized form, south of St Martin's and at the east side of Castleton. The plan shows what may be Holy Trinity Chapel at the west end of the bridge.

large size of Haverford would have increased the cost of such a venture. It should be noted that in many other boroughs extra-mural areas were permanently left undefended (cf. Carmarthen and Kidwelly). Moreover, there are numerous examples of medieval towns (especially in the more settled areas of England) that never completed their defensive circuits.[44] Despite what we know of walled Tenby and Pembroke, broadly speaking it was the privileged royal, not the seigneurial boroughs, that became defended.[45]

In 1274 Haverford was granted to Humphrey de Bohun III, but only after a dispute between the latter and William de Valence, who attempted to make Humphrey do homage to him as quasi-earl of Pembroke.[46] This dispute between the two appears to have rumbled on for some time, with William further claiming that the town's burgesses should answer pleas outside the borough and do suit at Pembroke. In consequence, royal justices adjudicated in 1276 apparently in William de Valence's favour. In 1284 a commission of oyer and terminer was instigated into the affair, and the King himself came to the town, possibly to try to settle this long-drawn-out matter, for letters patent were dated at Haverford in that year.[47]

In 1289 there was an important seigneurial change when Humphrey de Bohun III exchanged his two-third share in the lordship with Eleanor of Castile, wife of Edward I. The Queen was to live only until 1290, yet in the short time that she held Haverford, she spent considerable sums on rebuilding the castle, and for some unknown reason appears to have taken a particularly fancy to the place.[48] Unfortunately for the historian, no survey of the town appears to have survived, if indeed one was ever commissioned. Without such a survey the question of the precise extent and population of the town at this date remains elusive. Although no complete survey exists, we are fortunate that the inquisition post mortem into the estates of Roger Mortimer, who died in 1282, shows that he still held an interest in Haverford, which we know amounted to one third. His share of burgage rents amounted to £6 10*s*, which when multiplied by three gives a total of £19 10*s* for the farmed burgage rents. Since we know that rent for a single burgage was 12*d* per annum, then the number of burgages could not exceed 390, and was probably somewhat less.[49] This figure is nonetheless strikingly large for the period and suggests that Haverford was one of the largest towns in late thirteenth century Wales. This number of burgage plots could easily be accommodated along the streets known to have existed from medieval documents, if we accept that the property boundaries displayed on the late-nineteenth-century 25-inch OS maps represent fossilized medieval boundaries.

THE EXTENT OF HAVERFORD BY THE EARLY 14TH CENTURY

By the 1280s the first runs of extant property deeds emerge. These deeds are now housed at the County Record Office at Haverfordwest, and B. G. Charles's typescript schedule[50] has been extensively used to extract place-names of streets shown in Table 1.

Historic Name	Modern Name or place	First Mention
Ban(e)stret(e)	Barn Street	1300 *c.*
Batemanys Lane	Hill Lane	1471
Brygestret	Bridge Street	1312
Casteltun	Castleton	1325
Cathlet (Mill)	Cartlett	1298
Cokeystret(e)	City Road	1312
Cornestrete	?Tower Hill	late 13th *c.*
Durkstret(e)/Derkestret(e)	Dark Street	1285
Dewystret/Dowystret/Great Do.	Dew Street	late 13th *c.*
Parva Dowystret	Dew Street	1397
St David's Street	Dew Street (Rat Island)	1312
Gates of the town:		
East Gate	Swan Square	1478-9
North Gate	North St/Perrot's Road	1374
South Gate	Market St/Goat St	1406
St. Martin's	Church Street	1596
West Gate	Dew St (near Library)	1427-8
Gotestret(e)	Goat Street	1358
Gildhus [Council Chamber]	Guild House 1415 [?]	late 13th *c.*
Hill of St Thomas/Hilstret	Hill Street	1343
Hilstret(e)	Hill Street	1384
Horn' Lane	Horn's Lane	1572
Hystret/ Vico Alto	High Street	1300 *c.*
Kingesfeld	[Shipman's Lane?]	1340s
macellum	[meat stalls near St Mary's church]	late 13th *c.*
Mawdlens/Mawdyns [chapel]	foot of Merlins Hill	1535
[cf. *terra Leprosorum* in Prior foundation grants]		1210
Marketsret	Market Street	1367
Middle Street	Nr St Mary's	1427

Middle Street in St Mary St		1440
Pillerestret/Pillorie Streete	Market St/Old Gram.	1491
Portefelde	Port Field	13th C.
in vico Prioris/Prio(u)risrew(e)	Prior's Row	1383
Key(e) Street	Quay Sreet	1564
Regiam Stratam	[?King Street]	1498
Saynt Marystret	St Mary Street	1438-9
Schippistrete	?Quay Street	1370
Schotstret/le Schote	Part of Dew Street	1545
Shomakers streete	Part of Market Street	1587
Shortrew [Short Row]	Lower High Street	1427
Schytericheslake/Scyterich'	Shitter's Brook	1310

Table 1 Select list of names of Haverfordwest streets with the date of first mention in the Haverfordwest Deeds or listed in Charles *Non-Celtic Place-names*, p. 80, or his *Place-names of Pembrokeshire*, ii, p. 644.

The above table lists only the most prominent names mentioned in the deeds – there are many names that I cannot locate. It is clear that the present streets in the core of Haverfordwest were well established by the fourteenth century, and many are mentioned in the later thirteenth century bearing the names that survive to this day. The earliest surviving deeds start around the middle of the thirteenth century, and many relate to properties in Dew Street, High Street, Dark Street, Market Street, Barn Street, Goat Street, Bridge Street and the Quay. Some deeds relate to burgages and half-burgages at the extremities of the built-up area. It seems reasonable to suppose that by the late thirteenth century the central area near St Mary's was fully developed. With few Castleton burgages mentioned in the deeds it is possible that the smaller burgages there may have been abandoned in favour of larger plots in new areas. This is a common occurrence that can be witnessed at places like Kidwelly.[51]

The combination of evidence from surviving medieval deeds, the estimated maximum number of burgages in 1282, and the boundaries on the Victorian 25-inch OS maps, allows us to draw another map conjecturing growth by this date (Fig. 6). The most striking observation to be made is the large size of the town by this period. The nucleus had shifted away from the castle to a new focal point at the resited market around St Mary's. Here, immediately to the east, a guild hall was built, possibly the 'gildhus' referred to in the later

Fig. 5 St Mary's Church lies at the hub of the expanded medieval town with the surrounding streets forming a triangular plan. Within its graveyard and the immediate environs, the market functioned from the thirteenth century onwards, after the focus of commercial activity moved from Castleton.

(Crown copyright, Royal Commission on the Ancient and Historical Monuments of Wales).

thirteenth century,[52] which stood at this site, no doubt undergoing many rebuildings, until the middle of the nineteenth century.[53] Evidence for market activity is shown by the very many references to stalls and particularly to meat stalls (*macella*); indeed the market continued to function within and around the enclosure of St Mary's until a new building was constructed in Market Street in 1827.[54] The triangular layout of streets which formed this market area around the church is characteristic of many other medieval boroughs[55] and it may be argued that this constitutes evidence for conscious town planning on behalf of the medieval builders. Certainly there are elements in Haverfordwest's layout that appear regular enough to suggest areas were surveyed and laid out prior to their settlement. The regular dispersal of burgage plots north and south of High Street and the layout of streets along upper and lower Market Street, with the crossroads formed by Goat and Hill Streets is strongly indicative of such planning. Market Street itself came into existence before or as soon as St Mary's and St Thomas' churches were established. It is probably this street that is referred to as the 'great road' that lead from the market (*foro*) to the lepers' land (Magdalen's) in Robert fitz Richard's grant to Haverford Priory before 1210.[56]

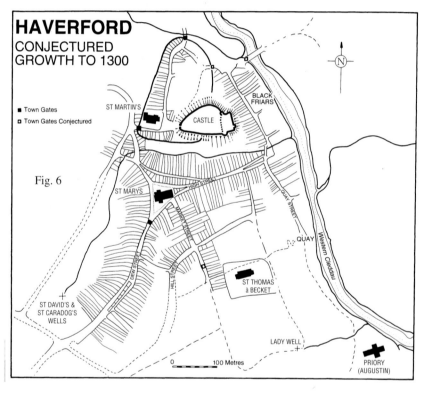

HAVERFORD
CONJECTURED
GROWTH TO 1300

■ Town Gates
□ Town Gates Conjectured

Fig. 6

At the lower end of High Street the road was wide enough for the development of small houses, and possibly shops, in the middle of the street. This became known as Short Row, a group of eight houses that existed until their removal during the construction of a new bridge and its approach road (Victoria Place) after 1834.[57] However, the original date for this development is uncertain.

A similar 'island', development took place at the upper end of Dew Street. This is referred to as Middle Row in a lease of 1664 and was probably the Rat Island removed by Perrot's trustees in 1845.[58] It may also be the *Parva Dowystret* referred to in 1397.[59] The development of Dew Street is itself of interest. I have already suggested that the burgages either side of the street may have been laid out over former open-field strips. This takes its name from the nearby holy well dedicated to St David (*Dewi*).[60] The street is also referred to in medieval documents as *vico Sancti David*, one deed in 1312 describes the dimensions of a burgage there as 42 ft (12.8 m) in length and 64 ft (19.5 m) in breadth.[61] This is a very small burgage, and the only modern properties of such small dimensions are at the Milford Road end. Such a burgage could, however, be accommodated in the area where Middle Row stood.

An interesting document of 1315[62] relates how a certain Walter Drinulle, chaplain, 'by common consent . . . and . . . use of the community . . . brought a certain subterranean way through the middle of three gardens for carrying water from the common well, enclosed with stone and lyme, called the well of St Caradoc near the well of St David to the street called Dowistret'. Both were situated close to Dew Street at a place call the Fountain. There is a Caradog's well about a mile to the south-west of the town,[63] but clearly the natural contours of the land would not allow the conveyance of conduited water from there to Dew Street. These two wells must therefore have been located near the north end of Fountain Row (NGR SM95061543) and the conduit itself in all probability ran near and parallel to Fountain Row as the document states that it only ran across three gardens to Dew Street.

The combined evidence suggests that the whole of Dew Street was built up by the early fourteenth-century, the burgesses being attracted no doubt by the large size of burgage plots there (modern properties are about 70 metres by nine metres), so that considerable infilling was already taking place with the emergence of Middle Row and the partition of many larger plots. An added attraction was that Dew Street, along with Hill Street, was located along the busy highway linking the market in the town centre with Portfield, the town's main open field.

Other areas of expansion included Bridge Street, which had in all probability come into existence prior to the founding of the Friary.[64]

The Friary of Dominican, or Black Friars, was certainly established before 1246, for in that year it received two donations from Henry III.[65] Although the founder is unknown, it could have been William Marshal II, who founded a Dominican friary in his vast holdings in Ireland at Kilkenny in 1225.[66] William Marshal I also founded a house of *Fratres Cruciferi* at New Ross, a town that also contained a Franciscan Friary.[67] Clearly the Marshals were great advocates of the mendicant orders, and are likely to have been instrumental in setting up the house at Haverford. It is not known where the house was originally sited, but in 1256 the Friars were given a grant of 15 marks (£10) for the transfer of their 'church and building to a spot more useful to them' out of the moneys collected for the crusade.[68] The rebuilt friary was located in the area east of Bridge Street extending down to the waterfront (NGR SM95431571). Fenton states that it was located at the site of the Black Horse Inn (now number 5). Whatever its precise position, the friary must have been quite extensive, as it contained the very considerable fraternity of 39 friars by 1285,[69] and continued to grow, as it expanded further in 1394. Then the friars acquired a number of additional burgages 'for the enlargement of their manse and close',[70] so it may well have eventually occupied the whole river side of Bridge Street. Close by, on what is now the Old Bridge, there was a chapel dedicated to the Holy Trinity[71] which is frequently mentioned in documents.

The friary also appears to have been an important place for pilgrimage, for it had an image of the Virgin with a miraculous taper.[72] In this context it is worth remembering that Haverford lay along one of the important pilgrims' routes to St David's.[73] The fact that holy wells dedicated to St David (and recalled now by Dew Street) and St Caradog existed at Haverford combined with the Taper at the friary is significant. The town was clearly situated along a transit point for pilgrims whose mission would have been heightened by a stop-over at Haverford, with its own holy attractions. The consequent need to provide lodgings would no doubt have encouraged an already thriving economy.

Bridge Street presumably originated as a route that linked the bridge (and Castleton) directly with the quay. There must have been a fording place or small bridge across the stream *Schytericheslake* ('Shitter's Brook'[74]) that ran down between High Street and the castle, which may explain the peculiar dog-leg that formerly existed between Bridge Street and Quay Street now masked by the open area at Castle Square (Figs 1 & 4). Bearing in mind that Victoria Place and New Bridge are modern developments, it is probable that the route from Bridge Street to the quay predates High Street.

In this part of the town lay the quay with its wharves and warehouses and also a pottery (recalled by Potter's Lane). The quay area appears to have been called Ship Street, but at the far end one entered *Vicus Prioris* or Prior's street. The Augustinian Priory of Black Canons also provided an impetus for growth. Founded, as we have seen, before 1210, the house was richly endowed by its patron Robert fitzRichard. The endowments to the prior and canons include the three parish churches within the town, the chapel in the castle, the tithes of wool and cheese, the tithes of all his mills and demesne lands and lands near and around St Thomas's and within the town.[75] The house was dissolved in 1536, and the inventory of goods, *Valor Ecclesiasticus,* shows that it was still well endowed holding the Manor of the Green or Little Haverford, with its demesne lands, two mills, Mawdlen's Chapel; the grange of Cokey, a tenement called Temperness, one called Butterhill, and various other lands elsewhere. It also held eleven churches or chapels in Pembrokeshire and Carmarthenshire.[76] The ruins have been consolidated and excavated by Cadw, and some of the architectural embellishments recovered attest the richness of the church and buildings around its cloister. [77]

By the early fourteenth century Haverford was approaching its zenith. Then its bustling streets and market place would have echoed with the voices of many tongues – English, Flemish, French, and also Welsh, for as we have seen Welshmen appear in property transactions. Its castle had been rebuilt by Queen Eleanor, the town walled (at least in part) and it was entered through five gates. It had a bridge and numerous mills and could boast three parish[78] churches, a large Dominican friary and a priory of Augustinian canons. It was well sited as a port at the tidal limits of the Haven, becoming a centre for textile and leather manufacture, including finished goods. Its export and import trade served a rich agricultural hinterland. But the shadow of the Black Death was close at hand, and in common with all towns of Europe, Haverford's population declined dramatically after 1349, indicated by a marked decrease in trade recorded in the customs' returns.[79] As late as 1473-4 (124 years after the Black Death) the town had still not recovered to its early-fourteenth-century apogee, for a survey showed about 167 whole or parts of burgages were then decayed (i.e. empty).[80]

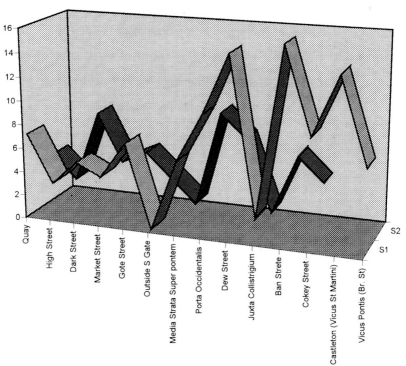

Fig. 7 Analysis of the location of decayed burgages in 1476-7.

What is revealing from an analysis of this survey (Fig. 7) is that the core of the late medieval town around St Mary's (including High Street, Dark Street, Market Street and Goat Street) remained well settled. But the peripheral streets, most notably Dew Street, Barn Street and within Castleton, had witnessed abandonment, which paints a picture of a town very much in or at the end of a period of considerable decline. Evidently, contemporary events were not helping a trend towards recovery, because a gold coin hoard found in the town in 1825 was probably buried as a result of the unsettled civil war of 1471.[81] Perhaps as a consequence of its run-down state

Haverfordwest was granted a charter of incorporation in 1479 for the town to have a mayor, sheriff and two bailiffs. In 1500 the Crown granted the fee-farm of the borough to the Corporation for a term of 72 years at an annual rent of £26 12*s* 4*d*., a figure B. G. Charles optimistically suggests could amount to 422 burgages (although many were certainly still empty).[82]

However, the administrative changes we can see in the late fifteenth century clearly made a mark. By the middle of the sixteenth century the town could be described as 'the best buylt the most civill and quickest occupied Towne in South Wales . . .' (Owen, 1903, 46).[83] Haverfordwest had turned the corner. The topography of the busy market town and administrative centre that we see today retains the unique plan elements that were indelibly stamped during the first hundred years of its history.

TERRENCE JAMES

HAVERFORDWEST CASTLE
c1110-1577.

The towering rocky bluff on which Haverfordwest castle stands is so excellent a site for a large medieval stronghold and occupies so convenient a position, overlooking a point at which the Western Cleddau, navigable to this height, could be bridged, that it is reasonable to imagine that it was occupied at an early date. In fact, we hear of it first in 1188 when Giraldus Cambrensis, in the retinue of Archbishop Baldwin, who was preaching the Third Crusade, visited the castle and met its lord, Richard fitzTancred. Tancred was a Fleming who founded the castle soon after the first Flemish settlement in Pembrokeshire in 1108. Giraldus describes him as the neighbour of the saintly Caradog Fynach of Rhos who died in 1124.[1] He was probably dead himself in 1130, leaving heirs under age.[2] Richard was the youngest son, which helps to explain his presence some 58 years later.[3]

Robert fitzRichard is mentioned in 1204. In 1207 he was confirmed in his rights by King John,[4] but in 1210 the king ejected him from his property, and in 1211 he died.[5] Though we have only an isolated authority for his downfall, it is clear that something of the sort happened, for in 1213 John granted the castle and lordship, for a substantial consideration, to the great William Marshal, Earl of Pembroke, to whom it was a most valuable acquisition.[6] In 1215, when Llywelyn the Great played havoc with the English garrisons in south-west Wales, we hear nothing of any threat to Haverford, and when the prince did attack the town in 1220, we are told that he burned it 'up to the gate of the castle' – a phrase which conveys both triumph and frustration.[7] The Welsh had already in this raid destroyed Wiston castle, where there is a low stone shell keep on a big earthen motte, and it seems probable that there was already a really strong stone castle at Haverfordwest to set their efforts at naught.

By 1219 the great Marshal was dead. He was succeeded in the earldom by his sons William II (d.1231), Richard (d.1234), Gilbert (d.1241), Walter (d.1244) and Anselm who died only a month after his brother without having been invested with the earldom. None of these had heirs, and the huge Marshal estates were partitioned between their five sisters, or their successors. Eva de Braose, the sister to whose share Haverford fell, once more to be severed from Pembroke and the earldom, was already dead. She, too, had only left three daughters, so that the lordship passed into coparcenary between Maud and Roger Mortimer, Eva and William de Canteloupe, and Eleanor and Humphrey de Bohun. This simultaneous tenancy seems to have lasted for a long time in part of the property, but the castle passed to Eleanor and Humphrey.

Fig. 8 Haverfordwest Castle (Sam Nicolson).

Humphrey de Bohun II, son of Humphrey and Eleanor and heir to Humphrey, Earl of Hereford, received seisin in about 1248. He took the Montfortian side in the Barons' War and, in 1265, William de Valence, the lord of Pembroke, took the castle from him. Humphrey himself died later in the same year, probably from wounds received at the battle of Evesham. William de Valence was given custody of the castle during the minority of his heirs[8] and, in 1273, he is found trying to make Humphrey de Bohun III do homage to him as quasi-earl of Pembroke.[9] Foiled in this, he surrendered the castle to the king, who granted it to Humphrey in 1274.[10]

In 1289 there occurred an important break in the castle's history, for Humphrey de Bohun exchanged with Queen Eleanor.[11] In the short period before her death at the end of 1290, the queen spent large sums on the castle, to which, for some reason, she had taken a particular fancy: we hear of £400 borrowed from two English notables of south Wales, and of sums of £360 and £47 paid for carpentry work. The learned authors of the *History of the King's Works* conclude:

> As the existing curtain wall and towers appear to date from the latter part of the thirteenth century, their construction may safely be attributed to Queen Eleanor, though her reasons for acquiring and rebuilding this remote Welsh castle remain obscure.[12]

From this time onward, the castle remained in royal hands for the most part. Edward I conferred it, among much other property, upon his son, Edward, later Edward II, when creating him Prince of Wales[13] at Caernarfon in 1301. Edward II granted it to Aymer de Valence, Earl of Pembroke, for life in 1308, and in fee simple in 1317,[14] so that the earl enjoyed something like the old power of the Marshals. When Aymer died in 1324, the latter of these two grants seems to have been forgotten, for he was treated as a life tenant and the castle reverted to the Crown. In 1331 Edward III granted it for life to his mother, Isabella of France.[15] The wicked queen lived until 1358. In 1343 her grandson, Edward the Black Prince, who had been granted the reversion after her life tenancy, ordered a survey of the castle, that was still, in large measure, a fairly new building. The report is not particularly informative:

the castle is of stone, covered with lead, and apparently used only for the residence of the lord and his ministers, for the defence of the lordship (*patriae*) and for the custody of prisoners; within the circuit of the castle there are two curtilages, worth 18.4d. yearly, together with the herbage of the castle ditch.[16]

The Black Prince was a competent and conscientious proprietor, but his *Register* records no expenditure on the fabric, and in 1374 he obtained a pardon for granting the castle to Thomas de Felton for life without licence. Felton was dead by 1381, and in 1383 Richard II granted a life-estate in the castle and lordship to John de Clanvowe, the constable, who died in or before 1391.[17] In 1393 followed a grant of a life estate to Thomas Percy, Earl of Worcester,[18] who was executed in 1403.

In 1405 the castle was in danger. The French expedition sent to Milford haven to aid the rebellion of Owain Glyndŵr, burned the town and attacked the castle. They were beaten off, and one of their leaders killed.[19]

After this the history of the castle is obscure, but in 1448 the tenant for life was Roland Lenthale, knight. The reversion was granted to William de la Pole, Duke of Suffolk and Earl of Pembroke. Lenthale died before 1451[20] but Suffolk can hardly have had any enjoyment out of the castle, for he fell from power in 1450 and was murdered on his way into exile. In 1455 the castle and lordship were granted, *inter alia,* to Edward, Prince of Wales, son of Henry VI, but in 1457 the castle was granted to his mother, Margaret of Anjou, while in 1460, Richard, Duke of York, procured a grant of it to himself.[21] He was killed in the same year in the battle of Wakefield, and any interests of the Lancastrians were extinguished in the York triumphs of the succeeding year. In 1462 it was leased for twenty years to William, Lord Herbert, who was created Earl of Pembroke in 1468, and beheaded after the battle of Edgcote Field in 1469. The lease passed to his heir and was unaffected by the grant of the freehold to Edward, Prince of Wales, later Edward V, in 1472.[22] In 1483 the castle was granted to Henry, Duke of Buckingham, for life[23] – an ironic limitation, for the duke was executed in the same year. In 1484 it formed a substantial part of the Pembrokeshire property belonging to Richard Williams, one of the ushers of the king's chamber.[24] The doomed King Richard III intended this as a precaution against invasion, for Williams was to command at Pembroke itself.

In 1488, after the Tudor victory, Henry VII conferred Haverfordwest on his uncle, Jasper Tudor, Duke of Bedford and Earl of Pembroke, and the heirs male of his body.[25] Since Jasper was also lord of Pembroke and of Cilgerran, we have for the last time a real Earl of Pembroke of the old style. When he died in 1495, the lordships returned to the royal line in the person of the king's younger son, Henry, Duke of York, the future Henry VIII.[26]

Apart from the appointment of officials, Henry did nothing with the castle, except for granting it, raised as a marquessate, along with other property, to Anne Boleyn, who held it for only four years.[27]

We must now suspect that we have come to the end of the history of the castle as a castle. In 1343, as we have seen, it was described as 'covered in lead', but a jury of 1358 found that it needed at least £100 worth of repairs. Nevertheless, during the fourteenth century the records suggest a castle properly kept up, and at the time of the Glyndŵr rebellion, we find a brisk programme of work – an old tower rebuilt, a new tower at the gate, a new stable, the ditch widened. After that, however, it was repeatedly granted away to life-tenants and the like, who had little incentive, and in many cases, little opportunity, to put the fabric in order, though there were small bursts of activity in 1472-3 and 1477-79.[28] The Great Sessions are recorded as having been held in the castle in 1563 and 1575,[29] but a survey of 1577, by Robert Davey, deputy Queen's Surveyor, describes a mere ruin:

> The Castell. The same hath bene a verie proper pyle buylt uppon a rocke and had the town in olde tyme on the north side thereof; but the towne now flourishing is all wellneere on the south side of it. Also, the Gatehouse or entrance thereinto is on the west side having had in it a porter's lodge, an utter gate, and ynner gate with ii portcullices, all now utterlie decayed (as the rest of the roomes hereafter touched tare). Also, within the utter gate and over the ynner gate hath bene th'eschequier, of xiiii foote square with a prison house under it. Also, there is on the said north side a Tower sometime consisting of divers roomes, and hath adioyning to it the walls of a stable w'ch was iiii^{xx}vi [four score and six] foote in length and x in breadth. Also, from the said stable forwarde on that side standeth a wall of xx^{ti} yards in length with a watch tower in the myddest thereof, from thence towards the

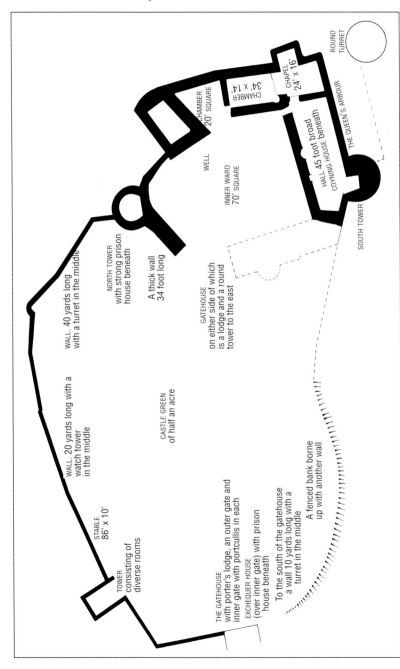

Fig. 9 Plan of Haverfordwest Castle as described in the survey of 1577.

north-east is a like wall compaswise of xl yardes longe, with a turret in the myddest thereof. Also, from the said gatehouse southwarde, a short wall of x yardes in length with a turret in the myddest; without this wall, a fenced bank borne up with another wall, & within that circuit a green walk. Also, the castell greene contains half an aker.

Also, concernyng the late inhabited p'te of the castell being utterlie decayed as before: the gatehouse or entrie thereinto hath in either side a lodge; under that gate is a vawte w'ch seems to have bene made for some privy waye into the town but none dare search the end of it. Uppon the east side of the said gate a round tower, and from that a thicke wall of xxxiiii foote longe. At the end of that another rounde tower, under which is a stronge prison house called Brehinock. The roomes within this mayne building in brief be these: a hall of xlv foote brode with a chymney in it, having under it a lardge roome (with a chymney) called the coyning house, out of w'ch goeth a stayer into a walke called The Queen's Arbour, in the east corner where there is a round turret, and at eche ende of the hall a tower; also, a chapple of xxiiii foote longe, and xvi foote brode; a great chamber (with a chymney) of xxxiiii foote longe, and xiiii foote brode; one other chamber (with a chymney) of xx foote square; one other roome for offices of xii longe & vii foote brode, with other small roomes, and a kitchen with iii chymneys. Also, within the circuit of these buildings, an ynner ward or greene of lxx foote square having a well in it.[30]

By the time of the Civil War, the castle was so far decayed that no real defence of it was ever made; town and castle simply changed hands according to the tides of war.[31] In 1648 it was ordered to be slighted;[32] it would appear that the defences of both wards were breached on the approachable side, and the fabric left to the weather and to casual stone-robbers. Worse was to come. By the beginning of the nineteenth century, the inner ward had been turned into a prison. The reaction of the local antiquary, Richard Fenton, is amazing to modern eyes:

> This superb portion of the castle is now converted into a county jail, and it is to be wished that all the other castles in county and corporate towns were converted to the same use; a change to be effected at an expense comparatively trifling to that of erecting a new prison, and without materially taking away from the picturesque and venerable appearance of the ruin . . . [33]

In fact, this progressive action on the part of the authorities ended in destroying the inner buildings of the main ward, rendering the whole castle a good deal of an eyesore, and providing Pembrokeshire with a gaol which the philanthropist John Howard considered to be an abomination. A new prison was erected in the outer ward of the castle, where its shell still stands, its interior converted, first into a museum and then a record office. The older prison, after long years of standing derelict and hideous, was cleared away in 1964 and the foundations of the original buildings opened up.

D J CATHCART KING

HAVERFORDWEST CASTLE
1577-1964.

An early account of the castle being used as a prison was given by Giraldus Cambrensis, when he and the Archbishop of Canterbury, on their way to St David's in 1188, stayed at Haverfordwest, probably with his kinsman Richard fitzTancred. Giraldus related a story about 'a notorious freebooter being held in chains in one of the towers' at the castle. 'Three boys, the son of the Earl of Clare, sent to Haverfordwest for his education, and two others, one of them the son of the castellan and the other his grandson,' were in the habit of visiting the prisoner, who made iron-tipped arrows for their bows, but one day, he snatched the boys and threatened their lives unless he was released.[1]

The survey of 1577, by which time the castle was 'utterlie decayed', reported a 'rounde tower, under which is a stronge prison house called Brehinock'. There is also reference in the survey to a prison under the Exchequer House at the inner gate of the outer ward. In addition to the prison at the castle, there was the county gaol at the Cock-house, situate at 'the north end of the Middle Row, between Saint Mary's Street and Dark Street', which was mentioned in deeds from 1342 onward. In 1640 the annual rental of 8s.0d. (40p) was received for 'the Cocke House being the County gaol.'[2] but from 1656 it was leased to the county, along with the armour house, for £5.10s.0d. (£5.50) per annum. When, later, a new county prison was built, the Cock-house was converted into a dwelling house and was demolished in 1844.

The confusion in the administration of justice is revealed in a dispute that took place at Haverfordwest on Saturday, 9 February 1572 when Robert Lloyd, the county under-sheriff, arrested one Rhys Awbrey and lodged him in the 'sheere-jayle', but it was discovered that he had made the arrest within the liberty of the town, and the mayor then ordered the town sheriff to arrest him and put him in the Town Gaol, which led to legal proceedings against the mayor and town sheriff.[3]

Towards the end of the eighteenth century, the public conscience was made aware of the terrible conditions in which prisoners were kept by the publication, in 1777, of *The State of the Prisons in*

Fig. 10 Haverfordwest Castle from the north-east, 1740: Samuel and Nathaniel Buck.
(*Pembrokeshire County Library collection*).

Fig. 11 Haverfordwest Castle from the north-east, 1890.
(*Pembrokeshire County Library collection*).

England and Wales by John Howard, Sheriff of Bedfordshire, who had made a general investigation of prisons in this country. He had visited Haverfordwest in 1774, when the county gaol was still in the Cock-house, and reported:

> This Gaol is also the Bridewell . The two lowest rooms are very damp dungeons, in one of these a prisoner lost first the use of his limbs and then his life . . . The upper rooms are dirty and offensive with small windows. No sewers, no courtyard.
>
> The county are applying for an act in order to build a new gaol.

The 'Act for building the New gaol and house of correction for the County of Pembroke,' in 1779, stated that:

> Whereas the Common Gaol of the County of Pembroke in Haverfordwest is greatly too small, inconvenient and unsafe and situate in a low, unhealthy and confined situation and being very ancient is greatly gone into decay and is so incapable of being repaired . . . it is necessary a new gaol should be built.[4]

It instructed the officers of the Quarter Sessions to treat with Robert Prust, who was mayor the previous year, for the absolute purchase of the castle in order to erect a common gaol therein, and confirmed that the Act would not affect the rights of the Duke of Leeds to whom, as Earl of Danby, had been granted certain revenues by Charles II. A letter written by John Higgon on 20 September 1886 stated that he had always heard that a grenadier in Cromwell's army, named 'Prust grabbed the ruins which being of no value he was allowed to retain and one of his descendants sold the old Walls to the County for £300 to turn into a Prison.'[5]

The gaol was built against the south wall of the inner ward of the castle by Griffith Watkins and John Webb, both of Haverfordwest, and was completed by 1 December 1780 at a cost of £1,200. The cells were 13 feet long and 6½ feet wide, with brick floors, and 3-inch-thick red deal doors. The windows were 2½ feet by 1½ feet. There were five felons' cells on the ground floor, and a debtors' prison and a women's bridewell on the first floor.[6]

When John Howard next visited the town, in 1782, he reported that he had 'had the pleasure to find a new gaol built on the castle hill instead of the ancient loathsome place of confinement.' He came again in 1788 and stated that 'the prison was clean and quiet; yet I am sorry to add, no divine service has been performed in the chapel for some time past.'[7] There were three debtors and four felons held at the gaol at the time of his visit. When he came in 1802 he noted that 'men, women, debtors and felons' were able to associate during the daytime in 'a spacious, airy courtyard about 108 ft (33m) square. The gaol had 'a chapel but no infirmary nor a bath.' The debtors were allowed straw on wooden bedsteads, but the felons had only straw to sleep on, even though the brick floors were sunk three steps below ground level. The gaoler, Samuel Howell, had told him that 'for a month together eight or ten prisoners have been crowded every night into each cell.'[8] This problem was relieved in 1816 when a debtors' prison was built against the wall between the North Tower and the gaoler's house.

In 1803 another prison reformer, James Nield, visited Haverfordwest. He found the twenty-three-year-old building less than satisfactory, and he gave a report that was a repeat of Howard's, adding that there were eleven felons and three lunatics in the gaol.

Revd Sir Thomas Gery Cullum, Bart., Bath King of Arms, visited Haverfordwest in 1811 and, 'happening to meet Mr Mathias, a gentleman and I presume a magistrate as the doors of the castle flew open at his approach,' thought the castle had 'nothing of interest remaining and what might otherwise be admired is defaced by the prevailing taste of the country in whitewashing all their buildings, both ancient and modern.'[9] He was thus echoing the observation of Mrs Morgan, who found the castle 'terribly defaced by the taste that prevails in this place of whitening all kinds of buildings.'[10]

There were some French prisoners of war held at the gaol in August and November 1813. French prisoners had previously been held at the castle following the abortive invasion at Fishguard on 22 February 1797. When news of the invasion reached the town, six nine-pounder guns were prepared for its defence but within 48 hours the French had laid down their arms and were marched to Haverfordwest where 415 prisoners were held at the castle for a time before being moved on to Pembroke and ships in Milford Haven. When the Duke of Rutland visited the prison the following August he noted that eight French prisoners, held back to give evidence in the discredited treason trial against local people, were given the free run of the fives court in the prison and had taken the ducal party 'into their mess room, where they sang the Marsellois Hymn, really in fine style.'[11]

In 1817 a committee of magistrates was formed to improve and make additions to the Gaol and House of Correction under the chairmanship of Henry Leach, who had suffered in French prisons after being captured on an armed merchantman. His committee's attitude towards prisoners may well have been influenced by his experiences. The committee's first report[12] described the conditions in the gaol and expressed its views on the treatment of prisoners, stating that it felt that:

> it was time to act upon the conviction which we all feel, that the plan of diminishing crimes by lessening the rigour of punishment is not the child of modern imbecility, or enthusiasm, but has been handed down to us by the wise and good in generations that are past. We have no right to deprive a prisoner of pure air; no right to ruin his habits by keeping him in idleness, his morals by compelling him to mix with a promiscuous assemblage of hardened and convicted felons, or his health by forcing him into a dirty cell with the victims of contagious and loathsome disease.

It was the intention of the members of the committee, who ultimately rebuilt the prison, not only to remove the criminals from society and punish them, but to convert 'our prisons from the abode of idleness and debauchery . . . to a place of industry and instruction.' Their optimistic and liberal view of prisoners was clearly set out in the report.

> Your committee solicit the aid and assistance of the benevolent of both sexes and they may be permitted to express their earnest hope that the inhabitants of the town and neighbourhood may be induced to extend towards the unhappy prisoner in the gaol a portion of that commiseration and kindness which they are so conspicuous for exercising towards the needy outside its wall. . . . Humanity cannot find objects more deserving of its care than those within the walls of a prison.

Within three years of the first meeting of the committee, a new prison building was designed and built on the outer ward of the castle. The new prison, designed by Mr Pritchett, a native of Pembrokeshire who had previously designed prisons and lunatic asylums, was a three-storeyed building erected in the outer ward. It was divided into eight wards, with two work rooms, one for males and one for females, eight day rooms and eight airing yards. In 1866, a system of pipes and grills was constructed to allow hot air to flow through the whole building. Later alterations increased the number of cells to 110. There was a large chapel, a small court house and a gallows within the main building.

An Act of 1822 provided 'for converting the Gaol and House of Correction of the county of Pembroke into a gaol for the said county and for the town and county of the town of Haverfordwest; and for applying the gaol of the said town and county of Haverfordwest to the purposes of a lunatic asylum.'[13] The Act provided that the debtors and other prisoners should be committed to and kept in the gaol for the county of Pembroke by the warrant of the town magistrates, and that they be maintained there at the costs and charges of the town, and that the town sheriff should be answerable for their safe custody. The town magistrates were empowered to visit and inspect the gaol, but its control and management and the appointment of officers and servants remained with the county magistrates. The gaoler gave security to the county and town sheriffs for the safe keeping of their respective prisoners.

The old town gaol, on St Thomas's Green, was converted into an asylum 'for the reception of Pauper and Criminal Lunatics belonging to the town and county of Haverfordwest and the county of Pembroke,' and was to be the first county asylum in Wales. The county magistrates were authorized by the Act to send criminal and pauper lunatics to the asylum at the expense of the county, but the control and management of the asylum was vested in the magistrates of the town. The old gaol was reported, in 1835, to be 'inconvenient as a receptacle for lunatics, both as to size and arrangement,' and there was no resident medical officer.

One feature of prison life which the reformers hoped to amend was the way in which prisoners occupied their time. The work they did was not to disadvantage law-abiding citizens, for example by manufacturing goods produced elsewhere in the town, nor were they to be trained in skills that could later create competition with local craftsmen. Furthermore, the work was to be suitable for all convicts, and aimed at reducing the cost of the prison service. To these ends, the Committee of Magistrates installed a tread mill which would turn the millstones of a flour mill. This provided work for up to 64 prisoners, men and women, weak and strong, upon whose health and condition the surgeon kept a regular check. The mill was designed and built by Sir William Cubitt, who had already installed similar mills in twelve other British prisons. The mill cost £302.10s.3d (£302.51) and £107.12s.11d (£107.65) was spent on its transportation and installation. The costs were soon recovered from grinding corn for private individuals, and flour for making the prisoners' bread, which was baked in the prison.

The effect of the treadmill as a deterrent soon became apparent. This had been optimistically foreseen by the Committee, whose only apprehension about providing the mill was that 'the number of prisoners may not, in future, be sufficient to enable it to do so much work as it is capable of performing; on this we can only remark that as the end of punishment is the prevention of crime, a result more perfectly more satisfactory could not take place.'

The mill was built in the south-eastern corner of the inner ward of the castle, on the site of the chapel. There were two wheels, five feet in diameter, one for males and the other for females. The conditions under which the prisoners were to work on the wheels were clearly set out in the prison rule-book. They worked for seven hours in winter, and for ten in summer, turning the wheel at a rate of 48 steps per minute for 15 turns, followed by five minutes rest, throughout the day, with an hour for lunch.

Detailed records survive of the quantity of flour ground at the mill from its inception until 1839. The early records contain interesting references to the buildings. In 1821, a passage was built to connect the mill to the cells, so that prisoners would not be able to communicate with each other and, in the same year, Cubitt supervised the construction of a window in the mill and made additional space for the prisoners to turn the wheel. In 1823, a complete flour-dressing machine with best approved wire was purchased, and work was done to prevent the men from getting over to the women's wheel,[14] and £24 was spent on general repairs. The miller was paid ten shillings a week.

Fig. 12 The 1820 prison building, from above the Governor's house, 1964: the tower enabled a warder to see into all the exercise yards.

(Pembrokeshire Record Office).

Fig. 13 The Governor's house, now the Town Museum.

(Pembrokeshire Record Office).

In 1867, plans to build a matron's house and new cells on the site of the 1779 prison were submitted to Whitehall for approval, and the Quarter Session minutes record that a mortgage of £1,200 was requested, to be spent on enlarging the prison. The plans appear to have been abandoned, but a new matron's house was built beside the rectangular tower.

Day books kept by the gaolers, surgeons, chaplains and visitors for the period 1820 to 1840, together with the daily lists of prisoners, records of work done at the mill and returns to questionnaires from the Government, provide glimpses of prison life during that period.

Soon after the new prison had been completed, there was an attempt to escape from the old prison cells, that were clearly still in use. A prisoner sent a letter with the gaoler's daughter to Mary Vaughan of Prendergast asking her to provide him with a saw and files. The gaoler allowed the letter to be delivered and removed the saw from a bundle subsequently sent to the prisoner. Later, while the prisoners were in chapel, the gaoler inspected the man's cell and found a rope twisted out of rags, and an examination of the cell bars revealed that they had been cut through with the mainspring of his watch, which was found to be missing. The prisoner was put in irons until the visiting magistrates considered the case and their conclusion was that alterations to the windows of the cells was necessary so as to avoid a recurrence.

On 22 March 1821, the gaoler noted in his day book that a lunatic prisoner had broken the windows in his cell and he had him chained upon the right hand and left foot. On the same day, the gaoler complained that 'the expense of furnishing the prisoners with woollen trousers is very great and will only be provided in case of absolute necessity.'[15]

The number of prisoners held at the prison varied from day to day. Normally, there were between twenty and forty, but at times the total rose to seventy or eighty. The most common crimes committed were felony and bastardy, but others were punished for leaving their service, family or apprenticeship, breaking the peace, smuggling, rioting, larceny and malady.

The last person known to be hanged at Haverfordwest was William Roblin,[16] who was charged with the murder of a gamekeeper at the New Inn at Deep Lake, on the Carmarthen road. Sentence was passed on Easter Monday, 23 April 1821, and Roblin was hanged in the presence of a great gathering of townspeople, 'and his body dissected and anatomised.'

The prison was closed in 1878 by order of the Home Secretary, and the prisoners were transferred to Carmarthen. The buildings were then occupied by the Pembrokeshire Police Force until 1963, and the main building was gutted in the following year and converted for use as a county museum, until it was removed to Scolton, and a record office. The old prison buildings were demolished.

In medieval times, the outer ward of the castle would have been an open space with buildings set against its boundary wall. The main gate stood below the present entrance to the castle and, according to the survey of 1577, it was a substantial building, comprising a gate house with porter's lodge, an outer gate and an inner gate, with a portcullis in each. Over the inner gate was the Exchequer House which, according to the survey, was fourteen feet (4.26m) square, and there was a prison house under it. To the south of the gatehouse was a wall, ten yards (9.1m) long, with a turret in the middle, and outside the wall was 'a fenced bank borne up with another wall, & within that circuit a green walk.' The outer ward, sometimes described as the Castle Green, covered about half an acre, and around it there were buildings set against a high boundary wall.

To the north of the gatehouse, along the curtain wall, stood a tower 'consisting of divers roomes', which may have been 'the new tower built next to the outer gate' in 1407-08,[17] and other towers on the north side are marked only by kinks in the wall. Excavation in 1981 revealed that the wall, at its base, was six feet (1.90m) thick but set less than two feet (0.5m) into the subsoil. Adjoining the tower, and set along the wall, was a large stable, 86 feet (26m) long and 10 feet (3m) broad, which may have been built in 1387-88.[18]

Outside the castle wall, to the north and west, was a ditch, to which there is reference in rentals and surveys of 1358,[19] 1577 and 1653,[20] that was 13 feet (4m) wide and may have been cut more than 6 feet (2m) into the solid rock. Excavation within a walled enclosure beyond the ditch, on the north side, in 1978 revealed that the site had been occupied by a smith during the early medieval period, but the remains of the smithy had been buried beneath a substantial deposit of silt and freshly dug stone which may have been dumped there when the ditch was cleaned out in 1407. The site was then abandoned and used as a garden until the middle of the twentieth century.

The North Tower has walls that are seven foot (2m) thick. Its entrance was at the first floor level, which would have been reached by means of steps from the courtyard. The curtain wall between the North Tower and the rectangular tower was built after the towers were completed. The butt joint between the wall and the North Tower was obscured when the wall was restored in 1978. The upper part of the wall was thickened with grey Boulston gritstone which effectively doubled its thickness and provided a walkway at parapet level between the two towers. There are a number of 'putlog', small square, holes in which the timber ends of wooden scaffolding were placed. The wall that joined the inner gatehouse to the North Tower was inexpertly 'restored' in the 1960s by the Pembrokeshire County Council and it was only by chance that further 'restoration' of the kind was halted. The wall is pieced at first floor level by a passage marked on the south side by a poor modern copy of the arch on the north side. Its purpose is not known but it provides a rather difficult access to a vaulted chamber within the thickness of the wall.

The rectangular tower appears to be the earliest surviving stone structure on the site and may well have been designed as a keep.[21] It is rectangular internally, while its east wall is curved externally, and is built of brown sandstone quarried on the site. The tower had at least three floors.

The gate to the inner ward was in a wall connecting the North Tower to the South Tower. The gate house had a lodge on either side and a round tower to the east. The gaoler's house, now the Town Museum, appears to have been built on the foundations of the west wall of the inner ward. The minister's accounts of 1407-08 record expenditure on a new drawbridge near the inner gate, which suggests that there was a ditch between the outer and inner wards and that it may have been part of the ditch dug around the original castle. Under the gate was a vault which 'seems to have been made for some privy waye into the town', according to the survey, 'but none dare search the end of it.' Excavation behind the gaoler's house in 1914 exposed a cavity, at least 17½ feet (5.3m) high, which may have been where, about fifty years previously, 'an inmate of the castle prison was wheeling a barrow' when the ground caved in under him.[22]

During the year or so in which Queen Eleanor had possession of the castle, in 1289-90, work was started on the east and south wings. The uniformity of their construction is so clear that it is likely that they were built as part of a single programme. They do not seem to have been built on earlier foundations and appear to form an extension to the castle on the strong, but precarious, position overlooking the river valley and the town. Their large windows indicate that the castle had become a grand residence for the lord and his officials, built at a time when defence was becoming of secondary importance. The evidence suggests that the castle was not radically altered, extended or rebuilt after the first decade of the fourteenth century, when the east and south wings and associated buildings were completed.

The east wing had two floors, the original being near the present level within the wing. The first-floor level, marked by a ledge along the wall, has two garderobe alcoves below which chutes, built within the thickness of the wall, opened into a cesspit that emptied through two arched openings in the east wall on to the rocks below. To the south of the alcoves, a window lit a 20-feet-square chamber, immediately south of the rectangular tower. Next to it was 'the great chamber (with a chymney)', lit by the three large windows that look over the town.

The Buttress Tower, at the south-east corner, had a chapel on the first floor, lit by a lancet window in the east wall. The chapel was used as a prison chapel in the old prison, built in 1779, but was presumably abandoned when a new chapel was erected in 1820. The room below the chapel probably had a vaulted ceiling but this may have been removed when a treadmill was introduced in the nineteenth century.

The main feature of the south wing was the great hall on the first floor, 42 feet (12.8m) long and 20 feet (6m) wide. It was lit by two large windows in the south wall and probably more overlooking the inner courtyard. Beneath was the Coining House, but there is no evidence that coins were minted at Haverfordwest and it is likely that this room was used for administrative purposes. It was lit by four windows, facing south, and it had a fireplace in middle of the north wall. The Coining House had a vaulted ceiling and a report by H M Office of Works, in 1937, stated that the medieval vaulting was still in existence.

At the west end of the Coining House stood the South Tower. A staircase lead to the upper rooms above, and another down to the Queen's Arbour, which may have been named after Queen Eleanor. South of the buttress stood a round tower that may have been connected by a short curtain wall. Beyond the staircase is a small area lit by four windows overlooking the town. The vault beneath a modern grill was a cesspit. The south wing was partially rebuilt in 1779 as a county prison and the level of the roof of the building is indicated by the groove along the wall between the first-floor windows.

Five types of stone were used in the construction of the castle, and they may be identified by their colour. Brown sandstone quarried from the rock on which the castle stands and varying in colour from a warm red-brown to a grey brown, is visible in the north and rectangular towers and in the north boundary wall to the outer ward, and it was also used extensively in the prison buildings. Grey gritstone, or Boulston stone, was used between the north and rectangular towers on the corbelled portion, and it is the main building material for the east and south wings. Grey-brown and purple Nolton stone was soft enough to be carved into the moulded jambs of windows, doors and lintels: it is so soft that much of it has weathered away. Squared blocks of Grey Limestone, which occurs naturally within five miles of Haverfordwest, are found scattered throughout the castle, in the band of brown sandstone at first floor levels, and as quoins of the alcove above the garderobes. Limestone from the Stackpole quarry was given by Lord Cawdor for building the 1820 prison.[23] Yellow sandstone was used for the moulded outer frames of the large windows and their tracery may have been of this material. It is also present on the outer bevelled corner of the Buttress Tower.

Up to the nineteenth century, none of this stonework was visible as the walls were lime washed, and, in the words of Mrs Morgan, 'that fine piece of ancient architecture' looked 'as bald as an antique bust would do with a plaster of Paris nose, or a bronze statue of the Grecian Venus with a white handkerchief.'[24]

MICHAEL FREEMAN

THE AUGUSTINIAN PRIORY

The ruins of the Augustinian priory at Haverfordwest have seen a transformation in recent years. Sited on the banks of the river Cleddau, on the southern outskirts of the town, overgrown fingers of masonry from transept and nave until recently stood alone to remind the passer-by of the former life of the monastery. Then, in 1981, the site was acquired by the Gild of Freemen of Haverfordwest,[1] who gave it to the Secretary of State for Wales, thus enabling an extensive programme of excavation and presentation to be undertaken. This work comprised the excavation and presentation of the church, cloister, chapter-house and slype, as well as an extensive area of medieval gardens which lay between the priory and the river. This chapter acts as a useful interim statement of progress on the site but is proffered with the proviso common to all interim statements that ideas may change as work progresses.

The plot of land granted to the Augustinian canons by Robert FitzTancred in about 1200 left a good deal to be desired as a building site. Convenient its position may have been on the side of the navigable river, not far from the town quay, but the topography of the site was that of a rough, sloping bank giving way to marshland, then, as now, subject to flooding from the tidal river as well as being crossed by numerous streams from the higher land to the west. The first task that confronted the builders was to create a flat site wide enough for the monastery and high enough to withstand flooding. This was achieved by cutting rock and gravel from the slope and dumping it to form a large platform some 2.5m high above the marsh. This platform had then to be supplied with a series of drains to divert the streams and thus to allow building proper to begin. The bank of the river, though it has certainly varied in the past, seems to have been in much the same position then as now, the main alteration being the relatively recent silting up of a turn in the river on the south of the priory. This creek, shown on early drawings of the priory,[2]

would have meant that the buildings and their garden would
originally have been bordered by water on two sides, the east and
south-east.

Fig. 14 The south-east view of Haverfordwest Priory: Samuel and Nathaniel Buck,
1740.

Excavations have shown that while some of the claustral buildings
were built up within the fill of the made up building platform, the
chancel walls at least were built directly on to the surface of the
marsh. The building platform was then raised at the same time as and
around these substantial masonry foundations which were equipped
with a battered plinth, the top of which stood just above the monastic
ground surface. The foundations of the transept walls, still massive,
were however built on to made up ground, albeit only some 200mm
above the marsh. The western end of the nave was built on to the
reduced subsoil as were the western range buildings. The junction
between the made up building platform and the cut subsoil, the point,
in other words, between the cut and fill, showed particularly clearly
during excavations in the cloister garden as an irregular line running
roughly south-east/north-west.

The form of the priory is conventional, with a cruciform church on
the north side of a square cloister, on the east side of which lay the
dormitory, the south the refectory and the west the storage range.
Two seasons of excavations in 1922 and 1924 by Clapham and

Rahbula,[3] demonstrated the presence of a series of buildings to the south of the refectory, which were identified as service buildings – buttery and kitchens – and the infirmary. Due to the natural constraints of space on the east and west, and presumably town buildings and roadways on the north, monastic buildings tended to spread southwards towards the marsh, though it has not been established whether or not any buildings are substantially later than others and, if so, whether extensions of the original building platform were required to accommodate these.

The original plan of the main claustral buildings seems to have been established from the start. No alterations or extensions to the basic shape of the church or the four ranges were revealed, though there were certainly internal changes and remodelling. The buildings incorporated the mixture of local limestone and gritstone, as do the

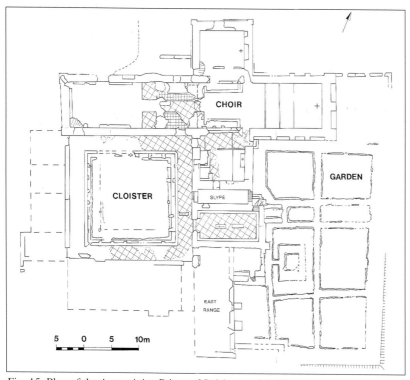

Fig. 15 Plan of the Augustinian Priory of St Mary and St Thomas.
(Crown copyright – Cadw: Welsh Historic Monuments).

other medieval buildings in the town, most notably the castle and the three churches of St Martin's, St Mary's and St Thomas's. External walls and the church walls generally were stoutly built throughout with good lime mortar, though some internal walls, such as the wall between slype and chapter-house, and walls around the claustral ranges, were found to be clay bonded, the facework alone being pointed with lime mortar. The church walls were approximately 1.5m thick, with the external batter on the foundation giving a basal thickness of 2.5m. Built apparently in horizontal bands, the walls were generally strong and were reduced by subsequent robbing rather than collapse. The claustral walls were considerably less well constructed, being only 0.9m-1m thick and, indeed, the west range walls seem to have been constructed on to the cut subsoil with little in the way of foundations at all. As was unsurprising on a sloping, marshy riverside site, there appears to have been a tendency for the eastern range buildings at least to subside, hence a number of secondary buttresses placed along the external east walls.

The church was laid out to a simple cruciform aisle-less plan and provides a classic example of primitive Augustinian planning. The stalls were sited in the crossing and, to allow free passage around them through the north transept, a single bay aisle was built in the angle of the north transept and nave with doorways to allow access and form a lower choir entry. Similarly a passage in the thickness of the wall was contrived in the angle between the north transept and presbytery to form the upper choir entry. The building, some 49m long, is of small-to-average length for the lesser monastic houses in Wales. Excavations have generally been non-intrusive below final monastic floor levels, but sufficient dissolution and post-monastic disturbances had been wrought on the interior to allow us to obtain information about earlier layouts. The earliest surface encountered, just above the platform make up at several points in the chancel, was a uniform flat surface without chancel steps, at the same level as the crossing and nave floor. Though it had a reasonably fine mortar surface, there was, at no point on this surface, any indication of impressions of tiles or slabs or any other flooring material and it may well be that this is merely a finishing smoothing at a uniform level throughout the church rather than a used floor in itself. The three chancel steps were at least an early, if not an original feature, though they had been remodelled in slightly different positions during the life of the church. The extreme eastern end of the chancel had seen considerable disruption, not least from the 1920s excavations, but there is little reason to doubt that the final position of the altar, immediately at the east end against the wall, remained the same through the history of the church. The tiled floor, where it survived, displayed much evidence of patching and wear and had evidently been laid many years before the dissolution. The pattern was evidently that of green and buff plain slip tiles laid in a diagonal grid. This was the basic floor type encountered in chancel, transepts and crossing, though there were variations in pattern, especially in the north transept and locally around the choir stalls. The floor of the tower was a mixture of tile and slabs while the nave floor was slabbed throughout in local slate, green, blue and purple, being laid with some apparent attempt at harmonized colour. These slabs would seem to have been not altogether appropriate for a hard wearing floor. They were thin and laminating, though were evidently still worth robbing after the dissolution, as most of the central, larger slabs were missing.

Beneath the rather patched, worn and composite floor of the 1530s church were found clear traces of an earlier, uniformly tiled floor. Only a matter of millimetres below the final floor, this tiled floor was

Fig. 16 Tile from the Cloister showing impression of a dog's paw.
(*Crown copyright – Cadw: Welsh Historic Monuments*).

found at every point of the church where later disturbance made it possible to examine it. It had again had tiles of the same dimensions as the later floor laid in a diagonal grid, but only the impressions in the mortar floor have survived. The tiles had evidently been removed either for reuse or patching, or for discarding. The three chancel steps were in slightly different positions in this earlier layout, but the altar step and the altar itself appeared to be at the same point.

Two major alterations, both perhaps connected and contemporary, occurred within the church during its lifetime. The first was the heightening of the transepts walls and the raising of the roof level, evidence for which survives in the fabric of the transept upper walls and windows. The second was the insertion of a tower within the church, at the east end of the nave. Early illustrations of the ruined church proved that there had been a square tower, but Clapham, when studying the standing structure in the 1920s[4] had found it difficult to understand how this had been supported as there survived no traces of springers for the tower arches at the crossing, the conventional position. The reason for this became clear during our excavations, when not only were the four bases for the piers revealed but also good remains of the southern arch which had fallen bodily on to the nave floor directly below. The tower was evidently inserted into the east end of the nave in the fifteenth century and formed the retrochoir between the rood and pulpitum screens. Its upper stages were accessed by a spiral stair built against the east side of the north-east pier and pulpitum screen. On its west side the rood screen had a central doorway flanked by a pair of nave altars, above which there seems to have been open tracery panelling. After the insertion of the tower, the lower choir entry doorway in the north wall of the nave was blocked and a tomb was inserted against it. The construction of the tower must have been disruptive and may be contemporary with the alterations to the roof levels throughout the church.

The nave was given a bench around all three walls; this had evidently been constructed before the latest floor, the slabs of which butted up against it, but sat upon the earlier one. One small piece of bath stone seating slab survived showing that that was the material with which it was finished. Similar benching ran along the low wall of the back of the choir, between the stalls and the south transept. Probably because of the topography of the site, the nave was built without a west doorway and instead the main entrance was midway along the north wall, reflecting the main approach to the priory from the north. Unfortunately now blocked as it lies on a modern property boundary, it was 2m wide, equipped with steps down into the nave. Though the north wall only survives to a height of around 2m the west front is more intact and stands almost to eaves height at its south-west angle. Access to the roof space was provided by a small spiral stair within the north west corner buttress, the bottom courses of which still survive. The lower parts of a fine west window remain and one and parts of the splayed jambs of three further windows survive on the south wall. At each end of the south wall there is a doorway into the cloister; the one at the east end was elaborately decorated with large undercut foliate dog-tooth ornament but only the lowest parts of its jambs now remain.

The transepts were built symmetrically as equal arms of the crossing, but show considerable differences in arrangement of windows and doors because of the monastic buildings which adjoin the south transept. The north wall of the north transept has three windows flanked externally by small niches for statues. The east wall had a wide recessed arch forming a large niche for an altar slab. Its rear wall had a single lancet window flanked by blind arches. The west wall has a pair of lancet windows which had shafts banded at intervals by annulets or shaft rings up the internal jambs. The south transept had perforce to have higher windows in the west, to avoid the cloister pent roof, and in the south to avoid the dormitory beyond. Because of this restriction and perhaps to compensate, the east wall had three windows with a single altar set below the middle window. There is a piscina and aumbrey set into the south wall and a doorway into the sacristy beyond. In the west wall there is a small doorway which gave access to the night stair to the dormitory, contrived within the thickness of the wall.

Quantities of wall plaster, much of it painted but unfortunately in small scraps, were found from dissolution levels within the church. The poor condition of this made it impossible to recreate any pictures or patterns but most seemed confined to geometric or linear decoration, 'masoning', in red. Again, quantities of window glass, not necessarily all from the church, were found in the nave and in adjacent stretches of the north claustral pavement; the large majority of the fragments was unpainted, though fragments of painted figures and heads did survive. The quality of the dressed stone from the church, now undergoing analysis, suggests that the building was quite richly ornamented, with the cream coloured bathstone imported for tracery and decorative features. The roof was slated and topped with clay ridge tiles and may have been covered with a lime coating in the characteristic Pembrokeshire fashion, to judge from the evidence of the collapsed roof slates found in adjacent areas outside the church.

The claustral ranges remain largely unexcavated save for the sacristy and chapter-house in the eastern, dormitory range. The small, narrow room immediately outside the south transept wall appears first to have acted as a slype, or corridor connecting the cloister with the riverside exterior of the priory. It was equipped with a door at either end, and covered with a plain barrel vault. Its slabbed floor was set over a sizeable stone lined drain which served to take water from the cloister drain to the river. A third door led into the south transept, and it was subsequently this door alone which remained accessible when the slype was remodelled into a sacristy. The two end doors were blocked, the drain from the cloister recut and enlarged and the slabbed floor relaid and a small cupboard was inserted into the south wall. Thus altered and accessible now only from the church, the room would have proved a strong and useful repository for the priory treasures.

The chapter-house was a plain rectangular room without any of the eastern-end embellishments which are often encountered at other monastic houses. It had from the start, however, a fine west door leading into the cloister, with a window on either side. Unusually it had a small side doorway in the north east corner allowing access to the riverside, but this was blocked in a drastic remodelling of the building which occurred in the fifteenth century. This included the insertion of a new ribbed vault the springers of which were supported on extraordinary massive corbels, one of which survived. This has seven human faces with common eyes carved on to the exposed front and the quality of the carving of this and surviving sections of the vaulting ribs gives some indication of the sumptuous decoration of the chapter house in its final form. The floor was tiled with green and buff tiles laid in a diagonal pattern, and in the centre were two graves. The most prominent was a tomb plinth which had evidently supported the effigy of a figure clad in chain mail with sword, shield and helmet. Thirteenth-century in style, and in so pre-eminent a position, this may be regarded as the tomb of an early and influential benefactor, presumably one of the fitzTancred family. The effigy had unfortunately been smashed and pieces of the sculpture were found widely scattered both in the post-dissolution fill of the chapter-house and outside the building altogether. Only about half of the effigy has so far been recovered. Immediately to the west of the effigy was a second grave slab set into the floor, which had survived relatively intact.

Sufficient standing masonry survived to the south of the chapter-house for us to appreciate that the ground floor buildings were covered with a plain barrel vault, here running north/south, unlike the sacristy and chapter house. This apparently plain room, equipped

Fig. 17 Corbel head from the Chapter House.
(Crown copyright – Cadw: Welsh Historic Monuments).

Fig. 18 Carved stone head from an effigy of a thirteenth-century knight, presumably one of the fitzTancreds, from the Chapter-house.

(Crown copyright – Cadw: Welsh Historic Monuments).

with a door from the south-east corner of the cloister, may well have been merely a store, but without excavation its function is impossible to determine. Above the sacristy, chapter-house and southern room, the canons' dormitory ran from the south transept wall to the small piece of surviving masonry on the south which formed part of the reredorter (latrine) wall. The opening of the drain leading from this to the east has been excavated, and it apparently ran along the south precinct wall to discharge into the river.

Neither the refectory range to the south of the cloister nor the western range has been excavated, but sufficient remained from the open trenches from the 1920s excavations for us to have some idea of their layout. The excavation of the cloister, of course, also provided information about their inward-facing elevations. A narrow doorway in the south-eastern corner of the cloister led into a passage or dark entry through the south range to where the kitchen and service rooms stood.[5] The main door into the refectory lay to the west. Close to it we were fortunate to discover several sections of the long lavatorium, or stone wash-basin along with sufficient wall-face to show where originally it had been positioned. The basin was set into the wall so that it protruded from the wall-face, set above a step in the pavement below. The half of the basin which projected into the cloister was worn as the canons inevitably leaned against it while washing; the section within the wall, however, was still covered with mortar and retained the rough tool-marks from its original dressing. A drain ran from the bowl outlet to carry water away into the main cloister drain. Suitably cleansed, the canons would have passed through the door to the long refectory for their meals.

Two further rooms ran from the refectory towards the south, and were interpreted by Clapham,[6] plausibly enough, as kitchen and buttery. Evidently covered by the usual stone vaults, they were small serviceable buildings, accessible to the townsfolk, who would have provided the labour force, by a cobbled path which led from the town around the western end of the church and cloister. Whether or not the rectangular building which lay to the south east of the complex is the infirmary, as Clapham suggested, remains to be seen, but its position, away from the centre and probably with its own separate water supply and discharge system, makes this interpretation also very plausible.

The west range, the crease of its roofline still visible against the nave wall, has not been excavated but seems to have consisted of a series of plain rooms equipped with four doorways from the cloister and at least one door to the roadway to the west. Uniquely at Haverfordwest, this range was built on to the cut natural subsoil rather than on or within built-up ground. It was poorly constructed, with thin, clay bonded walls set on alarmingly slight foundations. As it lay at the foot of the artificially steepened slope to the west, the discharge of natural water must have been a real cause for concern. A series of no less than four drains led from the west under the floors of the west-range rooms and the cloister pavement and into the cloister drain. Described by Clapham as the 'cellarer's range'[7] the west-range rooms were probably largely used for storage. Only one length of the interior wall remains to a significant height, the rest being footings, but they show no signs of ornamentation.

The cloister, in the centre of the priory at Haverfordwest, was fully excavated. The small square garden in the centre was surrounded by a pavement tiled on three sides and slabbed on the less significant western side. East, south and north pavements were laid with the same diagonal pattern of green and buff tiles as the chapter-house, and the floors in both were clearly laid at the same time as each other and, indeed, as the latest floor in the church, probably some time in the fifteenth century. The cloister walks were covered only with a pent roof and were subject to weathering as well as considerable passage of feet. The pavements were considerably cracked and worn, and displayed localized areas of severe subsidence and patching, unlike the contemporary floor in the chapter-house which was evidently more protected. Random slabs of local grey stone covered the floor of the west alley and incorporated the capstones of four drains. The slabs continued partly into the south alley to incorporate the step to the lavatorium and the capstones of a drain running from the south range through the main refectory doorway.

Between the cloister alleys and the central garth the sizeable main drain was carried around all four sides to form a water feature. The drain performed a vital function in this sloping, marshy site. Not only did it drain the west range and the natural springs and run off from the slope beyond, it was also the collection point for rainwater from the pent roof and the church and claustral range roofs. There must have been times when the drain resembled a raging torrent and when its generous depth and width were tested to extremes. Certainly, excavation of both claustral drain and its discharge drain under the sacristy floor revealed no pre-dissolution silting, and while it was in use the force of water evidently kept its stone sides and bottom clean. The drain was spanned at intervals by a series of small bridges which supported the buttresses of the cloister arcades. At the mid-point of the drain on the east, however, was a lower section of walling and stone supports, presumably for the bridge giving access into the garden.

Between the drain and the garden ran a slabbed pathway, with even some slabs surviving on the western half where the bright yellow subsoil made its line and position particularly clear. The garth seems to have been planted as a garden, for bordering this internal path was a narrow trench which was interpreted as the bed for a hedge. On the west, again most clearly visible, this trench was broken at the mid-point, suggesting perhaps, some symmetrical planting design. Unfortunately the opposite point on the west had been disrupted by later trenches apparently associated with repairs. The layout of the garden planting must therefore remain somewhat speculative. What was quite clear, however, was an octagonal depression in the centre. With too precise and clear an edge to represent a garden bed, and with an even, flat base, this was presumably a stone platform to support a central feature. It was not equipped with a water-feed or drainage, but may have supported a water stoup or cistern. The remaining area of the garden may have been grassed. Certainly the surviving garden soil cover was quite thin below the dissolution levels, and excavation revealed no formal dug beds. A series of hollows and depressions in the subsoil with a deeper survival of garden soil may well represent the positions of individual small trees or bushes, but they did not conform to anything which might be construed as a formal planting scheme. The most likely interpretation is of a grassed area with an informal planting of small trees, with a stone water cistern in the very centre and a path and low hedge running around the perimeter.

The cloister as it appeared at the dissolution, with bathstone dressings and pillars, was a remodelling of the original thirteenth-century cloister. Ironically, as much of the dressed stone from the earlier cloister had been reused in the remodelling, albeit as supporting basal stones or for corework fill, excavations allowed a more complete interpretation of this earlier layout than of the subsequently remodelled structure, which had been substantially robbed of its dressed stone. Fine abaci decorated with friezes of running animals, fish, clouds and vegetation were used to support later buttresses or as stone slabs for the pathway. Parts of cluster columns and capitals were reused in the core and dressed stones for heads of arches were used in the remodelled bridge-buttresses across the drain. The recovered elements of this first cloister arcade were either cut from the fine purple Caerbwdi stone from nearby St David's or a contrasting coarser-grained sandstone. Remarkably, some of the capitals and bases had been turned on a lathe. The overall design was of a series of open pointed arches each supported on three detached Caerbwdi shafts or intermediate buttressed piers of four-coursed sandstone shafts.

One of the most unexpected but exciting discoveries at Haverfordwest was that of the extensive medieval garden which lay between the priory buildings and the river. Clapham had discovered a low revetment wall running outside the church and had, not unreasonably, interpreted this as the canons' cemetery[8]. Indeed, in the first centuries of the life of the priory this may well have been the function of this area, as one monastic grave discovered beneath a disturbed section of one of the garden paths suggests. However, at the same time as the cloister within the priory was being remodelled, the decision was taken to establish a garden over this area. Showing scant regard for the problems of flooding and subsidence which had so exercised their predecessors, the canons designed a series of apparently raised garden beds, created in reality more economically by excavating down within and around the medieval building platform to make a network of sunken paths on a north/south-east/west geometric grid, bounded by the church on the north and the east range on the west. The raised beds thus created were then revetted with low stone walls which were probably topped with a decorative coping and the exterior of the walls rendered and lime washed. The series of low beds stood about 45cm above the paths, which were given a slabbed surface. The shapes of the beds were strictly geometric, rectangular or square, save for a chamfer in one and a dog leg in another to avoid pre-existing structures. The grid thus established allowed a straight walk from the church south, or, from the dormitory east, to the riverside precinct walls. Little now survives of the precinct wall, but it is to be hoped that it continued to be in good repair until the dissolution as evidently it would have been much needed to keep the now sunken garden paths safe from flooding. The establishment of these sunken paths also necessitated the removal of one of the primary corner buttresses on the chapterhouse, which, given the insertion of the new heavy vault in that room, could be seen as a somewhat hazardous undertaking.

The main grid of garden beds established was within the rectangular area between the presbytery, the east range and the river. Eight beds of differing shapes made up this rectilinear pattern, their dimensions largely determined by the need to fit with pre-existing features such as doorways, buttresses and building projections in the east range. However, it is perhaps not insignificant that the dimensions of the beds fit into ratios of three : 12x12m, 6x12m and 6x3m. In addition to the eight beds in the main area, a ninth bed was added outside the east end of the presbytery, and a tenth outside, and to the south of, a late building which projected east from the east range. All in all the ten beds so far discovered covered an area of some 50x20m.

The raised beds generally appeared to have been simple in their form, the low white retaining walls having supported a flat bed of the form frequently seen in medieval manuscripts, often with cultivated areas incorporated within a grassed verge or planted with decorative small trees. Unfortunately, as the area had for so long since the dissolution and the degradation of the precinct wall been subject to flooding and tidal action, the soil cover on the great majority of the beds was virtually non-existent. The redeposited subsoil of the medieval building platform lay almost directly under the turf. The only exception to this was at the very western edge, where the collapse of the east-range roof had given a stratigraphically intact, though porous, layer of slate and mortar over the garden soil on three beds. It was doubly unfortunate, therefore, that environmental samples from this section of garden soil proved to be negative, the conditions apparently being unfavourable for either pollen or seed survival. The bed outside the east-range projection remains

Fig. 19 Part of medieval garden, with raised beds, under excavation.
(Crown copyright – Cadw: Welsh Historic Monuments).

unexcavated as yet, and there is perhaps one more chance for useful environmental retrieval.[9]

One bed proved to be an exception to the normal plan. This displayed a more complex arrangement with an opening through its west wall which led to an internal path around a small central bed. The narrow raised bed thus created on the western side seems to have been more structural with a mortar and stone fill between the stone walls and, it is suggested, may represent the base of a turf bench, again a familiar feature in depictions of medieval gardens. Until the discovery of the tenth bed to its west, this ornate bed was the nearest to the projecting building and was supposed to be the garden referred to in a document of the 1530s leasing a room above the church to the friar of Haverfordwest along with the garden belonging to that room.[10] Now that it is appreciated that the room in question had separate garden beds both to the east and south, it cannot be certain which garden it is that Friar Maurice Johns leased from Prior Thomas Rogers, not long before the dissolution. It is possible that the full excavation of the tenth bed may make this clearer.

It is almost certain, however, that this late lease refers to the small two storey block which projects from the east wall of the dormitory. It is a late addition with, probably, its own separate entrance, and tracery from a perpendicular window which lit the east wall, was found in the rubble-fill within the room. This window overlooks the garden to the east and, apart from those in the dormitory above, is the only window which does. The function of the building cannot be known for sure but it was clearly designed for additional accommodation for a single person requiring some privacy. One would imagine that the prior himself required a rather more spacious residence and perhaps the building was constructed from the start as guest accommodation.

No attempt was made to excavate into the building platform of which the garden beds were composed, nor below the mortar surface of the garden paths, a surface which showed impressions of the slabs with which they were floored. Accordingly, the hypothesis that this area was originally the priory cemetery was not tested. One grave, however, was found in a disturbed area under one of the paths, the later medieval excavation of the path line having almost cut into the skeleton. The revetment wall ran over the body at its pelvic region, and had slightly subsided into the looser grave fill. The skeleton was perfectly orthodox in position and had evidently been buried in a coffin as a coffin nail was found. It seems unlikely that this grave, so far from the church, was buried isolated and alone and it seems likely that excavation would reveal further burials. Whether this hypothetical cemetery was itself contained within a wall with pathways, which may thus have led to its ready adaptation to the formal gardens, can only be surmised.

While it was not part of our strategy to investigate graves, nonetheless excavation to the monastic ground level within and outside the church inevitably revealed grave cuts and within the church later disturbances had cut through burials. Within the church substantial numbers of graves were encountered, both those cut through the early floor and subsequently floored over with no memorial slab remaining, and those cut through the later floor and covered with grave slabs. Most of these stones had been robbed after the dissolution, but two complete slabs remained along with the shattered remains of several others. Another slab survived set into the eastern pavement of the cloister as well as the two within the chapter-house. All these prestigiously positioned graves would have been those of benefactors and their families. A number of humbler graves were found to have been cut outside the church to the west and east of the north transept, and the presence of children's graves among these leads to the reasonable supposition that this area was used as a town cemetery for the adjacent extra-mural suburb of *Parva Haverford*, a fair distance from the other medieval churches of the town. The only eccentricity amongst the burials at the priory was one evidently post-dissolution grave cut through step masonry in the presbytery. The body had no evidence of having had a coffin, was positioned only roughly east/west and was apparently rather unceremoniously laid out on one side, with the head unconventionally laid towards the east.

The priory buildings were at least partially enclosed by a precinct wall. Sections of this remain, built against the western slope to act as a revetment wall against unstable areas of cut bedrock as much as to enclose the priory on this steep slope. The wall stretches are discontinuous, and may always have been so, as they seem not to form a straight boundary. Slight footings of walling survive intermittently below ground level on the south and east where the river and creek would have run. It would be interesting to know whether the priory quay lay on this south side against the precinct wall. It would certainly have been a more convenient and private position, near the service buildings and away from the main stream of the river to the east. Excavations on the present river side merely established that the medieval river bank had been washed away, repeated post-medieval tidal inundations having removed part of the medieval building platform as well as any medieval constructions which may have stood at the river bank. From the late nineteenth century onwards, river and tidal erosion ceased and there began an episode of silting caused by the establishment of the town weir, the new railway and road embankments and episodes of riverside dumping. This brought the bank out again into the stream, curiously enough, nearer to where it had been during the life of the priory. Priory Marsh, the extensive area of wetland on the river side to the south-east of Haverfordwest, still retains an isolated finger south of the priory, albeit hemmed in now by the embankments but still fed from run-off from higher land to the south and west. What seems to

Fig. 20 Reconstruction drawing of the Priory.
(Crown copyright – Cadw: Welsh Historic Monuments).

have been an open creek of water to the south of the priory precinct wall has largely silted up, and is now discernible only as a sunken area free from any vestigial traces of buildings.

The north wall of the church may have formed its own boundary to the outside world. What may be the remnants of a gate through the wall survive against the bank to the west of the nave and a cobbled road passed through this skirting the main priory buildings on the west and leading to the kitchens and service buildings on the south of the main complex. A smaller gate originally lay to the east of the church through the slight wall which ran from the presbytery wall towards the river, but this was made redundant when the ninth garden bed was raised to the east of the church and the opening was blocked. Whether or not a separate gatehouse and extension of the precinct wall lay on the north on the town side is unknown. Two later houses stand on either side of the modern entrance to the site, and either might lie on, or incorporate stonework from, a gate.

This description of the Haverfordwest Priory shows it to have been unremarkable in size or layout both in terms of Augustinian houses and Welsh monastic houses in general. Its position, just by the side of the thriving, busy mercantile settlement of Haverfordwest is characteristic of Augustinian houses in England and Wales, though the popularity of the Augustinian order in Wales was limited.[11] The two west Wales monasteries at the Anglo-Norman towns of Carmarthen and Haverfordwest, were similarly positioned and perhaps typical of the order as a whole, though Carmarthen itself was a conversion from the Benedictines. Neither house, however, was typical of the order's handful of houses in Wales. Llanthony, in the south-east, was a remote house far from any settlement, the tiny house at St Kynemark's near Chepstow remains obscure, while the cluster of isolated houses in north-west Wales were incorporated within the order by the late transfer of previous Celtic establishments to the Augustinians.

The history of the priory at Haverfordwest also is unremarkable. Though the foundation charter is lost, the date of its establishment must be around 1200, as a later charter confirming the grant of land refers to the founder being Robert fitzTancred. Giraldus Cambrensis makes no mention of the priory in 1188 though he visited the castle. Certainly nothing from the excavation record makes a date of 1200 unlikely. The norm for a moderately-sized Augustinian priory like Haverfordwest would have been thirteen canons – the houses of regular canons were generally more modest establishments than those of other orders – and there is no reason to suppose that Haverfordwest would have deviated substantially from the norm. Characteristically, numbers had slumped drastically by the dissolution when the prior and only two canons remained, though apparently four priests (not canons) were maintained, presumably to minister to its appropriated livings. Undoubtedly numbers had fluctuated through the 340 years of the priory's existence, due to a variety of external forces, but it is worth noting that at neighbouring Carmarthen twelve canons had apparently been resident until just before the 1536 visitation.

Both Haverfordwest and Carmarthen priories were urban communities as far as the term could be used in medieval Wales. Certainly Carmarthen priory owned considerable properties in the old and new town, and though less evidence survives for Haverfordwest it seems likely that it was from properties within *Parva Haverford* that the prior would have earned much of his income. All the priory lands lay within the cantref of Rhos – good sheep-farming land, though there are no figures for livestock for the priory in the 1291 valuation.[12] Among these lands were the grange of Cokey and the Manor of Green both fairly close to the monastery.[13]

Spiritualities were derived from the appropriation of churches within the town. Haverfordwest priory had been granted the churches of St Thomas, St Mary and St Martin at its foundation and the churches had certainly been appropriated by the mid-thirteenth century. By the end of that century the churches at Camrose, Llanstadwell, St Ishmaels, Dale and Haroldston had also been acquired. Omissions in the valuation in the 1291 result in our being unable to assess the income derived from the spiritualities, though it was clearly an important factor and by 1535 temporal revenue was below 30 per cent of total income for the house.[14] Augustinian canons had from the first been able to serve parish churches and it is possible that their own canons served in these churches. However, this practice became increasingly rare as communities became smaller and as early as 1256 the Haverfordwest canons obtained a papal indulgence to quash the vicarage ordained in their church of St Martin so that the church might be served by chaplains rather than their own members.[15] By the dissolution, four priests were maintained by the monastery to serve their appropriated churches.

Like all Augustinian houses, Haverfordwest priory was virtually autonomous. Though subject to the authority of the diocese, the Augustinians had no means of exercising a uniformity of observance. However in 1284 Archbishop Pecham undertook a visitation of Welsh dioceses as a means of exercising the authority of Canterbury over the Welsh church.[16] As luck would have it, the injunction for Haverfordwest is one of only five to survive for the two southern dioceses. Pecham noted irregularities in financial affairs and recommended improvements in auditing accounts, but this was probably not an indication of serious failings in the house. The recommendations were common to all five houses, a part of a general process for tightening of financial regulation which the modern reader will probably only too wearily recognize. More particular to Haverfordwest was his exhortation to the prior to show his presence more to the community at church and at mealtimes and spend less time entertaining his guests. Reading between the lines, the injunction suggests that lay people were being allowed into priory buildings rather too easily and meat was eaten rather oftener than the rule dictated.

The valuations of Haverfordwest show it to have been a moderately-sized house with a small but quite viable income. It appears to have been spared the vicissitudes of political fortunes meted out to so many other monastic houses in Wales and was never damaged by war or accident. It seems to have enjoyed the period of increased prosperity in the fifteenth century common to other houses in Wales,[17] for this was the period of the insertion of the tower in the church, the remodelling of chapter-house and cloister and the establishment of the gardens. The dissolution, however, brought the life of the priory to an end in 1536 along with the large majority of monasteries in Wales.

Excavations have revealed interesting insights into the methods employed by the dismantlers of monastic houses. After the removal of the portable items, such as the plate, of which Haverfordwest had a modest though respectable 94oz,[18] the lead was stripped from the windows and melted down in makeshift moulds. The extraordinary survival not only of one of the moulds set into the church floor but also of one of the ingots already stamped with the rose and crown stamp and awaiting transportation from the site, brings this process vividly to life at Haverfordwest. The tracery and dressed bathstone was removed from walls, the dressings roughly broken off, and the main blocks taken away for reuse. The circular mark left in the tiled floor under the tower when a bell dropped down again helps one picture the scene of destruction. Reusable slabs were systematically robbed from the nave floor, the western pavement of the cloister and the garden paths. The collapse of the roof happened shortly after this desecration of the building and subsequently sections of the walls seem to have been systematically robbed of stonework.

At the dissolution, both the priory and friary at Haverfordwest along with the knights' estates at Slebech and the Tironian house at Pill were purchased from the Crown by Roger and Thomas Barlow, brothers of William, bishop of St David's.[19] The priory site was never developed or built upon. It survived mostly as an open space through the centuries, used periodically for smithying and tanning, and for opportunistic stone-robbing, but largely left alone, grazed by animals, the stonework neglected under a mantle of vegetation.

Fenton, in the early nineteenth century, describes the 'grove of masts' belonging to the dockyard that grew up on the river adjacent to the priory[20] while we know from excavations that a smithy was built in the nave, and what is probably the smith's house still squats against the chancel wall, built probably to service the dockyard nearby. Yard surfaces, post-medieval boundaries and fence lines and a series of pits in and around the north transept and the cloister, some of which contained the carcasses of domestic animals, suggests a late usage as a tanner's yard. Ramshackle blockings of the west-range doorways into the cloister and apparently late subdivisions of the west range, along with the evident continuation of use and repair of the roadway outside the west range, suggests the adaptation of this range for low-status domestic use, perhaps for the accommodation of workers attached to the tannery. Later, the construction of a substantial stone surfaced roadway running across the sunken and presumably boggy area of the cloister from north to south rendered the western roadway redundant, but this later road continued in use until recent years as a public footpath, albeit with its substantial cobbled surface hidden from view beneath vegetation.

Since the completion of excavations, the site has been laid out for public display. The archaeological work on the priory has given us a clear indication in most areas of the materials of which medieval floors and surfaces were constructed. Accordingly it was decided that we should, wherever possible, use appropriate modern surfaces which would reflect both the medieval construction and the status of the different areas of the buildings. Inevitably there were constraints upon us, largely dictated by the new use, as a public open space, to which the site would be given. The surfaces therefore had to be able to withstand weather and the passage of feet without wearing away or becoming lethally slippery or waterlogged. The medieval floors themselves were far too flimsy to endure even a few years of exposure, and it was decided to raise floor levels over the entire site by some 150mm, burying the original surfaces with protective layers of terram, sand and chippings. Over this, floors that had originally been tiled received a surface of lime concrete set into diagonal bays subdivided by stone edging to reflect the mortar bed into which the tiles were set and the diagonal pattern in which they were laid. Slabbed surfaces were set with new stone, the layout of the slabs reflecting as far as was possible, the original pattern. In the nave, for example, where some slabs had survived along with considerable lengths of their impressions in the mortar bed, the layout could be quite faithful to the original. The slabs in the church were fine slate, while the western pavement of the cloister was paved with random slabs of local stone and this difference again was reflected in our choice of different stone types for the different areas.

The discovery of the medieval garden outside the priory, exciting though this was, presented us with a difficulty in that the site became very cramped, in terms of presentation; indeed part of one of the garden beds lay outside the property boundary altogether. Consequently it was decided to purchase a small area of land alongside the road embankment to allow public access all around the garden, and to give the garden beds a *cordon sanitaire* so that the priory could be viewed in its entirety from the riverside and from the south. While we have to accept that the ugly road bridge can never be disguised, we hope that our tree-planting along the riverside may serve to soften its impact. It is hoped that the final layout of the ruins and their interpretation will be a real asset to the town of Haverfordwest. It should complement the castle and the three medieval churches in the town and, we trust, will contribute to the appreciation of the historical dimension and the sense of place, of this remarkable west Wales town.

SIÂN REES

THE CHURCHES AND CHAPELS

THE CHURCHES

By the end of the thirteenth century there were three parish churches in Haverfordwest and, indicative of the early wealth of the town, the churches all have well-developed plans, complete with single aisles and towers. The architecture of all three churches provides no help in establishing the date of their foundation, as medieval Haverfordwest had a wealthy and growing population ensuring that all three churches were soon rebuilt and enlarged. It is possible that parts of St Mary's and St Martin's contain Norman work, but this is far from certain. Structurally, the earliest work that can be dated with confidence is the fine Early English arcade of St Mary's, built in about 1220. St Martin's seems to have been rebuilt in the fourteenth century, with some carved work typical of that period. Both St Mary's and St Martin's underwent remodelling in the early years of the sixteenth century, when the south aisle was added at St Martin's, and St Mary's was completely transformed by the addition of the clerestory with the fine carved oak roof, achieving almost cathedral status in its opulence.

In common with virtually every church in Wales, the hand of the restorer is all too evident. This is especially true of St Thomas's, which was rebuilt in the seventeenth century, and rebuilt again in 1853-5, leaving only the tower and part of the south wall intact. St Martin's was in a dire state of repair by 1862, when an extensive restoration was begun under C. E. Giles of London, which was largely completed by 1865. St Mary's was restored several times: in 1844 (Thomas Rowlands), 1860-63 (W. H. Lindsay), 1863-64 (C. E. Giles), 1882-89 (Ewan Christian), and 1903-05 (W. D. Caröe).

The Victorian zest for church restoration was founded in the Anglican Revival, which was embodied in the establishment of the Oxford Movement and the Ecclesiological Society in the 1830s which set out to recreate a church that was concerned with spirituality and its expression through ritual, rather than with social and political influence. The Ecclesiologists, who published their own journal, centred their arguments on re-establishing the Gothic style as the only suitable one for church restoration and building. For two centuries previous to this, new churches tended to be plain inside and, where funds allowed, detail was inclined to be classical. Repairs to medieval churches were nearly always of a destructive and makeshift variety: indeed, from the late eighteenth century, various commentators noted that virtually all of the medieval features of St Martin's had been destroyed over the years. As late as 1839-40 Thomas Rowlands destroyed the capitals of the chancel arch to install a flat plaster ceiling, and his work at St Mary's in 1844 was strongly criticized by *The Ecclesiologist*, which noted the poor seating and the quality of the repairs to the east window. Conversely, in 1867, the same periodical was warm in its praise of the works at St Martin's, complimenting C. E. Giles on his 'unpretentious' restoration.

The conservation of medieval church architecture began to be practised following the formation of the Society for the Protection of Ancient Buildings in 1877. Before then, some of the Victorian architects' zeal for restoration knew no bounds: both W. H. Lindsay and C. E. Giles wanted to get rid of the low thirteenth-century tower at St Mary's and replace it with a grand tower more suited to a county town. Ewan Christian's work at St Mary's, however, saw the careful preservation of old features wherever possible, while W. D. Caröe, in 1903-5, painstakingly removed centuries of limewash from the arcade, bringing to life once again the magnificent carved capitals.

St Martin's Church

St Martin's, the oldest of the three medieval churches in the town, was located within the early twelfth century settlement of Castleton. St Martin of Tours was one of the more popular saints in the early Norman period and many churches were dedicated to him. Nothing is left of the original structure, however, and the medieval detail that does survive indicates that the church was rebuilt in the early fourteenth century, the surviving carved work of which is of high quality. The font, often the only twelfth-century survival in a Pembrokeshire church, has been restored and repaired so as to make its dating tentative.

The early part of the fourteenth century, falling within the Decorated period of Gothic architecture, when medieval church architecture was at its most flamboyant, saw a flurry of church-building in the county and traditionally this is associated with the activity of Henry de Gower, Bishop of St David's 1328-47, who built the splendidly carved stone pulpitum at the cathedral and enlarged the Bishop's Palace on a scale unparalleled elsewhere in south-west Wales. Fortunately, a large amount of Decorated work has survived drastic restoration at St Martin's and enables one to ascertain the fourteenth-century plan of the church, consisting of nave, chancel and south porch, the latter being absorbed within the north aisle, built some two centuries later. That the porch is part of the fourteenth-century church is indicated by the fine Decorated niches, one on each side of the inner door, both with trefoiled arches and ogee heads. The sedilia is also fourteenth-century with ogee-shaped arches on hexagonal colonettes, which have circular bases. Typical of this date, and richer still, is the piscina alongside, which has ball-flower decoration and a crocketted ogee surround. The main surviving feature of the fourteenth-century church, however, is the fine tall chancel arch, which has three groups of small filleted and keel-shaped roll-mouldings. The capitals were destroyed in 1840, when a plaster ceiling was installed.

Late in the fourteenth or, maybe, early in the fifteenth century, the tower was built on to the north-western corner of the nave, rather than at its west end. The slender tapering tower is typical of towers of this date in the county, except that it has a spire. Although the present spire is of 1870, and is some fifteen feet higher than its predecessor, it appears that the tower originally had a saddleback, or steeply gabled, roof. According to information given by Henry Mathias to Edward Laws in 1888,[1] the spire was raised on top of the original saddleback roof, suggesting that it was a feature added at a later date. Saddleback towers are rare in south-west Wales: they were originally found at Castlemartin and Pendine churches, but such towers are more frequently encountered further east, in Glamorgan.[2]

The early sixteenth century saw the addition of the south aisle, separated from the nave by two arches and by a single arch from the chancel. The present arcade was rebuilt in 1862-5, but in the respond of the eastern arch is a fine Tudor arched hagioscope, or squint window, allowing a view of the altar from the aisle. The Tudor arch is typically sixteenth-century, as is the less typical carved bowl set below the hagioscope, with a rose on its underside. According to some,[3] this is a piscina, but its position is unorthodox. Henry Mathias referred to it as a stoup in 1888,[4] which is more likely, even if its location remains rather unusual. The date of the aisle is confirmed by the Tudor-headed arch into the chancel and the (restored) Perpendicular east window. The aisle incorporated the fourteenth-century porch at its west end, above which a priest's room was added, reached originally from a stair in the corner of the aisle, traces of which remain.

From the seventeenth century, the church entered a period of decay. Thomas Beaufort in 1779 referred to St Martin's as 'a large, old, ugly wretched church',[5] and Fenton, in 1810, noted that the nave was 'plain roofed', but of the windows 'there is no judging either of their size, shape or former tracery, as many are entirely stopped, and most, if not all of them contracted and otherwise transformed.'[6] Samuel Lewis noted in 1833 that the church had 'suffered so extensively by the insertion of windows and other alterations that little of its original character remains.' He also noted the existence of 'ancient' stalls in the chancel.[7] Apart from the alteration of several windows, there is no evidence of alterations made in the post-Reformation years, but it is likely that box pews and a double-decker pulpit were installed. In 1839 plans were made to carry out a scheme for reseating, including a gallery, and the building of a ceiling, under the superintendence of the architect Thomas Rowlands.[8] The gallery was not built, however, and work was restricted to erecting new pews. By now, the vicar was bemoaning the wretched state of the church,[9] as the roof had partly fallen in and the walls were in a poor state. Moreover, the tower was structurally unsafe and, despite spending £194 on building a buttress to prevent its collapse, the spire remained in a dangerous condition.[10] Matters reached a head by 1861, when an appeal was launched for the restoration of the church.[11] Work began in the following year by adding new roofs with steeper pitches, a new north chancel aisle, and new windows and furnishings. Initially it was intended to retain and repair the old nave arcade,[12] The architect was C. E. Giles of London, the builder John Davies of Haverfordwest; the clerk of works was Jesse Harvey of the Paper Mills.[13] During the restoration work, Sunday services were held in the National Schoolroom at Barn Street. On 28th September 1865 the church was reopened by Bishop Thirlwall of St David's,[14] the work having cost £2,000,[15] and it is evident that the appearance of the present church owes much to the work done then, described as 'an unpretentious and therefore pleasing restoration.'[16]

In many ways, the restoration was typical of the day, with the use of the early Decorated or Geometric style for the new windows of the nave and chancel, and an arch-braced roof for the nave together with a scissor-truss roof for the chancel. The plain open pews were installed, the large bathstone pulpit erected, and the font repaired and retooled. After some debate, the capitals of the chancel arch, destroyed by the 1840 ceiling were replaced with continuous mouldings to match the existing ones, rather than attempt a replacement of the lost capitals, an unusually careful step for church restoration of this date.

Despite fears about its safety, attention was not focused on the spire until 1866 when builders were invited to tender for its rebuilding.[17] The 'foundation stone' of the new spire was not laid until August 1869,[18] with Jesse Harvey again acting as supervisor, Giles and Robinson of London as architects and W. Payne of Milford Haven as builder. The structure was to be some 15 feet higher than the previous one, thus making it 47 feet in height, and built of limestone, with Forest of Dean stone bands. However, the days when the tower had to be rescued from collapse were not forgotten and a correspondent to the *Haverfordwest and Milford Telegraph* of 6 April 1870 advised that it would be unwise to add further weight to the tower. The contractor withdrew his services and it was left to Stephen Lewis, builder and monumental mason of Haverfordwest,[19] to complete the work on the spire that has graced Haverfordwest townscape ever since.

Attention now turned to improving the interior. The east window, depicting Christ with Saint Martin and Saint David, was installed in about 1880, and the south window was placed in the aisle in 1893 in memory of Revd Howard Leeds, chaplain at Pembroke Dock, who often visited St Martins, and died after falling from his horse, was designed by C. Godfrey Gray of Cambridge[20] In 1895, also as a memorial to the Rev. Leeds, the chancel was painted with frescoes by Godfrey Gray, who specialised in wall paintings depicting Biblical narratives and whose frescoes survive at Monkton Priory.[21] The incumbent from 1888 to 1907, Revd Martin Phelps, decorated the church with murals and frescoes, adding an inscription over the chancel arch, but his successor, Revd Arthur Baring Gould, removed much of this work, replacing the frescoes with 'honest whitewash', and also a reredos, erected in 1890, which he described as an 'aesthetic outrage'. The chancel screen, which Baring Gould believed to have been 'more suitable for supporting runner beans' had been taken down before his arrival.

Since the nineteenth century St Martin's has had a reputation for its High Anglican ritual. The Stations of the Cross in the nave were purchased in 1895 from a manufacturer in Munich.[22] The porch screen was set up in 1903 by Hugh Thomas, architect.[23]

In 1909, the south aisle was made into a Lady Chapel in memory of the late Revd Phelps,[24] which meant removing the Father Smith organ of 1704 (previously at St Davids Cathedral and installed here in 1881), from the aisle to the west end of the nave. The south-east window in the new Lady Chapel was erected by Heaton, Butler and Bayne, and the Gothic screen was by H. P. Thomas, architect.[25] The east window in the chapel, depicting the Virgin Mary, Mary Magdalene, Christ and Saint John was designed by Morris and Son of Merton Abbey in 1921.[26]

A modern addition to the church is the concrete and glass sculpture of the Virgin and Child by Stephen Sykes, who had worked at Coventry Cathedral.

A thirteenth-, or fourteenth-century coffin lid is inscribed with an elaborate floriated Latin cross. Of the other monuments, the best is that to Thomas Lloyd, of Danyrallt, who died in 1722: a small pedimented tablet, beautifully lettered, and with a shield above bearing his coat of arms.

St Mary's Church

St Mary's was probably founded towards the end of the twelfth century and although no datable features of the period survive, it is possible that the north wall of the church contains early masonry. The church was extensively rebuilt in about 1220 with a long nave, chancel and north aisle, together with a tower. The windows on the south side of the church appear to date from the later thirteenth century.

The west window, a triple lancet, the colonettes inside with bell-type capitals, is of the Early English period of Gothic architecture.

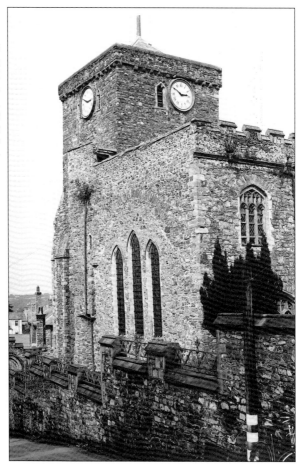

Fig. 21 St Mary's Church, showing gable line of original nave and thirteenth-century lancets.
(*Crown copyright: Royal Commission on the Ancient and Historical Monuments of Wales*).

There seems little doubt that the tower, which has a corbelled parapet and low added angle buttresses, also belongs to the early thirteenth century. In a county where towers date largely from the fourteenth and particularly the fifteenth century, the tower at St Mary's may well be among the earliest. The tower was capped by a timber spire until 1802,. The newel stair in the south west corner of the tower is a clumsy addition, probably added in the early sixteenth century, when the impressive lierne vault was added to the ground floor chamber.

The east window is puzzling. It consists of three lights, with quatrefoils in three roundels above. The detail within the arches with deep roll mouldings is early-thirteenth-century work, but the exterior appears to be an eccentric refacing of 1844, replacing what was probably a plate-traceried window. More unusual are the windows on the south side of the church, especially those in the chancel, each having two lights with an almost separated foiled circle above. These windows appear to date from the mid-to-late thirteenth century. This dating is strange, following so close to the splendid rebuilding of the church some three or four decades earlier. A possible explanation, which supports the notion that the north wall of the church is pre-thirteenth-century, is that the rewindowing of this part of the church was left until later, by which time the Geometric traceried window had replaced the commonplace plate-traceried ones.

The thirteenth-century work within the church is of a richness almost unparalleled elsewhere in south Wales, and is more exuberant than the Early English work at Llandaff Cathedral. The splendid arcade owes its origins not to any Welsh 'school' of masons but directly to the sculptors of the West Country centred on Glastonbury Abbey and Wells Cathedral, which may reflect the cultural interchange resulting from the sea-trade between Bristol and Haverfordwest and Tenby, where the fifteenth-century rebuilding of the church in the latter produced a building more akin to a West Country church than anything in Wales. The stone of the aisle and chancel arch was apparently imported from Brittany.[27] The arcade in the nave is four bays long with lavishly carved capitals and hood mouldings on head stops, as at Wells Cathedral. The piers are broadly cross-shaped with triple shafts in the cardinal directions, the middle shafts filleted. Between, are deep hollows and single shafts, the latter with continuous capitals, like the diagonals of the piers at Wells. The middle pier varies, being hexagonal in cross section, with no strong cardinal accents. The arches have three groups of deep roll mouldings, some with fillets. The capitals are of outstanding quality and, as at Wells, they mix stiff-leaf with profane subjects, including grotesque intertwined beasts, a pig playing a fiddle, an ape playing a harp and a lamb biting a serpent's head. The chancel arcade is of two bays, the pier with plain detached shafts and filleted ones between, the former painted black at some later date to imitate Purbeck Marble. The capitals are similar to these in the nave, including a figure with a pitcher, representing the thirsty soul. The eastern arch was added when the aisle was extended in the early sixteenth century, built in the style of the earlier arcades to match, but the carving is of much lower quality, the capitals with stylised foliage and flowers. The chancel arch is also *c*.1220, a fine and lofty structure, triple-shafted, with rich stiff-leaf capitals and deep roll mouldings in the arch itself: the trefoil-headed piscina in the chancel is of the same date.

At the beginning of the sixteenth century, St Mary's was transformed by the addition of the battlemented clerestory to nave and chancel and the lengthening eastwards of the aisle, which was given large panel traceried Perpendicular windows. Much of this work was built in local brown sandstone, showing well the former gable of the chancel, which is built of grey limestone. No doubt the stonework was lime-rendered and probably limewashed also, the present stonework having been stripped and repointed early in the nineteenth century. The clerestory allowed light to flood into the church, as did the large new windows on the north side. The church was completely reroofed in oak, that in the nave of shallow pitch, with large carved bosses at the intersections of heavily moulded beams: this may have been inspired by the fine oak roof, of a similar date, at St David's Cathedral. The roof rests on carved spandrels, supported on carved head corbels, female on the north and male on the south. At this date also, the ground floor chamber of the tower was given its impressive lierne vault.

With the creation of such a splendid church, it is not surprising that little new work was required until the eighteenth century. According to a plaque in the aisle, the roof was repaired in 1745, when it is likely that the chancel roof was largely reconstructed. as,

Fig. 22 St Mary's Church: arcade.
    (Crown copyright: Royal Commission on the Ancient and Historical Monuments of Wales).

after it had been restored in 1889, it was noted that the roof had been replaced some 150 years previously.[28] During this work, the remains of leadwork belonging to the original thirteenth-century roof were found to be still in excellent condition. In addition, a window was discovered in the north wall of the chancel, confirming that it predated the extension of the aisle.

In 1737 a west gallery was constructed, housing the organ. In 1797 the church, like St Martin's and St Thomas's, was used as a prison for French troops following the Fishguard invasion, and a contemporary account stated that the troops had 'wholly destroyed the inside of the church'.[29]

In 1802, the spire was demolished, largely to please Lady Kensington, who feared that it was about to fall onto her house nearby.[30] The churchwardens commissioned two structural reports, one by Griffith Watkins, architect, the other by John Webb and William Gwilliam, surveyors, following which it was resolved to remove the spire and sell the materials so as to build a new spire or cupola.[31] This was not done, however, and the tower retains its shorn appearance, despite several attempts to give the church a much more civic appearance, either by building a taller tower, or adding a spire.

At some stage, possibly in the early eighteenth century, the piers and capitals of the arcade were completely plastered over and the underlying riches were not revealed until some schoolboys accidentally knocked some plaster off in 1843.[32] Fenton noted that the capitals were 'almost hid and fairly blunted by vile whitewash, the incrustation of frequent daubings for several centuries'.[33]

In November 1843, a subscription fund was set up to carrry out a programme of restoraion[34] and plans for repairs, including the insertion of a new west gallery, were drawn up by the architect Thomas Rowlands.[35] As well as the gallery, new pews were planned, together with the restoration of the east window 'of exceedingly rich tracery and stained glass . . . destroyed by a thunderstorm many years ago'.[36]

Fig. 23 St Mary's Church: grotesque on capital of pillar showing an ape playing a harp.

(Crown copyright: Royal Commission on Ancient and Historical Monuments of Wales).

The church reopened on 30th August 1844, prior to completion, when it was noted that 'more than half the church's architectural beauties, hidden for ages [beneath the plaster and limewash] have been brought to light' and that the east window of the chancel had been restored and fitted up with stained glass, which was later replaced, in 1893.[37]

The Ecclesiologist, the vanguard of good taste in church-building reported in 1847 that the east window was poorly restored and that the pews were not all properly orientated to face the altar,[38] showing the slow influence of the Oxford Movement in west Wales. William Owen, the architect-improver of Haverfordwest, later stated that he had produced a 'model' for the improvement of the church and the reinstatement of the spire at about this time.[39] This suggests that the reinstatement of the spire may have formed part of the nineteenth-century improvements of the town.

In 1859 money was raised to carry out a major restoration, including the demolition of the old town council chamber which was located above the north porch, at a cost of £1,600.[40] By 1860 it had been decided to demolish the tower and to rebuild it twenty two feet higher in a Perpendicular style so as to give the church a 'minster-like appearance', plans for which were prepared by the architect W. H. Lindsay. In addition, the north and east walls of the churchyard were to be rebuilt, with a new entrance from High Street. The estimated cost was £1,800.[41] A lithograph of the church showing the proposed work was published, copies of which were given out as prizes at a fundraising bazaar held at Picton Castle in June 1860.[42] By the summer of 1861, it had been agreed to demolish the old town council chamber,[43] but as not enough funds could be raised, the improvements to the churchyard wall were carried out, and the tower was left untouched. The north porch was demolished and rebuilt in a vigorous Early English style in 1863, by which time Lindsay had died, and the work was carried out by C. E. Giles, then working on St Martin's Church. The old porch was an extraordinary affair surmounted by the town council chamber which oddly resembled a two-storeyed house grafted onto the church and reached by a vast flight of steps. Giles had bigger plans, however and wished to add a tall broach spire to the tower, reopening the blocked tower arch from the nave to expose the vaulted chamber to view and forming a small baptistery within.[44] A lithograph was published of the intended work, which shows a new tower, with large paired belfry lights, capped with a broach spire with polychromic stone bands.[45] The accompanying report about the interior of the church at that time reveals that the arcades were still painted, the seats consisted of 'common modern pews without even a central passage', while in the chancel, the fittings had been removed and the floor levels altered. It is small wonder that, with such obvious improvements needed within the church, the proposal to rebuild the tower was abandoned once again.

In 1876, a proposal was made to move the organ from the west gallery into the body of the church.[46] Whether or not it was moved at this stage is uncertain, but it was certainly located in the aisle by 1889.

In 1881, yet again, plans for restoration work and alterations were prepared by the architect T. P. Reynolds[47] and a structural report commissioned from Ewan Christian of London[48] who had been architectural advisor to the Ecclesiastical Commissioners since 1850. In 1884, tenders were invited for the restoration of the north aisle and north clerestory.[49] The restroration at the north aisle, reopened in the summer of 1886 at a cost of £1,600, being part of a programme of works estimated to cost £5,000.[50] In the next year, a new clock, made by Messrs Joyce of Whitchurch who had supplied the clock for St David's Cathedral, was placed on the tower, at the expense of the Trustees of Perrot's Charity.[51]

The restoration of the chancel, begun in 1887 under Ewan Christian was completed in 1889.[52] The roof had been extensively restored and the organ moved to its present location, where it was repaired and enlarged. It was noted that the organ had been erected in 1737, new pipes added in 1825, and was enlarged *c*.1860, retaining the original oak case. New furnishings included the present oak choir stalls, and a brass lectern, the latter by Hardman & Co.[53]

In 1893, the old charnel house, which stood to the north of the church, was demolished. The building was of two storeys, the lower storey barrel vaulted, and it had been used as a police station since 1851, when William Owen drew up plans to improve the structure.[54] The present north gate to the churchyard is actually a doorway salvaged from the charnel house and restored in 1912,[55] its detail, including small filleted rolls, indicating a fourteenth-century date.

By the turn of the century, the only unrestored part of the church was the nave and in 1903-5 a restoration scheme was carried out under W. D. Caröe, architect to the Ecclesiastical Commissioners. The roof was completely restored: the arcade cleaned and repaired; the floor renewed, and new pews together with an elaborately carved pulpit installed.[56] Work was halted in 1907 for want of funds, leaving the restoration of the chancel arch, the clerestory and nave windows to complete.[57] The west window was restored by Caröe in 1912[58] and, thereafter, the main additions to the church were several stained glass windows.

The earliest monument in the church is the defaced medieval figure of a pilgrim, the three scalloped shells on his scrip indicating that he had been to the shrine of St James at Campostella during the fifteenth century. Of several seventeenth-century monuments, two are of special note. The first is the brass to John Davids, who was mayor in 1642 and who died in 1651, which has fine lettering, and fashionable rusticated arches over a figure at prayer and a quartered shield. The second is to William Browne, mayor in 1665, who died in 1678, which has Ionic pilasters and a broken pediment containing a large winged cherub's head. The outstanding monument of the eighteenth century, signed by Christopher Horsnaile of London, is that of Sir John Philipps, Bart., of Picton, who died in 1736. This has free-standing composite columns with carved putti upon the pediment above, one clutching his temple almost in disbelief, and over the monument are suspended the funeral hatchments, the helm with visor uplifted and lambrequin. The sheer quality of this monument can be seen to best effect when compared with the most elaborate nineteenth-century memorial in the church, that to Sir Richard Philipps, Bart., the first Lord Milford and mayor of the town in 1766, who died in 1823, which was executed by J. Phillips of Haverfordwest. This is an ambitious piece of work, but it is over-large and disproportionate in its elements, which consist of urn-topped Corinthian columns flanking a huge shield. Other monuments of the nineteenth century range from the Greek style favoured by the 1820s, as on that of Joseph Maurice (died 1824) to the later Gothic style, as in the tablet commemorating Sir Richard Bulkeley Philipps, Bart., the second Lord Milford, who died in 1857.

St Mary's contains some very fine stained glass windows,

particularly of the period 1893-1930. Earliest however is that on the south side of the chancel, an instructive piece of early Gothic Revival glass of 1843, typically highly coloured. Even more vivid is the window of 1864 on the south side of the nave, by one of the prominent makers of the period, William Wailes. This depicts miracles of healing, the strong black-line drawing typical of High-Victorian glass. In contrast are the later windows, which look to the richness of late-medieval stained glass both in Britain and the Netherlands. In contrast to the earlier glass, the colours and modelling of figures became much softer. The master of this style was C. E. Kempe, whose firm was extremely prolific even after his death in 1907. The great east window of 1893 is by Kempe, based on Netherlandish late-medieval models, depicting the life of Christ in beautiful muted colours, the detail of the shading and line-work magnificently detailed. After Kempe died, the firm was continued by W. E. Tower: many of the windows in the church are signed with Kempe's wheatsheaf motif, with a superimposed tower for his successor. Although none match the east window in quality, some are extremely striking, such as that of 1910 on the south side of the nave showing Christ with Mary Magdalene, with rich deep colours and finely painted landscape backgrounds. The firm was changing to the use of less dense backgrounds and architectural surrounds in the south chancel window of 1929, of Saint Teilo and Saint Justinian, where much more clear glass is used. Later glass includes that of 1952 in the chancel by Powell and Co., depicting the Annunciation in harsh acid colours, with the use of a great deal of clear glass background, all features typical of that period. Latest of all is the west window of the aisle depicting Saint David, installed by Celtic Studios of Swansea in 1965, which is modern in its harsh and dominant black leading and elongated figure drawing.

Perhaps one of the most unusual features of the church is the free-standing stoup, probably of about 1500, which has a cusped square bowl upon a pedestal with colonettes. Of a similar date, or slightly earlier are the carved bench-ends, one depicting St Michael triumphing over Satan, the Archangel as usual with two pairs of wings and a sword.

The organ is early eighteenth century. It was given new pipes in 1825 and removed from the west end of the church to the north side of the chancel by Messrs Hill and Son in 1889. The original front faces the north aisle and the great diapasons speak into the chancel. The organ is much larger than any other in the county, with the exception of that at St David's Cathedral.[59]

St Thomas's Church.

The church was founded at a date following the canonization of Thomas à Becket, to whom it is dedicated, and before 1210, when it is first mentioned. The oldest remnant may be a part of the south wall towards the eastern end of the nave where the wall is unusually thick and may be of the thirteenth century. The tower is plain and typical of several built in the county during the fifteenth century, a date confirmed by the polygonal stair turret on the north side and the simple Perpendicular belfry windows, which although restored, are similar to those at St Peter's Church, Johnston. In Pembrokeshire, the use of traceried belfry windows is extremely unusual, the more common form being rectangular or plain arched lights. Typically also of Pembrokeshire church towers, the base of the tower is barrel vaulted in stone, a practice probably employed to strengthen a tall slender structure.

The church consists of a long and narrow nave with north aisle, north porch and chancel, the latter with an organ chamber and a vestry to its north. Virtually nothing is known of the appearance of the church previous to its effective rebuilding in 1854-5 and in 1880-1. According to a letter written by Henry Mathias in 1888,[60] the church was all demolished and rebuilt in the seventeenth century, save the tower and south wall of the nave. This was confirmed by when the congregation were preparing to undertake restoration work in 1851 by a report stating that 'the body of the church was rebuilt in comparatively recent times in the worst style and taste'.[61] While digging graves on the north side of the church, the footings of a north aisle were discovered[62] and the new work contemplated was the reinstatement of this feature, which in the event was not realised until 1880-8.

In summary, the pre-seventeenth-century church consisted of a nave, north aisle, chancel and tower. The tower, and possibly the aisle, may have been secondary additions. Except for the tower and south wall of the nave, the church was demolished in the seventeenth century and replaced with a smaller structure without its aisle. A late-eighteenth-century view of the church shows a considerably lower chancel than the present one.

The need for greater accommodation was apparent by 1820, when a gallery was built within the church, at the west end, to seat 175 persons, the plans for which survive at Lambeth Palace Library.[63] The certificate of completion was signed by G. Madox, probably a builder from Tenby, but the architect was Joseph Mathias. Shortly after this, the west door and window of the tower were inserted, in the Perpendicular style. In 1851, the church was in a poor state of repair,[64] and plans for restoration, which included the reinstatement of the north aisle, were drawn up by an 'experienced architect' who may have been E. M. Goodwin of London who, with his partner H. E. Coe, was responsible for the new church at Whitland, completed in 1853: correspondence reveals that Goodwin desired to use John Thomas, the builder of Whitland Church, for the new work at Haverfordwest.[65] The proposed new aisle was not realized and, instead, work appears to have concentrated on rebuilding the nave and chancel and providing new furnishings. When work started in 1853, the inscribed medieval tomb of Richard le Palmer was found underneath the pavement at the east end of the church and was cleaned and repaired.[66] The church was reopened on 29th May 1855 by the Bishop of St David's, who contributed £55 towards the total cost of £1,200, raised by voluntary subscription. New seats were provided, a new organ was installed, together with a white marble font, the gift of G. Lort Phillips.[67]

Following the rebuilding of the main body of the church, efforts were then directed to building new churchyard walls and railings, plans for which were prepared by William Phillips, church secretary and architect.[68] The work was completed in 1857, the iron railings and gates having been supplied by Stephen Green.[69]

In 1880 plans were prepared by E. H. Lingen Barker, architect of of Hereford, for the building of a north aisle, complete with porch and vestry and organ chamber, at an estimated cost of £580.[70] Lingen Barker was an architect capable of producing a competent, if dull, restoration at a cheap cost, but at St Thomas's his work is of a higher than usual standard. The elevation of the north aisle, with its

Decorated style windows rising to dormer gables and the two storey gabled vestry to the east is a striking piece of work. The work involved the insertion of the seven bay arcade between nave and aisle, the arches set on round piers. The church was reopened in the summer of 1881, when it was reported[71] that a stained glass window had been inserted above the altar, together with new floor tiles, a new pulpit and new candlesticks, the latter by Barwell of Birmingham. The cost had exceeded the original estimate and had risen to £1,200. The only major addition in the twentieth century was the superb Netherlandish style carved timber reredos by the architect, John Coates Carter.

The earliest monument in the church is the fourteenth, or early fifteenth, century slab with a Latin Cross carved in relief together with an inscription reading RICARD LE PAVMER GIT ICI DEV DE SAALME EIT MERCI AMEN. There are several eighteenth century monuments, ranging from the Baroque style of the early part of the century, such as that to John Bernardiston and family (*c*.1734), a splendidly large tablet framed by carved draperies, and Owen and Elinor Phillips (*c*1748), a more typical piece with scrolls and broken pediment signed by Thomas Beard of London, who was master of the Mason's Company in 1781, to the more pure Neo-classical monument to Elizabeth Eliot (1780). The latter is a very fine work, including a scene depicting a mourning female in a classical landscape. Of the nineteenth-century memorials, the best is that to the Chambers family (1852-72) with an unusually large statue of a praying woman on a tall pedestal, signed by Sanders of London.

The white marble font, given by G. Lort Phillips, has an octagonal bowl and a cover presented in 1969 in memory of William and Ethel Jacks. The pulpit, which has marble colonettes is a standard piece of its period, installed in 1881.

The earliest of the stained glass windows, is that on the south side of the nave, *c*.1868 by Cox and Sons, depicting the Crucifixion in the strong colours so favoured by the High Victorians. The east window is of 1881 by Mayer of Munich, also depicting the Crucifixion in sombre yet nevertheless rich colours, indicative of a movement against the intensely coloured glass advocated by the Anglican Revival of the 1840s.

St David and St Patrick's Church

A small Roman Catholic congregation in Haverfordwest began to worship in a converted cottage in Dew Street in 1845, when Father Peter Lewis who had, until then, ministered at Milford Haven, moved to Haverfordwest.[72] That the old cottage was inadequate was obvious by 1855, when it was reported that, despite recent improvements, a new building would be necessary.[73] By 1871, under the ministry of Father Cullen, the congregation began to raise funds for a new church. Builders were invited to tender for the demolition of the old cottage and the building of a church on the same site.[74] The present church of St David and St Patrick, designed by Richard Williams of Carmarthen, was opened on 26 April 1872, when Father Cullen was priest,[75] having cost £700 to build. The plan consists of nave with gallery and sacristy, with space for 250 worshippers. The altar and candlesticks were given by Lady Herbert of Llanover.[76]

In 1905, considerable improvements were made, including new windows, alteration to the roof and a new tabernacle.[77] With the growth of the air base at Brawdy, the number of Catholics in the locality rose rapidly, necessitating the enlargement of the church by adding an annexe to the north, opening off both nave and sacristy. This was completed in 1960,[78] thus forming the L-shaped plan necessitated by the constricted nature of the site.

The church itself is an extremely simple Gothic building, a gabled elevation facing Dew Street, complete with bellcote and traceried window set above the porch. Inside, the building is equally unpretentious, the nave separated from the sacristy by a triple-shafted arch. To the rear of the nave is a simple timber-fronted gallery, the nave having a simple arch-braced roof and two stained glass windows depicting St David and St Patrick. Within the annexe is the baptistry, the font erected by the parishioners in memory of Mother Eucharia, who died in 1967.[79]

THE CHAPELS

In 1900 there were ten Nonconformist places of worship in Haverfordwest: four Baptist Chapels (Bethesda, Machpelah, Hill Park and the Mission Chapel at Prendergast); two Congregationalist

(Albany and Tabernacle); the Calvinistic Methodist Chapel at Ebenezer; two Wesleyan Chapels (Chapel Lane and Prendergast), and the Moravian Chapel at St Thomas's Green. Two other chapels had long closed their doors by this date: the Quaker Meeting House, demolished in 1835, and the Primitive Methodist Chapel at Prendergast, closed in 1858.

Although several of the chapels in the town have early origins, the buildings themselves all wear a nineteenth century appearance, the result of several periods of rebuilding, alteration and enlargement. The huge increase in population in Pembrokeshire in the early nineteenth century, along with several revivals, most notably the great revival of 1858-9, caused many new chapels to be built, and practically all of the older ones were rebuilt or enlarged. In addition, the Methodists' split with the Anglicans in 1811 led to much building on their part. So fervent was the rebuilding, that no wholly pre-nineteenth century chapel is left in the county, and indeed, relatively few in Wales. The second half of the last century saw a vast rebuilding in towns throughout the country, and the Nonconformists were as preoccupied as anyone else with the issue of style.

Surprisingly little is known about the appearance of early Nonconformist chapels, but what is known, from illustrations and the occasional survivor, points to the logical fact that these buildings were plain, simple and utilitarian, closely based on those cottages, farmhouses and barns where the early dissenting societies met until the political climate, or adequate funds, allowed them to build a chapel. In rural parts, the majority of early-nineteenth-century chapels tended to be rather domestic in appearance, with the entrance located in one of the long sides, and little ornamentation, relieved only by the use of the round-arched window. They were either the product of local craftsmen working from copybooks, or copying recently completed chapels in the locality. Many chapels had twin entrances which some maintain are influenced by the architecture of barns, while the more logical explanation would be the easier ingress and egress for the congregation, making for a symmetrical facade and accommodating the pulpit which was often placed backing on to the entrance wall.

In Pembrokeshire, town chapels of this date tended also to be relatively plain. An exception to this rule was Tabernacle,

Haverfordwest, built in the Classical style in 1774, and probably the most elaborate of all Nonconformist chapels in the county at the time. Machpelah, of 1842, illustrates on a small scale the change in chapel planning in Wales from about the middle of the century, when the main entrance came to be placed on the gable end, rather than on one of the long sides. This allowed for some decoration of the façade which was by nature relatively small in area, and consequently cheaper to embellish. Albany has a gable end façade also, and is in addition a comparatively rare example of an early-nineteenth-century Gothic-style chapel, built in 1842 by the leading architect of the town, William Owen.

Albany leads the way into the second half of the nineteenth century. Not only is the chapel in a definable style, but it is the work of a professional architect. As the century progressed, it became increasingly rare not to employ an architect, even in rural areas. As the Victorians grew ever more obsessed with architectural styles, town chapels grew more and more ambitious. Whereas the Anglican revival in liturgy in the 1840s made it impossible for the established church to consider anything but the Gothic style for new buildings, the Nonconformists experimented with all styles. In towns, particularly, the days of the humble utilitarian chapels were over. Inside, the high box-pews and double-decker pulpits were replaced by more comfortable open pews, and larger pulpits to cope with increasingly demonstrative preaching. Galleries became increasingly elaborate, and the Nonconformists were ever keen to use modern materials and techniques, such as cast iron in galleries, brick for construction, and ventilators disguised as decorative plaster ceiling roses. Later, some congregations indulged in stained glass memorial windows. There seemed little reluctance to build increasingly elaborate chapels, and no denomination showed a preference for a particular style, nor were they concerned with stylistic purity. Tabernacle (Congregational), was re-modelled in the Classical style, whereas Albany was Gothic. Ebenezer (Calvinistic Methodist) was given a Classical facelift, and Bethesda (Baptist) received a highly decorative Romanesque front, but the second Baptist chapel at Hill Park was built in the Classical style, yet by the same architect as Bethesda. Many town chapels in Pembrokeshire are Gothic, yet few thought it an inappropriate style for dissenters. Clearly, the Nonconformists no longer liked their buildings plain.

Whatever the style, size, or location of the chapel, the basic interior elements remained constant. Altars being out of the question, the focal point in any chapel was the pulpit, from which the word of God was uttered. The Methodists retained communion rails in their chapels whereas, in other denominations, the sacrament was administered to the flock by the deacons or elders, whose place during the service was in the 'Big Seat', below the pulpit. Often, the Baptists chose to place baptismal pools under the Big Seat, the floor being removed for baptisms.

The revival of 1904-5 saw the last flurry of chapel building in Wales generally, but the amount of chapel-building in the later nineteenth century meant that few new chapels were needed in Pembrokeshire. The heyday of the chapel was approaching its end. In Haverfordwest, Machpelah is derelict; the Moravian Chapel closed in 1957 and was demolished; the Wesleyan Chapel closed its doors in 1985.

Albany Chapel

The story of Nonconformity in Haverforwest begins with Albany. A local tradition ascribes a date of 1638 for the meeting of the first group of Independents, at Haverfordwest and this date is inscribed on Albany Chapel, which seems unusually early but it is certain that a meeting room, known as the 'Green Meeting', was established on St Thomas's Green by 1651.

Among the clergy who were forced out of the church by the Act of Uniformity in 1662 for refusing to accept the Book of Common Prayer, were Peregrine Phillips, vicar of Llangwm and Freystrop, and John Luntley, rector of Llanstadwell and Nolton,[1] both of whom were to play an important part in furthering the Independent cause in south Pembrokeshire. Phillips, after his ejection, established an Independent cause at Dredgeman Hill, and in 1665 he became the leader of the Green Meeting, assisted by Luntley. Following the Declaration of Indulgence of 1672, Phillips was licensed to preach both in his own house, and in that of Richard Meyler, and he soon emerged as the leading light of the local Independent cause.

After meeting for some years at the Green Meeting, a chapel was built in 1691, two years after the passing of the Act of Toleration. The date stone facing St Thomas's Green gives the date of the first chapel as 1655, but it is difficult to believe that a purpose-built meeting house was erected at such an early date.

In 1839, the old chapel was demolished, and the foundations of the present building laid.[2] The architect was William Owen who, besides being a successful local architect, was a leading figure in the county, having been county surveyor since 1824, promoting in that year his scheme to improve the layout of Haverfordwest and building a new bridge over the Cleddau. Owen was three times mayor of the town, and sheriff of the county in 1859. He was a Congregationalist, baptized at Albany on 27 April 1797. He had already built Heol Awst Congregational Chapel in Carmarthen in 1827, which, though impressive in size, was still a variant of the standard early-nineteenth-century chapel, with its entrances along the long side, rather like a house or barn. At Haverfordwest, however, he provided something altogether more fashionable, in a simple Gothic style, with its entrance at the gable end.

The foundation stone was laid in October 1839 and, during the building work, the congregation worshipped at premises in Bridge Street until the new chapel was opened on 16 March 1841. The

Fig. 24 Albany Chapel.

(Robert Scourfield).

Fig. 25 Tabernacle Chapel.

(Robert Scourfield).

façade of the building was reversed from St Thomas's Green to face Hill Street, where several fashionable houses had recently been built, and set behind a small courtyard. The chapel is unusual by being top-lit, because of the abutment of the buildings each side. The interior probably had high box pews, and a small box-pulpit on a pedestal, as at Heol Awst, Carmarthen, and other well-preserved chapels of the period. It seems that there was no gallery for in 1873, according to the *Haverfordwest and Milford Telegraph,*[3] galleries were being built around the three walls to face the pulpit. Some members raised concerns about the cost of the project, but the minister, the Rev. W. Justin Evans replied, 'You build the galleries, and I'll fill them'. The architect responsible for the work of 1873 was D. E. Thomas, a local architect specializing in schools and chapels and his gallery, incorporating long bands of decorative ironwork is typical of the date, when architects were introducing more architectural detail inside chapels, moving away from simple panelled galleries and plain square pulpits. Thomas carried out further renovations in 1890,[4] which included new seating, and a large platform-style timber pulpit, with an oriel in the centre for the lectern. Such large pulpits began to appear in the later nineteenth century, perhaps as a result of the revivals, when the standard small enclosed pulpits of the earlier chapels were a hindrance to the more eloquent preacher. The local

Fig. 26 Tabernacle Chapel interior, evocative of a Roman basilica.
(Crown copyright: Royal Commission on the Ancient and Historical Monuments of Wales).

papers reported that the work was so thorough and well-furnished that there would be no need to carry out any more work until the chapel celebrated its tricentenary.

Fashionable, too, was the placing of a framework behind the pulpit, usually in the from of a plaster arch, often accompanied by a painted text, but here, in the form of a severely classical pedimented timber framework, guaranteed to give even the weakest preacher a presence in the pulpit. These Classical surrounds were favoured by several chapel architects from the closing years of the century. As yet, no architectural term has been successfully found to describe these features, which are, indeed, peculiar to chapel architecture: when D. E. Thomas installed it in 1904, the *Haverfordwest and Milford Telegraph* committed the heresy of calling it a reredos.[5]

Thomas's work was evidently satisfactory for, in 1908,[6] he returned to build the schoolroom, which abuts on to one side of the chapel. The building was designed to seat 250 persons, with entrances both from the street and from the chapel lobby. The reporter of the *Haverfordwest and Milford Telegraph* struggled to describe the new building, deciding that it was a mixture of Renaissance, Gothic, and other periods of English architecture, which just about covered everything![7] This 'free style' of architecture was typical of the Edwardian period, which sought to rid itself of the shackles of Gothic and Classical: Thomas was particularly adept at working in the style.

Renovations were carried out in 1917[8] by Arthur Thomas, architect, and a war memorial tablet was unveiled in 1922. New gates and railings were erected in 1925. A major renovation was carried out in 1965, when the large Gothic window over the lobby, blown out by a storm, was blocked in, the stepped front gable was removed, and a new ceiling constructed.

Tabernacle Chapel

Tabernacle was originally founded by the Calvinistic Methodists. The Calvinistic Methodist movement in Wales can be dated to 1735, the year of the conversion of both Howell Harris and Daniel Rowland. Harris preached from the lime kilns at Cartlett in Haverfordwest on 17 March 1743, and a society was formed, which met for 30 years, until a chapel was raised in 1774. The real impetus for growth came following the visit of the famous evangelist, George Whitefield to Haverfordwest in 1768. Whitefield, the leader of the Oxford Methodists, held strongly Calvinist views, which appealed to the Welsh Methodists who saw no reason to restrict themselves to licensed preaching houses, and as such were regarded by many Anglican clergy with great suspicion. However, they had no intention of establishing a denomination separate from the Anglicans, but unconsciously, given the fact that they saw fit to build their own meeting houses from the outset, they did not always restrict their preaching to licensed premises and began to oversee local societies by holding group meetings, evolved a church which was essentially Presbyterian. The split was inevitable, but a long time in coming. Many wished for a break at an early date: men like Harris were bitterly opposed. The early Methodist leaders were young men, and enthusiastic itinerant preachers. Harris preached all over Wales, travelling up to 150 miles a week; Rowland, and Howell Davies the 'Apostle of Pembrokeshire', were renowned preachers, while the hymns of William Williams, Pantycelyn, were extremely popular, and soon permeated other denominations.

The sermon preached by Harris at Haverfordwest in 1743 led to the setting up of a society in a house owned by a Mr Wheeler in Cokey Lane (City Road). The society was led in its early years by Howell Davies who, following a disagreement with Harris, became the effective leader of Methodism in Pembrokeshire after 1747.

When Whitefield addressed an open-air congregation in Haverfordwest in 1768, he reported that it numbered some 15,000 and that 'tears flowed like water from a stony rock'. Similar scenes were witnessed during his visit of 1769. One may be forgiven for accusing Whitefield of a little exaggeration, but it was soon apparent that Mr Wheeler's house was too small, and a chapel was needed.

In 1774, two gardens near Mr Wheeler's house were purchased, and the first chapel was built, with a remaining debt of £600. The chapel, judging from early nineteenth century illustrations, was a grand classical piece of architecture, with a pediment in the centre bay and, with windows on both storeys, the influence of the simple Neo-classical villa is all too evident. The building must have astonished the majority of Nonconformists in the county, many of whom were still meeting in houses and outbuildings. The interior was divided by columns to resemble a nave and aisles, and roofed with a plaster vaulted ceiling, according to the report of the *Haverfordwest and Milford Telegraph* on the ordination of Revd H. C. Long in 1864.[9]

The 'Whitefield Methodists' gravitated towards Congregation-alism and, following a vote taken in 1790, the Congregational faction won the day. The Methodists, under Nathaniel Rowland, son of Daniel Rowland and son-in-law of Howell Davies, left to re-establish the Methodist cause at premises in Bridge Street. One of the stalwarts of the Congregational side, Benjamin Davies, a draper in Short Row, bought out the mortgage of the building and, after some weeks, reopened its doors as Tabernacle Congregational Chapel.

The interior of Tabernacle was restored in 1819[10] and, in about 1835, fine iron gates were erected. By 1870, discussions were taking place with regard to enlarging the chapel, following the completion of the fine schoolroom in 1864.[11] In June 1872, the chapel advertised in the *Pembrokeshire Herald*[12] for architects to produce plans for a remodelling of the chapel, to seat 750 persons, at a cost of £1,500. Lawrence and Goodman of Newport, Monmouthshire, were engaged to draw the plans. In February 1873, the tender of James and John Allen of Pembroke Dock of £1,541 10s 0d was accepted. The new building, which was opened in 1874, was among the most striking of the Classical-style chapels in Wales. The aisled plan, complete with an apse housing the pulpit, is evocative of a Roman basilica. It is interesting to note that the basic plan of the old chapel was reused, most notably by the subdivision into nave and aisles by arcading, now supported on tall cast iron pillars with Corinthian capitals. Even the plaster barrel ceiling seems to hark back to the ceiling of the old chapel. No expense was spared in furnishing the chapel, with lavish use of cast iron for the balustrading of the galleries, which run around the three sides of the building. The strong swirly foliage pattern of the ironwork has no parallel in Pembrokeshire, and the pulpit is similarly unusual in having iron balustrading. The contemporary stained glass windows in the apse, depict suitable texts, together with the lily and the vine. The crowning glory is the splendid coffered plaster ceiling. A new organ, made by Sweetland of Bath,[13] was installed in 1879, and in 1881 a hot water heating system was provided at a cost of £92. The *Pembrokeshire Herald* of 3 April 1903 contained an advertisement for tenders to restore the interior, which was completed by September under A. H. Thomas, architect, including repainting, and revarnishing the seats.[14] A memorial window installed in the lobby to commemorate the nine members of the chapel who had lost their lives in the 1914-18 war was unveiled on 2 September 1920.[15]

Bethesda Baptist Chapel

In 1649, John Miles, having been immersed by total baptism in London, returned to Wales, to establish a Baptist Church at Ilston, near Swansea. When he left for America, his place was taken by William Jones of Cilymaenllwyd who, in 1667, founded a chapel at Rhydwilym, which effectively became another Ilston.

By 1740, Baptist ministers were preaching in Haverfordwest, and in the same year, a house was taken at the top of Prendergast for meetings to be held.[16] The Baptists believed in baptism by total immersion, but it was not until 1777 that the first such baptism took place in Haverfordwest, in the Western Cleddau, just above the Old Bridge.

The cause grew under Revd Benjamin Davies, minister of Molleston, who resided at Denant, the family home of his wife. He preached often at Prendergast, where the inadequacy of the meeting house became ever more apparent. A site at the foot of Barn Street was purchased for £200 on 12 May 1789,[17] and a chapel was erected by the end of September at a cost £308 6s 0d (£308.30). The chapel was able to sustain its own membership and, in 1789, sixty members are recorded, drawn from Molleston, Rhydwilym, and Llangloffan. Benjamin Davies became minister in 1798, and during the 18 years of his ministry, the membership swelled to 200. Davies died in 1816 and was buried outside the chapel and a tablet within the building bears his name.

The chapel was rebuilt in 1816, the new building measuring 45 feet square,[18] and it was at this time that the chapel was named Bethesda. The following years saw a falling away in membership, and there followed a rapid succession of ministers between 1817 and 1837. In that year, Benjamin Davies's son, Revd David Davies of Evesham, was invited to be the minister, and he returned to

Pembrokeshire to build up a much-depleted congregation. He was also responsible for establishing a Baptist College in the town, which flourished until its removal to Aberystwyth in 1894.

According to the *The Welshman* of 11 March 1842,[19] the chapel was damaged by a gas explosion which occurred under the floor of the building, damaging the seats and ceiling and, after repairs, it was reopened in the following August. A vestry was built behind the chapel in 1856,[20] but within a few years, there was a demand for a new chapel to be built to accommodate the increasing congregation.

On 12 April 1878, the *Pembrokeshire Herald* contained a notice to architects to apply for the rebuilding of the chapel, and the building of two vestries, the cost to be not more than £1,800. The walls of the old chapel were to be reused where possible. The successful architect was the favourite of the Baptists across the whole of south Wales, George Morgan of Carmarthen, who had built chapels of various styles in the area – Gothic at North Road, Milford Haven, and Classical at Carmarthen, both for the Baptists. He chose the Romanesque style for Bethesda. The style is characterized by large wheel windows, round-arched openings, and much carved stonework. He had already built a chapel in this style at Bethany, Pembroke

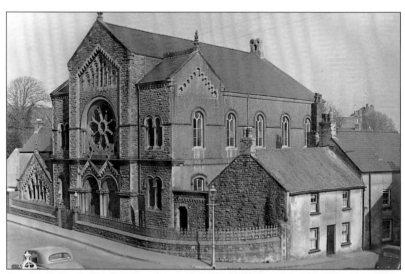

Fig. 27 Bethesda Baptist Chapel, completed in 1880 at a cost of £2,199.

(Pembrokeshire County Library collection).

Fig. 28 Hill Park Baptist Chapel, built to serve the Welsh-speaking community, 1858.

(Robert Scourfield).

Dock, in 1877, but the congregation had not been able to afford an expensive dressed stonework, so he used simple stucco external detail instead. The congregation at Haverfordwest wanted something more elaborate and they may have known of Morgan's recently completed, grandly Romanesque Baptist Chapel at Abergavenny.

Foundation stones were laid on 10 October 1878,[21] each stone recording the date of the previous chapels on the site. The builders were Morgan and Thomas of Haverfordwest and the stone carving was carried out by E. Powell of Abergavenny. The walls were faced with hammer-dressed limestone, with bathstone detail. The total cost came to £2,199, including all interior fittings, the schoolroom, and the forecourt railings, with over £1,000 of which in hand before the work began. The chapel was opened in 1880.[22]

The interior has seating for 900 persons, with a gallery around three sides. The gallery front, of cast iron with pierced detail, is a speciality of George Morgan, and demonstrates the Nonconformists' willingness to combine modern materials with ancient architectural styles. The pulpit, set within a shallow apse may well be an echo of that at Tabernacle, but the feature found increasing favour in larger town chapels where, very often, the organ was sited behind the pulpit. Behind the pulpit at Bethesda is a carved stone surround in a quirky Gothic style, intended to provide a dramatic frame for the preacher. The decorative glass windows were made by Cox & Son, a well-known firm of stained glass manufacturers. Typically of later-nineteenth-century Baptist chapels, the baptismal pool is underneath the platform of the 'Big Seat', a much more comfortable means of baptizing than in the open air, especially as the chapel had the luxury of central heating. The pipe organ, sited in the gallery, was installed in 1893.[23]

Hill Park Baptist Chapel

By 1857, Bethesda was thriving under its new minister, Revd Thomas Davies, and there became an increasing desire to build a chapel to cater for the Welsh-speaking Baptists in Haverfordwest, one of whom, James Rowlands, had rented a house in Back Lane in which Welsh services were held every Sunday morning at 9.30, following which worshippers attended the 11 o'clock service at Bethesda. The story goes that while on the way to Bethesda one Sunday, as they drew near to the bottom of Prendergast Hill, Rowlands declared that this would be a suitable site for the building of a chapel. He approached the owner and purchased the site freehold. Rowlands then proceeded to build a chapel, the building and site costing £1,400. He was well-placed in one important aspect to carry out the building of a meeting house, for he was also an architect and designed the chapel himself.[24]

The original chapel, which now survives as the schoolroom, though simple, was an ingenious building, unlike anything previously built in the county. The chapel was located on the first floor, approached by exterior steps, which were entered from a covered colonnade, which ran along the front of the building.

The first service was held on 27 January 1858 and, with members transferred from Bethesda and chapels in north Pembrokeshire, such as Llangloffan, and Beulah, Little Newcastle, the membership stood at 140 in 1866. The official opening took place in October 1858,[25] and despite a promising start, without having to go through the usual dilemmas of finding money for purchasing a site, and raising a chapel, the Welsh-only services ended in 1880,[26] but when the services became English, the congregation steadily increased again. With this increase came the problem of insufficient space for the congregation. Two solutions posed themselves: either to excavate the floor of the chapel and erect a gallery; or to build a new chapel on the adjoining plot of land, which had recently been purchased.[27] On 4 April 1888, it was resolved to take the latter option, and the obvious candidate for the overseeing of the work, was George Morgan of Carmarthen, the favoured architect of the Baptist denomination. An advertisement placed in the *Pembrokeshire Herald*[28] drew tenders of £2,012 from Robert and William Williams, and £1,477 from an Aberystwyth contractor.[29] The lower tender was accepted, which later proved to be a misjudgment. The foundation stones were laid on 12 September 1888 and work on the new chapel proceeded well, but just after the roof went on, the wall at the pulpit end collapsed. When it was rebuilt, it was found that the opposite wall was six inches out of true. Morgan ordered the builders to rebuild this wall also, but by now, the contractor had exceeded his budget and was no longer able to pay the builders' wages. Some of the builders left the site, and a number of suppliers were threatened with heavy losses, while the contractor declared himself bankrupt. One of the timber merchants took court action against the minister and three of the deacons, and at the hearing, Revd Jenkins vowed to devote the offertories of three anniversaries to raise the necessary amount.[30]

In July 1889, tenders were invited for finishing the building, and the tender of Messrs R. and W. Williams was accepted. The chapel was completed and the opening ceremony took place 26 and 27 July 1891.[31] The total cost amounted to £2,026. The new chapel was relatively plain, and the entrance front is largely concealed from public view. Due to the narrow site, the only prominent elevation is one of the long sides, and to embellish this would have been an extremely costly exercise. Morgan therefore provided the same solution as at the schoolroom he was building at the same time at Heol Awst, Carmarthen, namely, the use of simple cement-moulded arches on tall pilasters to liven up an otherwise plain elevation. The interior is in many ways typical of a late-nineteenth-century town chapel, the three-sided gallery incorporating bands of decorative ironwork, similar to the one Morgan had designed for Priordy Chapel, Carmarthen, and the pulpit was set in an arched recess. For understandable reasons, the interior of Hill Park is much less elaborate than that of Bethesda.

Six members of Hill Park lost their lives in the 1914-18 war and, whereas many chapels perpetuated the memory of the fallen by erecting a tablet or coloured glass window, the members of Hill Park took the unusually practical decision to enlarge the vestry beneath the schoolroom, within the former chapel. This involved lowering the floor level by digging out tons of solid rock, which was the reason why the idea of enlarging the old chapel had been abandoned.[32] A new side entrance was made, and a commodious schoolroom was opened in 1921. In 1933, the chapel was renovated, including the purchase of an organ, a reconditioned instrument which had been obtained from an English country house.

Mission Chapel, Prendergast

The Upper Chapel, as it was known, was established as an offshoot of Bethesda in March 1862,[33] with services held in English. The chapel stood on the east side of the road, between the Church Hall and the Cardigan Road junction. Few records survive of the building, which was built following several years of meeting in a private house nearby. Even after the change to English services at Hill Park Chapel, the 'Upper Chapel' continued in use. By 1923 it was being used as a mission room, and had accommodation for 300 but it was later demolished.

Machpelah Baptist Chapel, Portfield

Machpelah was built in 1842 under the ministry of Revd David Davies of Bethesda, as a mission chapel to serve the growing area of Portfield. It also served as a cemetery for the Baptists. The prime mover for the new chapel was William Rees, solicitor and deacon of Bethesda.[34] The chapel is a simple and small building, rather domestic in appearance, with a slate hung elevation and an entrance at the gable end. By 1851, there were approximately 70 members. When the Royal Naval Air Station was located at Brawdy services were held for naval families, and following that, the chapel was used for harvest festivals and Christmas services by the members of Bethesda. The chapel was closed in 1988, and is now stripped of its fittings.[35]

Ebenezer Presbyterian Chapel, Perrot's Road

The early history of the Calvinistic Methodists in Haverfordwest is associated with Tabernacle Chapel, until that chapel was taken over by the Congregationalists in 1790. Nathaniel Rowland then continued the Methodist cause in premises in Bridge Street where a small congregation met until 1807, when he was excommunicated by the Newcastle Emlyn Methodist Association for drunkenness. Rowland then proceeded to claim the Bridge Street property as his own[36] and the congregation was reduced to meeting in a corn loft at

Fig. 29 Ebenezer Presbyterian Chapel built in 1817, rebuilt in 1885.
(Crown copyright: Royal Commission on the Ancient and Historical Monuments of Wales).

Fig. 30 Wesleyan Chapel, originally built in 1772, 'far the neatest church in Wales', according to John Wesley. Closed 1985 and now an antiques showroom.

(Robert Scourfield).

Prendergast. In 1817 a site was obtained on a lease in Perrot's Road and a chapel built there. One of the key figures in the founding of the new chapel was a young man, Revd Thomas Harries, who was destined for the Anglican church, but had been refused ordination by the Bishop of St David's.

The chapel of 1817 was enlarged in 1844, and was reopened in November of that year. In 1871 the chapel had its own permanent minister in Revd Thomas Davies, and serious thought was given to the renovation of the building. Special services were held in 1873 in order to raise funds, but it was not until 1885[37] that builders were invited to tender for the work, under the supervision of the architect, D. E. Thomas of Haverfordwest. The proposal was to build two schoolrooms, one on top of the other, to face Perrot's Road and full advantage was taken of this to give the building a handsome Classical façade, the lower floor rusticated, the upper floor with Tuscan pilasters, and a small pediment in the centre. The elders of the church had planned things carefully, for once the schoolrooms were completed in 1886, the upper room was used for services, while Thomas was engaged to renovate the interior of the chapel, which reopened on 5 May 1889, the cost of the entire scheme being over

£1,600.[38] The leasehold of the site was purchased by John Philipps of Southfield for £93 and the building debts were finally paid off in 1906.

The interior of the chapel has an iron-fronted gallery at one end, similar to that at Bethesda. The chapel was renovated again in 1967-69, mostly by voluntary labour, under the ministry of Revd Arwyn Thomas.[39]

The Wesleyan Chapel

John Wesley made 14 visits to Pembrokeshire between 1763 and 1790. He was not the first to preach Wesleyan Methodism in the county, however, for in 1762, Thomas Taylor, a young Yorkshireman began preaching in the English-speaking south of the county. Wesley preached at Haverfordwest on 24 August 1763, where he had 'not seen so numerous a congregation since I set out from London, and they were one and all, deeply attentive.'[40] When he visited the town in 1767, he noted that 'the work of God in Pembrokeshire had been exceedingly hindered, chiefly by Mr [Howell] Davies's preachers',[41] whose Calvinism, centred on the doctrine of predestination, was abhorrent to Wesley, who believed in universal salvation

Following Wesley's visits to the county, the Pembrokeshire Circuit was formed in 1771. By 1781, there were sixty members at Haverfordwest, forming the largest congregation in the Circuit, which was reorganized in 1794, and again in 1805. They built a chapel in 1772 and, on 18 August of that year, Wesley preached at 'the new church' which he described as 'far the neatest in Wales'.[42] The chapel was known as the 'Wesley Room' well into the nineteenth century.

The chapel was rebuilt in 1818, and the *Carmarthen Journal*,[43] in an account of its reopening on 22 April that year, described the building as handsome. Handsome it must have been, for the cost was £1,800, the building seating between 800 and 900 worshippers. The chapel was enlarged in 1835, so that it measured 71 feet by 42 feet, with new pews provided in a gallery, and with a schoolroom underneath. This suggests that an extra gallery was added behind the pulpit. In addition, new vestries were added on the north side of the chapel. The reopening services took place 25-6 October 1835, an outlay of £463 having being made. The freehold of the site was purchased in 1849, and extensive repairs were carried out in 1859, when the inner lobby was rebuilt, a new communion rail fitted, and new stairs made to the pulpit.

Testimony to a growing congregation and Sunday School attendance was the building of the present schoolroom, on the north side of the chapel in 1873. An advertisement was placed in the *Pembrokeshire Herald* on 4 April 1873 for tenders to build the schoolroom under the supervision of D. E. Thomas, the Haverfordwest architect, who was at the time installing the galleries at Albany. The foundation stone was laid in May 1874,[44] the contract price for the work being £800. The schoolroom was almost as large as the chapel itself.

An extensive restoration programme was carried out in 1880-1,[45] again by D E Thomas, which involved the complete refitting of the interior, and probably the recasting of the façade in a chaste Classical style, possibly retaining the original twin doorways, which may have survived from the 1818 chapel. Tall end pilasters were created, elaborate surrounds placed around the doors and windows, and a prominent tablet placed in the parapet. The interior, now sadly gone, was extremely fine, with a gallery around three sides, supported on wooden Ionic columns, but best of all was the magnificent pulpit, which was highly carved, and had concave sides with fluted pilasters: probably this was the richest pulpit of its date in the county, and without doubt, the chapel interior was one of Thomas's most important commissions.

The rebuilding campaign did not end there, for in 1910, the old vestries of 1835 were demolished and rebuilt, occupying the angle between the chapel and schoolroom. *The Haverfordwest and Milford Telegraph* of 8 June reported that the foundation stone had been recently laid, the architect being Henry Budgen of Cardiff. The vestries were opened approximately a year later, at a cost of £1,195.[46]

The chapel suffered minor bomb damage during the 1939-45 war, and the chapel was restored in 1951. Owing to concerns about structural problems, the chapel was closed in 1985, the members transferred to Albany Chapel, and the Wesley Room became an antiques showroom.

Primitive Methodist Chapel, Prendergast

A small number of Methodists, who were drawn towards revivalism and evangelism, broke away from the Wesleyan church in 1810, and called themselves Primitive Methodists in the belief that they were reviving Methodism by removing the dogma with which Wesleyanism had surrounded itself and by sending out field preachers in the manner of Wesley. Their services were simple and plain and appealed above all to the labouring classes. In Pembrokeshire, their activities were restricted to the south of the county,[47] flourishing particularly around the colliery villages of Saundersfoot and Jeffreston. The chapel at Haverfordwest was the most northerly point of influence. The Pembroke Mission was set up in 1823, with its station at Pembroke Dock being the centre for outlying societies.

James Roles was appointed a missionary into Pembrokeshire and he preached on two Sundays at Haverfordwest 'to a very large congregation'. A preaching room was erected at Prendergast in about 1836, but it was not used exclusively as a place of worship. By 1843 there were only 20 members at Haverfordwest and the meeting room was closed in 1858, due to its distance from Pembroke Dock and the reluctance of ministers to cross the Cleddau in rough weather. By the late nineteenth century, the number of societies in the county had dwindled but the cause remained strong in the Saundersfoot and Cresselly area, until 1932, when the Primitive and Wesleyan Methodists formally united.

The Quaker Meeting House

The Quakers were well established in Haverfordwest in the seventeenth century. In 1657 George Fox, accompanied by John ap John, toured through south Wales and came to Haverfordwest where he received a welcome and had 'a great meeting'.[48] The Pembroke County Monthly Meeting was held regularly at Haverfordwest and at Redstone, where the first Yearly Meeting for Wales was held in 1682.

A small group of Quakers, including William Bateman and his wife, were imprisoned in 1661 for refusing to agree not to attend further Society meetings.[49] Due to increasingly severe persecution, many Welsh Quakers left for America after 1681, when William Penn obtained the grant of Pennsylvania from the king. The loss of so many members to emigration was an important factor in weakening the cause in Wales. Whereas many meeting houses were abandoned throughout the eighteenth century in the county, there remained a Quaker presence in Haverfordwest well into the next century

The first known meeting place of the Quakers was the Quay Street home of William and Sarah Bateman, and at a later stage, they were meeting at a warehouse in Quay Street. A meeting house is mentioned in 1729, but its location, if not still in Quay Street, is not known. Evidently the premises were not very suitable, for efforts were made from 1730 onward to find new premises. In 1745, the Quakers were building a new chapel on the corner of Quay Street and High Street, the seats and other useful materials having been transferred from the old premises.[50]

With the general decline in the Quaker cause across the county, only two people were attending weekly services by 1821,[51] and in 1829, the monthly meetings held alternately at Haverfordwest and Milford Haven, were abandoned altogether. In 1835, the Meeting House was demolished, to make way for the new Shire Hall.

The Moravian Chapel

The Moravians, who had fled from their church in Bohemia and had found refuge in Saxony, sent their missionaries to London by 1728. The first Welsh Moravian was William Holland, a native of Haverfordwest, who became a member of the Moravian Church in London in 1742, a little while before his friend John Gambold. Gambold was the son of the rector of Puncheston, and while studying at Christ Church, Oxford, he became acquainted with Charles and John Wesley, and was much influenced by John Wesley's ideas, becoming one of the 'Oxford Methodists'. Gambold resigned his living as an Anglican clergyman and entered the Moravian ministry in 1744 and, in 1753, he was elected as one of its Bishops.

William Griffith of Penmorfa, Caernarfonshire,[52] one of the original members of the London congregation, who seems to have been sent to Wales as a missionary, was the first Moravian to preach in Pembrokeshire. He preached in Haverfordwest in 1746, and a few years later, James Beaumont, a west of England evangelist, and John Gambold, were expounding the Moravian message in the town.

The first Moravian convert in Haverfordwest was John Sparks, who had been influenced by the preaching of Howell Harris in 1743.[53] A small society met at his house until premises were acquired in Quay Street, within a warehouse.[54] The Moravian congregation at Haverfordwest was officially incorporated in 1763, with its own Swedish pastor, Lorenz Thorsten Nyberg. John Gambold was pastor from 1768 until his death in 1771.

The Moravian cause drew in members of the Calvinistic Methodist gathering at City Road, and meetings began taking place in a warehouse at Quay Street. In 1764, a property was purchased on St Thomas's Green, and a house was converted to a temporary chapel, before the foundation of a purpose-built chapel in 1773.[55] The Moravian chapel at Haverfordwest was the earliest in south-west Wales, and it established a branch at Laugharne, which moved to Pendine in 1810, and also at Tenby in 1827.[56]

In December 1853, the *Pembrokeshire Herald* reported that the chapel had been reopened after renovations, complete with new windows, porch and gallery and the same newspaper noted in 1877[57] that £110 was needed for new seats. From old photographs, the chapel is shown as a simple building with tall round arched windows on the long sides, with the manse around the corner in Upper Market Street.

The last minister was Revd George Harp, and when the chapel closed in 1957, it was the last of that denomination in Wales, although still with 29 members. The chapel and adjoining houses were demolished in 1961, the name of the sheltered housing occupying the site, Moravian Court, perpetuating the memory of the cause. Against the members' wishes, the adjoining burial ground ceased to continue in their ownership, and the gravestones were removed and buried.[58]

ROBERT SCOURFIELD

THE BUILDINGS IN CONTEXT[1]

The combination of relatively rich documentary sources, a still-readable medieval topography and some key surviving buildings makes Haverfordwest a most rewarding town to explore, even if the final results are somewhat tantalizing. Haverfordwest's changing status as planted borough, lordship centre, effective county town, combined with its constant role as port and market, led to an accumulation of buildings of a special type which were very different from the buildings of the surrounding countryside. The challenge for the architectural historian is to deal with vanished and surviving buildings alike and also to bring out the quality of the layout of the town as a social and occasionally ceremonial space. It is not enough to know where and when particular buildings were constructed (though this may be hard enough), we need to try and understand why they were built. The structure of the chapter is broadly chronological, and I have tried to relate the domestic, religious and public buildings of Haverfordwest to their economic and social contexts in three well-defined phases of the town from medieval borough to assize town and reformed corporation. I have refrained from discussing Victorian, Edwardian and later buildings because they are described elsewhere.[2] However some detailed notes on public buildings (signalled by an asterisk in the present text) have been placed in an appendix.

I. THE LATE-MEDIEVAL TOWN

Late-medieval Haverford had an accumulation of notable and interesting buildings. The castle was the administrative centre of the lordship although its accommodation was allowed to become ruinous in the sixteenth century. Exceptionally for a Welsh town, there were three parish churches, one sited outside the walls, two religious houses (the Augustinian Canons without the town and the Black

Friars within) and several characteristically located chapels. There was a chapel at the bridge end for travellers, a Maudlin chapel and leper hospital on the far boundary of the town, and a mortuary chapel in which was kept (it seems) a taper dedicated to Our Lady. Alongside the navigable river were sited the town quay, several mills, and a fish weir. Late-medieval Haverfordwest was one of the few Welsh ports that participated in more than coastal trade. Ships from Portugal and Gascony with cargoes of wine and salt docked at the quay and the influence of the town reached down the haven. There were several important open spaces within and alongside the town. Gardens belonging to the friary and priory bordered the river. On the east side of the river was a marsh (Friars' Meadow) where archery butts were placed in the sixteenth century. On the west side of the town was Portfield – the town common of some 1000 acres which survived unenclosed until the nineteenth century. Those entering or leaving the town by the stone arched bridge (rebuilt *c*.1530) passed a wooden cross which marked the boundary of the borough.[3]

The common seal of Haverford depicted the two faces of the town: the closed walled and gated castle town and (on the obverse) a ship representing the open port and market centre. There were disasters when Haverfordwest needed to be defended – in the early thirteenth century and again in the early fifteenth century – but the borough seems to have been more of an open than a closed town. The town walls may have been more appearance than substance and do not suggest a siege mentality (see p. 22 above). Certainly Leland in the 1530s was more impressed with the walls and gates (which included an iron portcullis) of Pembroke and Tenby. The cloth woven in the town from a mixture of different coloured wools, referred to by Giraldus, could have served as a metaphor for the cosmopolitan nature of the town.[4] The relative openness of Haverfordwest was reflected in its architecture, which included buildings that were more national than vernacular in character.

The earliest public building for which there is documentary evidence is the 'guildhall'* ('gildhus', thirteenth century) presumably created for the burgesses and the gild merchants. Its building history is obscure but by the second half of the fifteenth century it had assumed the form regarded as conventional: a hall for the assembly of burgesses set over a vaulted arcade which served as a market or shambles. In 1469 the 'archys', probably three in number, of the 'vaute' under the guildhall were rented for shambles at 6d annually. The intrinsical and other courts allowed by charter were held in the guildhall and a separate Council House* may have developed for the mayor and principal burgesses towards the end of the fifteenth century after the incorporation of the town in 1476.[5]

It is impossible to be certain about the range of domestic buildings contemporary with the religious and public buildings of the town. It is not even clear what the dominant building material in the town was. A few fragmentary medieval stone-built domestic structures have survived but it is probable that contemporary timber- and clay-walled buildings have entirely vanished. The surviving domestic remains are slight and may be unrepresentative. In Haverfordwest, unlike the towns of the eastern Marches, domestic buildings have to be reconstructed from the bottom up rather than the top down. In Ruthin and Presteigne, for example, greatly altered medieval houses can still be identified from their ornate and smoke-blackened roofs.

Fig. 31 The vault known as 'The Crypt'.

(Crown copyright: Royal Commission on the Ancient and Historical Monuments in Wales).

In Haverfordwest, no early roofs have been discovered but (as in Pembroke) there are several vaults or cellars in the market area which predate the houses built over them.[6] However, vaults are difficult to date closely unless associated with good (moulded) architectural detail. A few cellars have pointed vaults but others are barrel-vaulted and possibly quite late. One remarkable and unquestionably early vault of *c.*1300, known now as 'The Crypt', survives on the south side of High Street opposite St Mary's church in the market centre of the town. Here the vault has two aisles with chamfered ribs springing from two cylindrical columns. A pointed doorway (possibly reset) gave access to the semi-basement from the street. Its name (acquired relatively recently) suggests a religious building but this fine vault should be compared with surviving late-thirteenth-century domestic vaults at Chester and other mercantile towns.[7] The vault may well have functioned as a store in relation to the market. Sometimes a vault might be leased separately from the building above; a 1369 agreement relates to a half burgage called 'le vawte' in 'le Heystret'. It is impossible to say what kind of house was raised over The Crypt. It is not even clear if its superstructure was built of stone or timber; a reference (1405) to a chamber of earth in St Mary's churchyard suggests that there was a clay-building tradition in the town. The Chester Rows show nevertheless that quite elaborate medieval timber houses (with complex building phases) were raised over comparable stone vaults. It seems clear from documentary evidence that houses of recognizable medieval plan existed in Haverfordwest. A deed broadly contemporary with the vault (1317) names the rooms of a burgage house in Haverfordwest as a hall (*aule*), chamber (*camera*) and solar (*solarium*). This may be reasonably interpreted as an orthodox medieval house with an open hall and storeyed end.[8]

This vault in High Street was presumably a survivor from the famous destruction of Haverfordwest by Owain Glyndŵr and his French allies who breached the town's walls in 1405. At the beginning of the fifteenth century when an attack on the town was a real possibility there were hasty attempts to strengthen the walls (which included demolishing a chamber built over one of the gateways) but when the attack came the outer defences were useless and the suburb – but not the inner castle town – was destroyed.[9] If Haverfordwest was essentially a timber town the absence of any early houses would be explained, in part at least, by the burning of the town. Stone vaulting would of course have survived the burning of a timber superstructure. It may be that a stone town rose from the ashes of early-fifteenth-century Haverfordwest. Indeed it is quite probable that there has been more than one change in preferred building materials with stone houses succeeding timber dwellings and (as we shall see) a reversion to timber for prestigious buildings in the sixteenth century.

The prosperity of Haverfordwest, like many medieval towns, was based fundamentally on cloth production. Haverfordwest drew in wool from the surrounding countryside, processed the yarn, and exported the woven cloth. Weavers, carders, dyers and spinners are all mentioned as occupations in the medieval town. Some of these processes would have needed special buildings – sheds, mills, workshops, stores and shops – but they have been swept away.[10]

However particular interest must attach to numerous fifteenth-century and later references to 'rows' in the town streets: Middle Row (1453); Short Row in High Street (1472), Prior's Row (1418). Rows, a word with multiple architectural meanings, generally referred to terrace-like adjoining houses or shops, sometimes all of one build, which were to be found in many English market towns. Some of Haverfordwest's rows were specifically referred to as 'middle streets' (*media strata*) because they were sited in the middle of principal thoroughfares. Philip Lea's plan of the town in 1693 (see p. 23), although schematic, does show the back-to-back structures of 'Back and Front Short Row' in the middle of High Street.[11] It seems probable that Haverford's rows were in origin groups of adjoining shops or workplaces, probably only one room deep and one storey high, occupied by members of the various craft guilds. The ordinances of the company of feltmakers, hatters and haberdashers refers to the custom of erecting a 'show of wares' directly over the shop or 'boulke'. The balk was the (tie-) beam immediately above the open front of the shop. 'Paradise', first referred to in 1503, may have been a superior storeyed version of these shops or booths; in 1537 it was a burgage with a small chamber and loft (*solarius*).[12]

It is not possible to reconstruct in convincing detail the cycles of prosperity of Haverfordwest despite the survival of some rentals and accounts.[13] However the architecture of the parish churches does provide a thought-provoking guide to major phases of investment in building which one assumes corresponded to periods of affluence or to the confidence of patrons in the medieval town. It is quite clear from the surviving architecture that two expensive building phases, separated by 250 years, are represented in St Mary's Church: the first half of the thirteenth century and the last quarter of the fifteenth. These periods of rebuilding coincided with two major events: the virtual refounding of the town after its destruction by Llywelyn and, secondly, the 1479 charter of incorporation granted by the Prince of Wales (Edward V) as lord of Haverford (with the subsequent royal confirmations). There was a broadly similar building chronology at Tenby parish church.[14]

To deal with the first period: the rapid recovery of the town after the burning of the town by Llywelyn in 1220 is clear. Four charters were granted to the town by William and Gilbert Marshal, successive earls of Pembroke.[15] These charters of course may have been aspirational, intending to encourage prosperity, rather than indicating an actually successful town. However, it is clear that the first half of the thirteenth century witnessed some exceptional building work at Haverfordwest. The *Annales Cambriae* recorded that in 1223 a major new church dedicated to St Thomas was begun at Haverfordwest. This may be a reference to the parish church of St Thomas, although it is hardly a major church, or to the Augustinian Priory church, or conceivably a mistake for St Mary's. Certainly St Mary was a major church and it was radically reconstructed – perhaps wholly rebuilt – at this period. St Mary's was an ambitious aisled church. Its nave and chancel were separated from the north chapel and aisle by a series of sophisticated clustered columns with carved capitals which would have been acceptable in a major church. The decorative treatment of these columns can in fact be paralleled in the cathedral churches at Wells and Dublin. There can be little doubt that the work at Haverford was directly inspired by the early-thirteenth-century innovative building work at Wells. This went beyond a general correspondence to some direct borrowings in the treatment of the wryly humorous figures which emerge from the stiff-leaf foliage of the capitals. St Mary's was not only a demonstration of the readiness of patrons to invest in expensive building work, it was also an expression of Haverfordwest's economic and cultural connections with Ireland and the west of England.[16]

This Gothic church was expensively enlarged and embellished over 250 years later, apparently marking the recovery of the town from a long period of decline.[17] In the last quarter of the fifteenth century the main body of the church was raised and traceried clerestory windows introduced to light the nave and chancel. A new 'Jesus aisle' was created by enlarging the old north aisle. The open pitched roof over the nave and chancel was replaced by a fashionable panelled ceiling with extravagant bosses at the intersection of the moulded ribs. This flat roof was in a national rather than a vernacular style which might be adopted by any important and wealthy church. Comparable roofs are strung along the western seaboard from Cheshire to the west country. In Pembrokeshire the new work at St Mary's was superior to the contemporary but rather vernacular waggon roof at Tenby and was to be surpassed only by the (later) nave ceiling in St David's Cathedral where astonishing pendants took the place of bosses.[18] This work cannot be dated precisely but it is probable that the enlargement of St Mary's followed the borough's 1479 charter of incorporation which gave new status to St Mary's as the corporation church. This date is consistent with several surviving grants which reveal the concern of burgesses to beautify their (new) church: in 1488, John Miles gave to the church two seats in the north aisle which he had erected at his own expense; in 1509, William Dier gave two latten 'chandlers', or standard candlesticks, to be placed in the chancel before the high altar. Presumably, new stalls for the mayor and corporation were created at this time. The flamboyant bench end of the mayor's stall displaying the royal arms and a figure of the Archangel Michael (the mayors were elected at Michaelmas) is a precious survival. Coats of arms of donors and patrons were incorporated in the glazing of the new clerestory windows and still survived, if somewhat grimy, in the late sixteenth century. Donors were customarily recalled by name every Sunday, when the souls of church benefactors were commended by the priest from the pulpit.[19]

Externally, the most striking feature of St Mary's was the new bell-tower with leaded spire which was reconstructed at the north-west end of the church. This new tower completed a trio of towered churches in the borough. The plain-vaulted towers at St Martin's and St Thomas's may have been more venerable structures but St Mary's was unquestionably the finest of the three (with a lierne vault) and belonged to a broad phase of late-fifteenth- and early-sixteenth-century tower building in the principal Welsh towns, including Cardiff and Wrexham.[20]

Haverfordwest had become a town of bells. In addition to the bell-towers of the three parish churches there were two bells in the Friary tower ('steeple') and presumably others at the Priory. A separate sanctus bell was perched on the chancel roof of St Mary's in an ogee-arched bellcote. The peals and tolling of these various bells helped structure daily devotional and secular routines and announced important events, arrivals and departures. The solemn significance of bells was clearly expressed in 1465 by the will of John Bulton, burgess of Haverford, which left elaborate instructions for his funeral mass and annual commemoration. Bulton required that his knell should be rung annually at the feast of St Thomas with three peals from the five bells of St Mary's.[21]

John Bulton also bequeathed an income (5s. 8d. annually) for the 'sustenance of Our Lady's taper which was to burn before her perpetually'. This was presumably the origin of Our Lady's taper at Haverfordwest which eventually came to Cromwell's attention and was extinguished by Bishop Barlow in 1538, after burning for two generations.[22] Haverford's taper must have been akin to the more illustrious taper at Cardigan: a perpetually burning wax candle placed in the hand of a statue of Our Lady. The location of the taper is uncertain, but it seems likely that it burned in the chapel dedicated to Our Lady above the vaulted charnel house* in the corner of St Mary's churchyard.

It may be, as Sir Glanmor Williams has suggested, that the Englishness of south Pembrokeshire may have encouraged the reception of Protestantism, but the visual shock of the Reformation cannot be doubted. There had been a major investment in religious buildings and their furnishings in Haverfordwest in the generation before the Reformation. Given the number of religious buildings in Haverfordwest the impact of the Reformation was inevitably very marked and the town's architectural face and routines of life were radically changed. The priory and friary were dissolved and the various chapels turned over to secular uses. Presumably a fair proportion of the silver objects and 63 bells listed in the Edwardian (1552-3) epitome of church goods for the hundred of Roose came from Haverford.[23] But there were secular compensations for the town. In Wales, Protestantism and the Acts of Union arrived together and it is clear that the Acts of Union brought new status, civic ritual and buildings to the early modern town of Haverfordwest.

II. THE EARLY MODERN TOWN

In the mid-Tudor period Haverfordwest emerged as the pre-eminent town within south-west Wales and was rivalled only by Carmarthen. Of the two other Pembrokeshire walled boroughs, Pembroke was in decay and Tenby was small and remote. The decay of Pembroke was graphically noted by Leland in the 1530s and its ruined houses still shocked observers fifty years later. Whereas Haverfordwest had successfully expanded beyond the Castleton, the east suburb of Pembroke once 'almost as great as the town' had atrophied and Leland found it 'totally yn ruine'. Haverfordwest prospered and by 1577 it had become, according to the surveyor of the lordship, 'the best buylt, the most civill and quickest occupied Towne in south Wales'.[24]

At the Act of Union the bishop of St David's had pressed the claims of Haverford as the new shire town arguing that it had a central position within Pembrokeshire. In the event Haverfordwest's peculiar status as a town and county in itself (first granted by royal charter in 1479) was confirmed and the borough granted its own Court of Great Sessions. The special status of the borough turned Haverford into a ritual space when the judges of the Great Sessions were on circuit and arrived at the limits of the town and county.[25]

The judges and their escort were met at the boundary of the borough by the mayor, sheriff, aldermen, bailiffs and serjeants with their maces and escorted over the bridge into the town where the sessions were held in the Guildhall. The Great Sessions for Pembrokeshire and Haverfordwest were held at the same time by the same judges, but a special ceremonial was devised to emphasise the judicial separateness of the two counties. Although the sessions were held in the Guildhall, the proclamation of the sessions for Pembrokeshire, and all the judgments for the shire, were made in the outer court (the Castle Green) of the partially ruined castle which was deemed outside the limits of the town. These must have been crowded and solemn occasions, especially when the judgments of life and death were made by the scarlet-robed judges. However, these carefully structured proceedings were at the mercy of the weather. It was recommended that a separate shire hall should be constructed within the castle for the Great Sessions and the courts of the lordship. This was never accomplished, and the charter of James I (1610) empowered the judges to hold the sessions for Pembrokeshire in Haverford's Guildhall, temporarily exempting persons attending the court from the jurisdiction of the borough.[26]

Haverford had become in effect if not actually in name the shire town and it became convenient to locate shire buildings within Haverfordwest, notably the county prison (housed in the Cockhouse*), the Workhouse* (for the punishment and employment of rogues and vagabonds) and the Armoury* which stored the arms and gunpowder of the militia in the vaulted charnel house and secularized chapel. The division of responsibility for the upkeep of these buildings, especially where they were owned by the town, was never entirely clear. The dilapidation of the gaol and workhouse was a constant item among presentments to the Court of Great Sessions and repairs to the town hall eventually became a bone of contention between shire and borough. It is revealing that the town hall was never fashionably rebuilt in timber as were other shire halls at, for example, Llanidloes, Brecon and the quintessentially stone-built town of Dolgellau. It may be that the shire could not be persuaded to contribute towards the cost of a new guildhall. The old hall drifted into disrepair in the mid eighteenth century and was deemed dangerous to those attending the sessions. The fine subsequently imposed on the town, if estreated, may well have helped pay for the modest new pedimented and stuccoed stone-built shire hall (still of traditional plan raised over a basement) which replaced the old guildhall about 1761.[27]

The mayor and twenty-four members of the common council, generally drawn from the town's merchants, were a powerful and increasingly status-conscious group who were able to dominate the town until the early nineteenth century. The wealth and respectability of the seventeenth-century mercer-burgesses was proverbial (according to Fenton) and their ranks were swelled by the younger sons of the principal county families. The dignity of the corporation was emphasized by ordinances of 1630 which required the members of the common council to process with the mayor to and from St Mary's church wearing their gowns. This show of aldermanic power was consciously intended to add 'authority and grace to the government of the place' and work 'a more awful obedience into the inferior sort of people'. Within the church mayor and common council sat as a body in the stalls flanking the chancel; a practice followed in some other Welsh boroughs, as at Conwy. Privilege of burial within the corporation church was increasingly restricted to aldermen and other members of the common council and their wives, rather than the meaner sort of burgesses, essentially tradesmen.[28] It is probable that the older monuments in the church were swept away at this time; Dineley was able to find only one inscription of note in 1684. The surviving memorial brass to John Davids, depicting the former mayor in his gown, is a good expression of mid-seventeenth-century aldermanic pride.[29]

The burgesses were organised into craft guilds with their own regulations and halls. The Feltmakers' Hall and Shoemakers' Hall are both referred to in the 1580s.[30] Fundamentally, the guild and town ordinances restricted trade to burgesses and guild members. Non-burgesses attempting to trade in the town could be prosecuted at Haverfordwest's Court of Great Sessions. The domination of the town by the common council was complete so long as the trade of the town was protected and the privileges of the burgesses observed. Departures from this unspoken bargain provoked rebellion. Numerous burgesses 'rose in mutiny' in 1633 when the mayor and common council proposed to grow corn in the town field which was used for common grazing. It was grimly said, 'they that sowe there shall never reape.' The visit of the Commissioners for Excise to the corporation in 1646, and their entertainment in the Guildhall, provoked an 'Amazonian' riot by poor women, presumably brewers and alewives, afraid of the imposition of new taxes. They laid siege to the Guildhall and the commissioners were forced to retreat for fear of their lives while the mayor made a futile attempt to pacify the protestors.[31] A sustained mid-seventeenth-century challenge to the established order came from the Quakers in the aftermath of the Civil War with the growth of radical dissenting congregations. Public buildings, particularly the parish church and the shire hall, provided public spaces for challenging orthodoxy and authority. In 1659 William Bateman and several tradesmen publicly challenged the doctrines of the preacher at St Mary's and Bateman was later prosecuted for holding conventicles at his house where 'strangers' and townsmen 'to a great number of persons met'. In 1662 thirteen

Fig. 32 St Mary's Church. Bench end of the stall for the Mayor and Sheriff displaying royal arms and figure of the Archangel Michael .

(Crown copyright: Royal Commission on the Ancient and Historical Monuments of Wales).

Fig. 33　Brass commemorating John Davids, mayor in 1642.

Quakers were fined and imprisoned for a memorable display of lack of deference when they refused to remove their hats in the sessions at the Guildhall. The rebuilding of the council chamber within St Mary's was a signal of the common council's determination to re-establish their authority at the Restoration. The location of the new highly visible council chamber, crowning the north porch of the corporation church, was an unmistakable statement of the identification of the borough's ruling élite with the Anglican church and their determination to exclude dissenters from the burgess roll.[32]

Haverfordwest was accounted not only 'civil' and populous but also the best-built town in Elizabethan Pembrokeshire. There was probably a solid inheritance of mid-Tudor and earlier burgess houses, shops and rows. The houses of substantial burgesses at the Acts of Union were stone built and already storeyed. An interesting and amusing series of depositions concerning the boundaries of the town preserves incidentally a description of a house which stood at the entry to the town. Crucially, the house straddled the boundary between one jurisdiction and another so that the hall and inner parlour, separated by a gabled stone partition ('pinion'), lay in different lordships. In 1534 the abbot of St Dogmaels was arrested for debt by the town's sergeant-at-mace while dining in the hall. His host exclaimed, 'Beshrew the Serjeant! If we had known this we might have stept into the parlour and been out of his libertie.'[33]

It is not unreasonable to suppose that this house, contemporary with the open timber halls of the Welsh border, was something like the surviving Tudor Merchant's House at Tenby: stone built with the principal rooms (hall and parlour), all with fireplaces, on the first floor, reached by internal stairs (rather than external stairs) from the ground-floor kitchen. Sixteenth-century inventories are rare, but we

Fig. 34 Staircase at seventeenth-century Clibborn House, Quay Street, demolished *c.*1930, from *Nooks & Corners of Pembrokeshire* by H Thornhill Timmins (1895).
(*Photo copyright: Thomas Lloyd*).

can gain an impression of the furnishing of a storeyed and heated townhouse from a mid-Tudor legal action which lists the goods of a south Pembrokeshire burgess. The furnishings included tables and benches ('fourmes'), presumably for the hall and kitchen, two 'skews' or fireside settles (a significant detail), bedsteads in the chambers, and tubs ('le kyvys') from the service-rooms. Still more revealing are the valuable and portable six panes of glass and the 'sprewse chest full of evydens'.[34]

Haverfordwest's ruling élite, which included six of the county's *generosi* listed by George Owen, lived in grander houses, one of which had the revealing name 'Great House'. The great houses were subjected to campaigns of fashionable modernization. In 1697 Mr. Barlow's house in Haverfordwest was 'new modelling' by an architect, the otherwise unknown Mr Hancocke, who was also working at Orielton, Picton, and constructing a 'water follye' at Landshipping. A sketch of a grand stair with barley-twist balusters provides a glimpse of the town's fine seventeenth-century interiors which have now been entirely swept away.[35] However, remarkably, a

Fig. 35
No.15 High Street,
sixteenth-century house.
(Crown copyright: Royal Commission on the Ancient and Historical Monuments of Wales).

fragmentary sixteenth-century mansion with some revealing period detail has survived in 15 High Street behind a nineteenth-century refronting. The plan of the house is uncertain but several important armorial fireplaces survive as well as the stone mullions of a five-light principal window. This was almost certainly one of the windows filled with armorial glass which George Owen noted in the town houses of Morgan Voyle and Jenet Jermyn in 1574. The heraldic fireplace at 15 High Street suggests that this house belonged to the Voyle family who had built up an extensive estate between 1550-70 and served the corporation as mayor and sheriff. The Voyles were proud of their descent from Cuhelyn Fardd of Cemais and Morgan Voyle registered the family pedigree and arms with Lewys Dwnn at the end of the sixteenth century.[36]

The great house in High Street seems to be a unique survivor although here and there in the town corbelled chimneys and blocked windows provide tantalizing hints of early building. Drawings and early photographs reveal how drastically the external appearance of town houses changed in the eighteenth and nineteenth centuries. It is initially a shock to discover from photographs that some of the houses near St Mary's Church which survived into the second half of the nineteenth century were elaborately jettied, timber-framed dwellings which would not have been out of place in Shrewsbury, Chester, the towns of the West Country, or, indeed, London.[37] But on reflection one need not be surprised. Haverfordwest was a trading town and drew on a widely spread and distinctive urban domestic architecture which survives today only in faded towns like Totnes. The visual record show that a variety of two- and three-storey houses with single or double jetties existed in Haverfordwest.[38] It seems clear that these were timber-fronted rather than fully timber-framed houses since the fireplace was placed in a stone lateral wall. Nevertheless, the timber fronts were elaborately treated with moulded jetty beams and ornamental gable framing. The striking contrast between stone building and timber building was apparent to contemporaries. George Owen's remark to the effect that mason's work was getting worse and worse while carpenters' work was better and better was a reference both to the decay of masonry castles and to the appearance of magnificent timber houses in the walled towns of sixteeenth-century west Wales.[39]

Although most of the early modern houses have been altered, documentary sources do disclose some of the vocabulary used to describe houses. A technical craftsmen's terminology of *wynd-beams* (probably tie-beams or collars), s*yntorn* (centering) and the like is recorded in building accounts.[40] More broadly, an everyday vocabulary relating to houses and streets is revealed in the presentments of the grand jury. The curtilage in front of a house was called a *forefront* and distinguished from the *backside* where there was a yard or a garden. Many houses, especially those occupying burgage plots, were built with a gable end or *pinion* facing the street rather than a long elevation. The *outward pinions* of decayed houses sometimes threatened to fall into the street. Some houses had a pentice or *half-roof* which provided a covered walk at the front of the house. Some modest half-roofs on the outskirts of town can be glimpsed in Bucks's mid-eighteenth-century engraving but more ambitious half-roofs, presumably supported by posts, were built within the town and sometimes obstructed the highway. A half-roof

Fig. 36 Heraldic fireplace at 15 High Street suggesting that it was the home of the Voyle family.

(Crown copyright: Royal Commission on the Ancient and Historical Monuments of Wales).

had stopped up the highway at the entrance to Ship Street in 1688, according to a grand jury presentment. Other obstructions included *pairs of stairs* (presumably framed stairs) housed in outshuts which projected into the street. These stair projections seem to have been a particular feature of the rows where permanent stairs had replaced ladder access to lofts. Beyond the curtilage of the house, sometimes bounded by the *forefront hedge* or wall, was the street with its gutter or *channel* and occasional pavement. Borough ordinances required burgesses to pave the streets in front of their houses and to bury drains and to keep the streets clean. Nevertheless, rubbish accumulated in the streets in great *mixens* or dungheaps or was thrown into the town stream, the appropriately-named 'Shitternslake', which formed foetid and dangerous pools when it was not cleansed and scoured. The accumulation of rubbish in Shitternslake was so great in 1696 that the grand jury claimed that it threatened the lives of the poor people of the almshouse.[41]

The Corporation's responsibility for the maintenance of public buildings was helped by the income from Sir John Perrot's gift to the town (1580) which was specifically intended for the repair of the town's bridges, walls, quays, conduits and other communal structures. There were many campaigns of repair to the quay but it is a measure of its importance that the townsmen as a body repaired the quay in 1616, each burgess providing a day's labour. The town's defensive structures were less important. It was probably with some relief that the common council acquiesced to Cromwell's order to deface the castle as the alternative was the maintenance of a garrison in the town. The town's walls and gates seem to have been silently eroded during the eighteenth century and had disappeared by the turn of the nineteenth century. The visitation of the plague in the mid seventeenth century had provided the last occasion when the townsfolk withdrew behind their walls and gates.[42]

Haverfordwest was fundamentally an open, trading town and its prosperity depended on its port, markets and fairs, although there were inevitably changes in the types of commodities traded.[43] Haverfordwest was technically a creek of the port of Milford and subordinate to the main customhouse at Pembroke (which, it is interesting to note, was furnished with a selection of Tudor royal portraits which overlooked the green baize tables).[44] The tidal river

Fig. 37 'The oldest house in Haverfordwest'.

(Pembrokeshire Library collection).

provided a relatively cheap method of carriage (cheaper than road) for incoming and outgoing goods and ships of quite large tonnage could dock at Haverfordwest. Bucks's *East View of Haverford* (1748) shows a range of shipping along the river from two-masted seagoing vessels to flat-bottomed barges moored at the bridge causeway. The barges probably had a central trading role but it is largely hidden since the trade of non-sea-going vessels were not registered in the port books of the customhouse. Bucks's mid-eighteenth-century engraving shows a range of substantial and relatively new warehouses of three or more storeys along the three quays, including the wool market which still survives. Smaller and older two-storey warehouses with chambers over the vaulted basements, mentioned in sixteenth-century sources, were scattered along the river front and adjacent streets and survived until relatively recently.[45]

The market was fundamental to the prosperity of Haverfordwest and its burgesses. By charter, the town was allowed two weekly markets which were held on Tuesdays (a small market) and Saturdays (a great market) and the number of fairs increased with the necessary but expensive process of charter renewal. A Bartholomew Fair established by the 1610 charter was held like the weekly markets in and near St Mary's churchyard. George Owen memorably described Haverfordwest market as one of the 'greatest and plentifullest' markets within the Marches of Wales and listed some of the food sold there: meat (beef, mutton, pork, bacon, veal, kid and coney), domestic fowls (goose, capons, turkey) and wildfowl, and for fish 'it passeth all others in Wales'. Many marvelled that the victuals 'seen at noon should be shifted away ere night'. But how was all this organized? The market was not a planned architectural space but a kind of ordered anarchy where stalls for different kinds of produce had established niches. There were few permanent buildings beyond the meat shambles (great and little) under the Guildhall, provided with stalls and trestles, and an arcaded corn market-house which was rebuilt in 1701 according to a plan by a Colonel Wheeler. A low, flagged wall with a pent-roof, obscurely called "Penniless Bench" served as the fish market. Beyond this there were no special market buildings but only booths and stalls which temporarily filled the four or five streets near the Guildhall. a flesh market was held in the churchyard and it seems probable that frames were placed over the churchyard wall from which joints were suspended; a length of wall serving as the 'pork bench' was still recalled in the late nineteenth century. In Pillory Street there were stalls selling garden stuff and roots, salt butter and salt meat. A separate hen market was noted in St Mary Street in 1536. The market was under the control of the mayor who appointed a clerk of the markets who collected the tolls, kept the approved weights, measures and common beam. Ordinances regulated trading in certain commodities to fixed hours and a clock, first mentioned in 1564, was maintained by the corporation.[46]

Conflicts connected with the markets were inevitable. Traders who competed with burgesses (who paid no tolls), particularly petty chapmen and peddlers, were regularly rounded up, fined and excluded from the market. Clerks of the market were suspected of extortion and keeping false measures. By the second half of the eighteenth century the chaotic market was something of an embarrassment to the common council. The presence of numerous butchers' stalls in the churchyard was found increasingly offensive. The butchers and other traders were excluded from the market in 1773 by the churchwardens and ordered by the mayor to remove to the streets on the north side of the churchyard. Great confusion ensued 'as persons who had goods to sell did not know where to expose them, and their customers did not know where to find them'. The butchers claimed a prescriptive right, took legal advice and returned to the churchyard but 'the battle of the market' signalled the beginnings of the improved town.[47]

III The Improved Town

The impetus for improvement derived partly from the development of Haverfordwest as a leisure town for the gentry. Bucks's engraving shows that an assembly room had been established in the town by 1748. A bowling green with a handsome gazebo adorned Castle Green and a promenade developed along the banks of the river with a view of the priory ruins. The calendar of social occasions included the spring and autumn assize weeks, the Portfield races, the hunt week, and the balls connected with these events. Mrs Morgan in her *Tour to Milford Haven* left a memorable account of Haverfordwest's assembly-room balls in assize week which were attended by persons of fortune from the town and country. These opportunities for professional and gentry families to meet for pleasure and business earned Haverfordwest the self-congratulatory title 'Little Bath'.[48]

The battle of St Mary's churchyard market showed that the determination to shed the more rumbustious elements of the early modern town and improve its appearance reached back to the 1770s. New public buildings expressed a practical concern for improvement.

John Howard's condemnation of the shire prison (*The Cockhouse*) with its dangerous 'dungeons' and 'offensive upper rooms' hastened the building of a new gaol within the castle where the gaoler was installed in a splendid new bow-fronted house. Fenton admired the result which not only preserved the picturesque and venerable appearance of the castle but also removed a nuisance from the town, and advocated that other corporate towns should follow Haverfordwest's example. Nash's later gaols at Carmarthen (within the castle) and Cardigan (a new site) were superior to Haverfordwest's and may have prompted a further round of improvements to the prison. In 1820 the gaol was enlarged and the division of prisoners into their separate classes 'perfected'. The market was finally tidied up in 1825 when a lavish new market-house was opened with shambles for an army of eighty butchers as well as stalls for the sale of poultry, butter and vegetables.[49]

There was probably a competitive element in the construction of these new public buildings. Pembroke, Haverfordwest's nearest trading rival, had in 1819 embarked on an ambitious and comprehensive scheme of improvement which involved the demolition of the old shambles and adjoining properties in order to build a new town hall, council room, and school room, separate corn

Fig. 38 Western Cleddau and Old Bridge.   (*Pembrokeshire Library collection*).

Fig. 39 Haverfordwest quay and warehouses.   *(Sam Nicolson)*

and fish markets, and a new marketplace with standings. By 1822 this complex was uncompleted and deteriorating and the corporation claimed damages of £1,000 from the contractors. With Pembroke's ambitious scheme semi-ruinous, Haverfordwest resolved to build a new market-house which was opened in 1825 and accounted 'one of the greatest improvements ever made in the town'. Despite the success of the new market it was characteristic of the unreformed old corporation that the accounts of the building committee were found to be completely chaotic. The 'convenient and substantial' building probably cost about £5,000 (including the purchase money) but no one could be sure since the only sources of information were the statements of the builder and the guesses of the committee.[50]

The town at this point was largely inhabited by 'shopkeepers, mechanics, and persons of moderate independent fortunes' attracted by 'the cheapness of living'. A few wealthy gentry families remained resident in substantial townhouses which included Foley House, built for Richard Foley in 1794, now the most complete of John Nash's early pre-picturesque houses. Haverfordwest was visited by numerous tourists who were agreeably surprised at the size of the town ('larger than Bury St Edmunds' according to Mrs Morgan) and its picturesque qualities when approached from the bridge. A cascade of sparkling lime-washed houses tumbled from the hilltop castle to the riverside. Sir Richard Colt Hoare noticed 'a suite of small hanging gardens neatly laid out with fanciful little buildings'. The whole effect was very pleasing – 'a most eligable acsidentiary achievement'. Nevertheless, once inside the town, visitors discovered that the streets were narrow, irregular, and ill-paved as well as impossibly steep in places, inducing in newcomers an undignified gait something between sliding and walking. Despite a leavening of good houses and shops, the 'slovenly' appearance of the streets and the absence of regular pitching and paving combined (as the Muncipal Boundaries' Commissioners woundingly expressed it) to deprive the town 'of an air of respectability'.[51]

The solution was to straighten out, clean up and modernize the town. The new status of Haverfordwest as one of only 178 new municipal corporations, granted by the 1835 Municipal Reform Act, accelerated schemes for improving the approach to the town by building a new bridge, for supplying the town with water, and for lighting the town with gas. Some paving of the town was undertaken by public subscription. The abolition of the Court of Great Sessions in 1833 after nearly 300 years provided a break with the early modern town and was the key to the improvement of the town. Formerly the judges had approached the guildhall by a circuitous dogleg from the old bridge. The judges of the new assize courts, it was said, "did not long put up with the stuffy, ill-ventilated old building which had served their predecessors." A scheme was rapidly put afoot to build a new shire hall at the other end of High Street. The neo-classical shire hall, completed in 1837, was an enormous building, eventually able to seat 900, and was soon a theatre for the trials of Rebecca rioters. A square was formed opposite the shire hall and a bridge erected by special act of parliament which provided a new point of entry into the town. A fundamental break with the past was made with the demolition of the old guildhall which (as Lewis's influential *Topographical Dictionary* noted) had obstructed the venerable parish church. The result of this replanning was a grand entry into the town over the new bridge directly into the principal street with St Mary's Church forming a *point de vue* at the end of the thoroughfare.[52]

Fig. 40 Foley House.

(Crown copyright: Royal Commission on the Ancient and Historical Monuments of Wales).

Fig. 41 Toll Gate.

(Pembrokeshire Library collection).

The driving force behind the improvement schemes was William Owen, an able architect who was four times mayor. Owen, the son of a Haverfordwest cabinet-maker with premises were in Short Row, was appointed county surveyor in 1824 and used his influence to push forward a coherent scheme of improvement which took over two decades to complete and involved not only the construction of key public buildings but also the replanning of the town's principal street. The responsibility for improving the approach to the town was vested in Commissioners but Owen apparently personally financed the new bridge, eventually recouping the outlay from tolls. Owen was an industrious, self-made Smilesean figure who personified the break with the town's old ruling élite and eventually acquired Hermon's Hill, the largest house in Haverfordwest.[53]

The replanning of the town hall involved radical changes to domestic buildings. The old rows were entirely swept away. In many places (the Boundary Commissioners noted) 'bad houses have been pulled down, and good houses built in their stead', including the urbane Castle Terrace (1832).[54] The change in the appearance of the heart of the town is beautifully illustrated by two drawings made in the 1830s, after the removal of the rows, and not long before the demolition of the old guildhall. The drawings illustrate the old and the new architectural character of the town appropriately seen through windows of different periods (Figs. 42 & 43).[55] In the first drawing a row of three jettied timber-fronted houses are viewed through the leaded panes of a mullioned and high-transomed window of seventeenth-century type. The houses are in various states of repair. The upper house still retains its decorative framing, but the framing of the lower houses has been rendered over. The fine applied window of the central house, supported on moulded brackets, now sports modern sash windows. The jetty of the house on the left, supported by chamfered posts, provides a convenient covered walk which is terminated by the underbuilt jetty of its neighbour. To the right of the picture is the old gated and probably redundant guildhall. The improving county town is framed in the second drawing by the moulded glazing bars of a sash window. The view looks further down the High Street (glimpsing the type of deep bracketed eaves popularised by Nash) towards the proposed new shire-hall and new bridge. The old narrow burgess houses with their confusion of roofs

Fig. 42 Drawing, probably by Thomas Ellis, of Short Row School, showing three jettied timber-fronted house and the Guildhall, with its fine gates and piers.

Fig. 43 Drawing, probably by Thomas Ellis, showing the south side of High Street.

and timber gables fronting the street have given way to tidy long-fronted stone-built houses. Many of these houses have professional or business premises on the ground floor, and the family apartments on the upper floor are signalled by a series of pretty bow windows. The scene is recognizably the beginning of modern Haverfordwest.

*   *   *

I have tried to describe the continuities and changes of the architectural face of Haverfordwest through a series of chronological slices. Some changes in the nineteenth century involved fundamental breaks with the past: the demolition of the Guildhall and the relocation of the market ended the continuity of half a millennium of trading and town government in the historic space around St Mary's church. The arrival of the railway sealed the fate of the old port in mid century, and the sale of the old Council House in 1862 and its subsequent demolition completed the break with the old corporation. Nevertheless, against the odds, the town's historic topography and some key historic buildings have survived Victorian and twentieth-century redevelopment. It is pleasing to know that there is a rich and largely undisturbed archaeology beneath the town and that there are still architectural secrets behind the nineteenth-century street fronts.

RICHARD SUGGETT

APPENDIX:
NOTES ON SELECTED BUILDINGS

This appendix provides notes on the town's public buildings, now mostly demolished. An unpublished lecture by my former colleague, A.J. Parkinson, 'Early Buildings of Haverfordwest' (RCAHMW, 1979), has been a particularly valuable source for these notes.

The following abbreviations have been used:

Charles 1955: 'Haverfordwest Accounts 1563-1620', *National Library of Wales Journal*, ix (1955-56), 157-79.

Charles 1967: *Calendar of the Records of the Borough of Haverfordwest 1539-1660'*, ed. B.G. Charles, Cardiff 1967.

Charles 1992: *The Place-names of Pembrokeshire*, Aberystwyth 1992.

Phillips and Warren: *The History of Haverfordwest with that of some Pembrokeshire Parishes*, Haverfordwest 1914.

Warren 1914: *The History and Antiquities of St Mary's Church, Haverfordwest*, Letchworth 1914.

H'west Deeds: Haverfordwest Deeds and Documents transferred to the Pembrokeshire Record Office from the National Library of Wales; schedule by B.G. Charles, 1960. NLW Microfilm 355-63.

The Guildhall. References from the late thirteenth century onwards (Charles 1992, 648). The stone built town hall set over vaulted shambles and regarded as the shire hall after the town's 1610 charter. The medieval guildhall does not seem to have been rebuilt in the 16th and 17th centuries and many repairs are recorded in the borough accounts (Charles 1955, 175-6). Grand jury presentments in 1748 and 1761 that the guildhall was dangerous and ruinous (NLW, Great Sessions file formerly in Wales 28/190-II and 4/817/1/I). Failure to repair led to a fine of £400 (Phillips & Warren 93). The town hall was rebuilt in the 1760s but rendered redundant when the new shire hall was completed, and demolished in 1837-8 (Phillips & Warren 99). The drawing by Thomas Ellis (1822, reproduced by Joyner, *Artists in Wales*, 33) shows a gated stuccoed neo-classical building with a clock. Another drawing 'from memory' (copy in NLW 1411C) shows the arches of the shambles. The South African war memorial now stands on the site (SM 9522 1557).

The Shire Hall, at the lower end of High Street, replaced the Guildhall after the abolition of the Court of Great Sessions. Neo-classical designs by William Owen, completed in 1837 (Colvin, *Biographical Dictionary of British Architects*, 3rd edn. 1995, 718.) Plan: NLW, Picton Castle 4663. (SM 9541 1561).

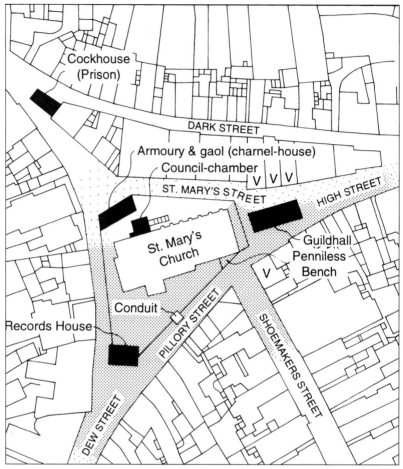

Fig. 44 Plan of the town in the environs of St Mary's Church.

The Council House. The meeting place of the mayor and common council where the corporation chest was kept. A building distinct from the Guildhall, first referred to in the sixteenth century Repairs to the building suggest that it was an upper chamber, perhaps over a vault, but its location is unknown (Charles 1955, 173-6). The Common Council seems to have first met in the 'new' Council House, built over the north porch of St Mary's Church in 1661 (Phillips & Warren 84). Depicted in Bucks's engraving (1748); photographs show a rather Georgian building with large sash windows regarded with horror by *The Ecclesiologist* as 'an ugly structure' (1848, 253. Sold by the Corporation in 1860 and demolished (H'west Deeds 1400-22; *Arch. Camb.* 1902, 118-20).

The Record House. The records of the town and county of Haverfordwest, and of the county of Pembroke, principally the sessions records, were kept at Haverfordwest. The early history of record keeping is obscure. In 1661, immediately after the Restoration, there was concern 'to preserve ye records of the town and county' and £10 was ordered to help pay for a place 'convenient between the Shirehall and yard of St Maries' (NLW, Great Sessions 4/791/2/1). This was considered in 1696 a 'very improper place', being a house 'not inhabited nor any fire kept in it except in sessions time' which might lead to the loss of records and thus 'injurious' and hazardous to the counties (Great Sessions 801/1/6/33). A purpose-built records house in Gothic style was constructed in the late eighteenth century (1791?) on the south side of the churchyard. The pillared records room was raised over a rib-vaulted (fireproof) ground-floor storey used as a butter-, later, fish-market. William Henry Black reported that the Great Sessions records occupied three very large double presses and the records were subsequently removed to the to the Public Record Office (*First Report of the Deputy Keeper of the Public Records*, London 1840, 106,115). The building, regarded as medieval, survived into the mid twentieth century but was demolished in 1951 despite its status as a listed building. Wartime photographs by the National Buildings Record (1941) and reconstructed plan by A.J. Parkinson in the NMRW. (SM 9517 1553).

The Cockhouse. A stone-built vaulted prison to the north of St Mary's Church. References to the Cockhouse begin in the fourteenth century (Charles 1992, 647). The name was probably a humorous reference to the height of the storeyed stone building in relation to the booths of Middle Row (cf. the Cock-tower at Cardiff). The 1610 borough charter continued the use of the Cockhouse as the county gaol for Pembrokeshire. The grand jury in 1623 considered the Cockhouse 'too litle for the receipte of prisoners of men and women togeather'; the lower room, probably vaulted, measured only 10 feet by 14 feet; the upper room (loft), 10 feet by 15 feet (Great Sessions 4/782/2/31). Enlarged in 1656 (Charles 1967, 150) and subsequently, creating six rooms. The two 'dungeons' and 'dirty and offensive' upper rooms were condemned by John Howard in *The State of the Prisons* (London, 1777, 465-6). Closed with the construction of the new County Gaol and demolished in the nineteenth century. (SM 9515 1562)

(New) County Gaol. The new gaol for the county of Pembroke was built within the inner ward of the castle after a 1779 enabling Act. Agreement between the county and contractors to complete the gaol by 1 December 1780 for £1,200 (NLW, Francis Green Transcripts, ix, 216-7). Descriptions by John Howard (1782 and 1788) and James Nield (1803) and in NLW MS, 1408B, 12. Accommodation for felons, debtors and a bridewell, chapel and gaoler's house. Prison enlarged in 1821 (from 22 to 86) with the closing of the town gaol when 'the proper system of classification of prisoners perfected' and a treadmill built (British Parliamentary Papers, *Crime and Punishment: Prisons*, vol. 9 (Shannon, 1970, 520-1, 634-5.) The surviving buildings now form the County Record Office, with the Town Museum in the Governor's house. (SM 9534 1574).

House of Correction. Authorised by the 1576 Poor Law Act for the punishment of vagabonds and setting the poor to work. Established in Haverfordwest in 1614 (Charles 1967, 48). Subsequent presentments at the Great Sessions until the mid seventeenth century. The instruments of punishment and work (looms and cards) viewed by the grand jury in 1623 (Great Sessions 4/782/2/35/, 77) and a schedule of stock compiled in 1637 (H'west Deeds 1259). Sited near Bateman's Lane (1637).

Town Gaol and Bridewell. A prison distinct from the Cockhouse and located in the Charnel House in the early 18th century, probably taking the place of the Cage under the Guildhall. Description by John Howard (*The State of the Prisons* 1777, 466). A new town gaol and bridewell was built on St Thomas's Green *c*.1800. Description in 1819 parliamentary papers (British Parliamentary Papers, *Prisons 8,* 520-1) before closure in 1822. The building was adapted as a lunatic asylum by the Act of 1822 (*Acts of Parliament concerning Wales*, ed. Jeffreys Jones, Cardiff 1966, 1655). The subsequent 'forty years of mismanagement' are chronicled by T G Davies (*Journal of the Pembrokeshire Historical Society,* 5 (1992-3, 79-84). Closed in 1866 after the joint counties asylum at Carmarthen opened.

The Charnel House and Armoury. Fifteenth-century references to the chapel over the Charnel House (Charles 1992, 647). A storeyed building on the north side of St Mary's churchyard with a vaulted bone-house on the ground floor and a chapel over dedicated to Our Lady where, probably, the taper was kept (p.127 above). Appropriated by the Crown at the Reformation and turned over to secular uses becoming the shire armoury. According to the will of Thomas Canon (1587), granting the lease to the corporation, there were two rooms above the vault for keeping and cleaning the shire armour (Warren, 1914, 24-5). Subsequently used by the corporation as a gaol and police station. Upper chapel demolished in 1891 but the vaulted chamber survived (Warren 1914, 25). The chapel can be seen in a mid-nineteenth-century proposal for reinstating St Mary's spire (NMRW). The thirteenth-century doorway serving as the north-west gateway into the churchyard is said to have come from the chapel. (SM 9518 1558).

SIR JOHN PERROT AND HAVERFORDWEST[1]

> Know ye that I, the said Sir John Perrot, for the love which I bear towards my beloved and faithful neighbours, the burgesses of the town and county of Haverfordwest, and for the mayor, sheriff, bailiffs and burgesses of the said town, have granted for them and their successors . . . messuages, lands, tenements, burgages and hereditaments . . . situate and lying as well in the town and county of Haverfordwest as in the said county of Pembroke . . .[1]

With these words, Sir John Perrot formally and publicly declared his intention to endow the town of Haverfordwest with such lands, rents and properties that, free of all charges, would yield sufficient funds for municipal improvement. The indenture was drawn up, signed by Perrot himself, sealed and one half delivered on 20 September 1580 to the grantees, the remaining half of the document was retained by the grantor.[2] Those to whom the grant was made, namely the mayor, Maurice Canon, the bailiffs, Thomas Tanke and Jenkin Davids, the sheriff, Richard Bateman and eight of the most prominent members of the town's ruling council, were entrusted with the responsibility of ensuring that 'the rents and profits to be annually derived from the premises' were to be expended on

> . . . the repair of the streets, bridges, walls, conduits of water, and for other dilapidations of the said town as well as to the rebuilding of the new quay . . . and all other works which may be needful or suitable for the improvement of the said town.[3]

Not without good reason, it seems, has the grantor been hailed universally as 'undoubtedly the town's most generous benefactor',[4] without whose munificence 'the provision of such public services as

Fig. 45
An anonymous
engraving in
mezzotint of the
portrait of Sir
John Perrot
dating from the
late eighteenth
century.

*(Reproduced by
permission of the
National Museum of
Wales).*

the inhabitants enjoyed would have been even more difficult and
uncertain'.[5] Yet Perrot's was but one among a number of donations
which sought, by various means, to enrich a town singularly
fortunate in having so many benefactors willing to part with their
wealth on its behalf. In 1581 William Walter established a fund 'for
such uses as the Corporation should think fit'. Unfortunately, as a
Charity Commission report concluded in 1831, 'they have
accordingly thought fit to pocket the lot!'.[6] Similarly, Sir Thomas
Canon (1599 and 1638), William Vawer (1606), Thomas Lloyd of
Cilciffeth (1613) and James Haward (1646) were moved by the spirit
of philanthropic adventure to endow the town with funds for projects

ranging from the repair of its churches, Guildhall and the setting up of a free grammar school, to the relief of the poor and sick generally and five of the most impoverished burgesses in particular. Nevertheless, where Perrot's generosity is remembered that of his fellow-townsmen has all but been forgotten, their funds dispersed or lost whilst his endowment continues to function to this day under the auspices of the trustees of the Sir John Perrot Trust. In an ever-changing and technologically-preoccupied world often quick to forget its roots and past history, the fact that the donation of a man long dead continues to have meaning more than four centuries after its bestowal is remarkable in itself and certainly worthy of investigation. As indeed, is the life of the man who, by his apparent selfless benevolence, ensured for himself a posthumous memorial forever linked to the town he purported to love.

Sir John was not the first (Sir Thomas d. 1461) or last (Sir Herbert d. 1683) Perrot to have close and intimate dealings with the town and county of Haverfordwest. The family's association with Pembrokeshire's premier borough was of long standing and can be traced back at least to the early fifteenth century, possibly beyond, and it continued for a further century after his death. The reason for this enduring connection with, and fascination for, the town and its affairs is not difficult to fathom for it was, in the opinion of one who knew it well, the affecting squire of Henllys, George Owen, 'a good town, wealthy and well governed'.[7] It was a sentiment evidently shared by shire resident and visitor alike for in the opinion of one who surveyed it on behalf of the Crown in 1577, Robert Davey, Haverfordwest was 'the best built, the most civil and quickest occupied town in South Wales'.[8] Certainly, it was among the largest and wealthiest urban centres in Wales and its weekly market, after Carmarthen, much the most prosperous. 'The market of Haverfordwest is thought to be one of the greatest and plentifullest markets (all things compared), that is within the Marches of Wales, especially for the plenty and goodness of victual,' wrote a clearly impressed and Pembrokeshire-proud George Owen.[9] The facts of it 'being seated in the midst of the shire and most convenient for trade' and thus 'greatly frequented of the country people', added to its attraction.[10] Indeed, without fear of exaggeration it is true to say that all roads in the county, such as they were, led to or radiated from

Haverfordwest so it was nigh on impossible to avoid the town. Unsurprisingly, it became a useful base in which enterprising families like the Perrots could further their commercial ambitions by tapping into the wealth of the shire.

Here, within its walls, medieval fortifications which still stood proud in the sixteenth century, town and country met and mixed, bound by their common interest in trade and the creation of wealth. Such activities often necessitated regular attendance at the town's fairs, markets and chamber of trade and more secure accommodation than that afforded by lodgings was increasingly sought by rural-based gentlemen. Certainly, George Owen was scathing in his description of some Welsh towns as being quite 'indifferent for intertaignements' which suggests he was, in the words of one historian, 'lamenting the inadequacy of comfortable lodgings, and the difficulty sometimes of finding any accommodation at all'.[11] Consequently, town houses were acquired and though they might only be used for a few days or weeks a year, some of them developed into magnificent mansions in their own right. In view of the proximity of Haroldston and although he was a substantial owner of properties within the borough, Perrot did not require either the comforts or convenience of a 'town house', at least not in neighbouring Haverfordwest. On the other hand, if his London base, Syon House, be taken as an example of his requirements in this respect, then they were such as to suggest that had he been disposed to reside inter-mural, a new rather than an existing building would have been an absolute necessity.[12] The ownership of town houses also enabled the occupiers to better their prospects of becoming members of the burghal community which, in Haverfordwest as elsewhere, jealously guarded its privileged status. It has been estimated that out of a population of between 1500 and 1700 in the 1570s, only 100 were burgesses or freemen of the borough, of whom 24 of the more powerful and influential sat in council.[13] From this latter 'ruling' or aldermanic group were nominated the chief officers of the town, namely the mayor, bailiffs and sheriff. The lesser officers of gaoler, sergeants-at-mace, beadle and chamber reeve were appointed by the mayor and common council usually from among the town's burgesses.

Haverfordwest was a cosmopolitan centre which afforded its citizens and visitors alike the experience of meeting and trading with merchants, and others, from as far afield as Ireland, France, Spain and the English south-west. The town's link with Bristol was especially strong: the Port Books of the second half of the sixteenth century note that near 90 per cent of the incoming coastal vessels hailed from the west country port.[14] The wealthier residents and merchants of Haverfordwest too had ships of their own and full use of a quay which could accommodate vessels of up to 40 tons. Perrot was the proud owner of a ship, called appropriately *The Perrot*, which plied its trade in home waters, exporting grain to Gloucestershire and further afield in importing wine from France, salt from Spain and most spectacularly of all, upwards of 19,000 tons of fish from Newfoundland.[15] In fact, the fishing industry was especially vibrant and it was said that the town's market 'for fish . . . passes all others in Wales . . . both for plenty and variety'.[16] Dependent though it undoubtedly was on its maritime trade via the navigable river Cleddau and its use of the landing points on the Haven, the town's prosperity owed much to the fact that it was almost entirely land-locked and surrounded by an agriculturally rich and fertile hinterland. To its market would come those intent on buying and selling livestock and others fortunate enough, in a largely subsistence economy, to have agricultural surpluses to dispose of. As owner, lessor and lessee of several shops in the boroughs of Haverfordwest, Pembroke and Tenby, Perrot had the means to sell directly much of what was produced on his 15 manors. Clearly, there were fortunes to be made and, not unsurprisingly, the borough's mercantile élite were among the richest, best connected and most travelled in south Wales.

The town's commercial significance and geographical convenience notwithstanding, Haverfordwest served also as the county's social and political centre. Having long outstripped Pembroke in terms of its size, wealth and importance, the Acts of Union of 1536-43 ensured, quite unintentionally, that henceforth it, rather than its one-time rival the old caput of the medieval earldom, would serve as the county seat. In acknowledging and confirming its status as a county in itself, as granted by charter in 1479, the Crown, by the act of 1543, had invested Haverfordwest with an importance and dignity which Pembroke, already in decline, could hardly match let alone surpass. That the latter had been eclipsed if not entirely ignored: is highlighted in a letter written in 1575 by Perrot to the Council in Wales and the Marches in which he states that:

> The Justices of the Peace when any commission cometh unto them do most commonly assemble in Haverfordwest, a town in the midst of the shire yet no part of the shire saving the castle, but a mere shire town of itself . . .[17]

When sitting in quarter session the county's J.P.s would most commonly assemble' in the Shire or Guildhall which doubled also as the venue for the Court of Great Sessions which met twice yearly. Here too would meet regularly the principal officers and common council of the town and it was here where borough courts and elections, both local and parliamentary, were held. Located near St Mary's church, in which yard the town market set out its stalls, the Shire Hall must have been an imposing building of at least two stories for beneath it stood the shambles the cleaning of which was undertaken and paid for by the town's authorities.[18] Needless to say, the income generated from trade, tolls, taxes and fines most commonly manifested itself in better-built buildings and wider facilities.

Haverfordwest was a thriving town. Its weekly markets, annual fairs, regular judicial sessions and irregularly-held elections ensured that the town played host to a steady throng of visitors, suitors and customers. Its many inns and alehouses were often filled to capacity, which may account for the frequency with which suits for violence and riots were heard both in the local courts and further afield in the Court of the Council in Wales and the Marches and in the London Courts of Star Chamber. Indeed, violence was never far from the surface and, while there was a criminal element in the town, the authorities were often no whit less 'criminal' in deed and intent. Witness the treatment meted out to Thomas Read, a husbandman from Ilmeston in Somerset, who, when passing through the town on his way to Ireland, was charged with spying! He was imprisoned temporarily in the town's gaol, whence 'he was conveyed to the house of William Walter, and stripped of all his clothes and money [and] being brought before the Sessions, he was found not guilty, and it was ordered that his money should be returned to him'.[19] Unfortunately for this hapless visitor, his tormentors, Francis Vaughan, Walter Roche and William Walter, Justice of the Peace, refused to offer their victim anything in the form of an apology or restitution. Perrot too had earned a well-deserved reputation as a brawler in his youth, being brought up on charges of affray committed in the streets of London. In the streets of Haverfordwest he left such matters to his servants who are frequently to be found in court records for inciting violence, brawling, rioting, and more seriously, wounding. In fairness to Perrot's retainers, many of whom wore their master's livery sporting the distinctive family crest, 'a parrot on their sleeves' according to one eyewitness, were as much victims as perpetrators in many instances.[20]

Politics, economics and sociability were indivisible elements in the make-up of those that comprised the class universally ascribed the label 'gentry'. They were an ambitious, competitive and forceful group who command the attention of historians largely on account of their remarkably complete domination of almost every facet of every-day life. Their power-base lay almost exclusively in the countryside and their social circle revolved around their country houses, but, increasingly, the opportunities afforded by the town to meet, make money, find sport and entertainment drew them in. Almost inevitably drawn to its environs like a magnet, those with pretensions to grandeur sought out the high and mighty and kept company with them, no doubt hoping either to attract their patronage or else forge an alliance. Many a great Haverfordwest family began their rise to prominence in such inauspicious and sometimes humble circumstances. By the sixteenth century, Haverfordwest had become a component part of the gentry's social life. Nor was this an accident for the town deliberately cultivated the rural élite for profit and social cachet, but at the same time, was careful to exclude them, bar a minority like Perrot, from membership of the common council. According to the most recent chronicler of the town fortunes in the sixteenth and seventeenth centuries, B.G. Charles:

> It was common courtesy to provide a meal or a bottle of wine for benefactors like the Perrots or dignitaries like the Bishop of St David's or the Deputy Lieutenants if they chanced to visit the town, which cost money but doubtless paid dividends also.[21]

Activated less by their sympathy for their citizens 'who were at a loss for distractions,'[22] and more on account of profit and reciprocal goodwill, the Corporation maintained a company of waits or musicians to entertain townsfolk and visitors alike even clothing them at the public's expense. Tudor Haverfordwest was at once an exciting and dangerous place: a congested, busy and populous urban centre full of pomp and colourful ceremony, politics and high society, crime and violence, sport and general entertainment. It could not fail to make an impression on those who visited it or who were intimately involved with it. In short, it was a town worthy of endowment.

Sir John Perrot's 'gift' to the town lies at the heart of his relationship with Haverfordwest and to uncover the motive behind the one may lead to a better understanding of the other. However, the task is fraught with difficulties for though a public figure of considerable eminence and stature, variously, Lord President of Munster (1571-3), Lord-Deputy of Ireland (1584-8), deputy Lord Lieutenant of Pembrokeshire (1587), Privy Councillor (1589-90) and twice MP for Pembrokeshire constituencies (1562/3 and 1589 but thrice MP for constituencies elsewhere 1547, 1553 and 1559), he has left no diary and little in the way of personal correspondence.[23] Consequently, we are left to ponder on what he did as opposed to what he intended to do. But to assess the true character of a man by his actions alone is only to half-understand him, yet in a period which yields so few of its secrets we have no choice but to infer much from deeds rather than from words. This is critically important in the case of a man, like Perrot, on whom much that is written has come to us by way of his enemies, principal among them George Owen, the antiquarian squire of Henllys, who has left a vivid, but ultimately unflattering, portrait of his distant kinsman. It was Sir John's singular misfortune to make bitter enemies of men who wrote so copiously and eloquently of their life experiences, and whose works have survived largely intact serving to colour and influence the views and opinions of later generations. It is an issue that highlights clearly the problem confronting historians who attempt to uncover the root causes of human motivation, especially when the subject in question has, with history's connivance, been drawn to a different scale to those around him.

We may accept at face value, as countless others have done, his desire to endow the town on account, as he himself said, of 'the love which I bear towards my beloved and faithful neighbours, the burgesses,' but to do so is to ignore the fact that with a number of them he was on chronically bad terms. It was not long before his supporters had been in bitter dispute with his 'beloved neighbours' over the election in 1571 of John Garnons as Member of Parliament for Haverfordwest. Although a majority of those who turned up to vote, at what turned out to be a stormy meeting at the Guildhall, did so in favour of Garnons's opponent, the latter's election was thwarted by the returning officer, who sent in a false return. It is not clear to what extent Perrot was personally involved in the affair (he was away in Ireland) but it is known that Garnons was his preferred choice and that the returning officer, the sheriff of Haverfordwest, Edmund Harries, looked to him for patronage.[24] In a subsequent court of inquiry Garnons was absolved of blame and allowed to keep his seat, which, in the event, lasted a little more than ten months, while Harries was fined and imprisoned for fraud. The unsuccessful candidate, Alban Stepney (or Stepneth) of Prendergast, succeeded in capturing the seat in 1572 and was to hold it through two subsequent elections until unseated by Sir John Perrot himself in 1588.[25] Needless to say, Stepney is hardly to be counted among Perrot's 'beloved neighbours' nor, indeed, are the majority of those who voted for him. They, significantly, were among the town's most privileged élite, no more than 100 burgesses in all, of whom 90 turned out for the election in 1572. The high turnout was unusual in itself and should perhaps be taken as a mark of Perrot's unpopularity for the average attendance at such elections seems to have been considerably less at around 20 to 25. Fewer than two dozen of those eligible to vote did so in the election of 1597 at which Perrot's son and heir Sir James was returned as the member for the town.[26]

Whether he was personally involved or not – and there are grounds for believing that his was the guiding hand behind Harries's deception – Perrot had a history of often violent confrontation with members of the burghal community stretching back nearly 15 years. In 1558 he was in dispute with Thomas Catherne of Prendergast over the latter's election as member for the county of Pembroke which Perrot claimed had been secured by deception.[27] In 1561 he was doggedly pursuing a number of the town's burgesses, Thomas Catherne and John Rowe prominent among them, over accusations of obtaining title to lands, again by deception.[28] In his capacity as Queen's Commissioner for concealed lands, he was charged with the task of rooting out and recovering, on behalf of the Crown, those properties appropriated from the former priory of St Thomas the Martyr. His zeal was due in part to the fact that he stood to gain from either the leasing or purchasing of those properties once title to them had been proved. Since the majority of the premises lay within the bounds of the town and county of Haverfordwest the resulting court case was convened in the Shire Hall and consisted of local jurors. Despite 'packing' the jury with his tenants and/or men known to be favourable to him, seven of the 17 refused to find in favour of the Crown. At least three of the seven, townsmen all, were members of the burghal élite, having held office in the borough and were thus men of standing and substance. Nothing daunted, a furious Perrot hauled them before the Court of Star Chamber in London, accusing them of obstruction and gross misconduct in having 'wilfully, obstinately, and perjuriously refused and utterly denied to find and present the said lands to be concealed'.[29] The fact that little tangible evidence had been presented to the original court of commission in Haverfordwest by either Perrot or his fellow commissioners, was conveniently set aside by the plaintiff. Unfortunately, the verdict of the court is missing, but that Perrot won may be inferred from the fact that 19 years later most of the properties then in dispute were among those donated by him to the town. Doubtless, the surviving members of the seven were struck by the cruel irony of their erstwhile foe's 'benevolent' endowment.

If it can be argued that the form of address adopted and expressions used by Perrot in his charter to the town were utterly conventional and of little account in determining motive, then we have to turn to the grant itself in order to gauge the level of his purported 'love' for the town and its inhabitants. The grant consisted of 34 separate items of property amounting in all to some twenty two and a third burgages and one messuage within the town itself, 131 acres of agricultural land and garden on its periphery together with a tenement and 'its appurtenances' in Camrose. Perrot's donation is estimated (in truth, it has perhaps been underestimated) to have been worth in excess of £30 annually, a substantial sum by contemporary standards and one which compares fairly well with other grants of that period.[30] Moreover, the perpetual nature of the grant ensured that, if managed effectively, it was likely to yield more as time elapsed. Unfortunately, apathy and neglect combined with evidence of mismanagement and misappropriation of funds conspired to ruin the value of the endowment and by the early 1780s Perrot's legacy was fast disappearing. It was saved by the timely intervention of the town council which met in October 1831 to decide its fate, whereupon it was concluded 'that it was a highly improvable estate' in 'that for the last fifty years not a single sum has been expended for either of the purposes intended'.[31] With public support it was rescued and re-established in 1834 as the Sir John Perrot Trust, its future security bolstered by its being recognized by Lord Brougham's Commission on Charity Funds. In 1912 the Trust was said to be worth £427 7s. 10d. annually; by 1962 it was valued at around £2,750, and in 1997 it was reported to yield about £55,000; a fine legacy indeed.[32]

The unprecedented scale of the gift might well betray a deeper and truer sense of Perrot's feeling and regard for Haverfordwest as distinct from its inhabitants with whom he was often at loggerheads. He may have suffered in part from the Welsh 'disease' which tends not only to root one firmly in the locality in which one was born and brought up but which tends to colour one's view of the world. It is a phenomenon which is best, if inadequately, defined in terms of the longing or *hiraeth* one feels when parted from one's hearth. Certainly, Perrot's contemporary, George Owen of Henllys, never shirked from expressing his deep love for his native county and its people: 'In speaking in praise and worthiness of the people of this county, if I shall seem fervent therein, yet should I therefore partly deserve pardon (the love and affection of my county egging me thereto)'.[33] It is important to remember that to the people who lived in these localities, be it county, hundred, parish or town, they were more than just administrative or geographical 'divisions', they were real places where they lived, worked, worshipped and died. Not unnaturally, there developed in some a deep love of country, in others a strong bond of local or regional loyalty; still more might be drawn to their birthplace by reason of some indefinable sentimental attachment. But in all there evolved some sense of communal identity. These 'patriotic' attachments to region, locality or community were often deeply rooted and not easily dislodged, a fact

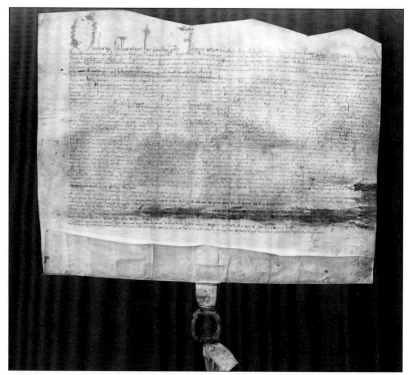

Fig. 46 Sir John Perrot's Deed of Gift to the Mayor and Corporation of the town in September 1580.

(Reproduced by permission of the Haverfordwest Town Council: photograph by Paul Harrison).

which early impressed itself on those who sought to unite in government the disparate, formerly 'marcher', elements that made up the newly created county of Pembroke following the Acts of Union (1536-43). Some, like George Owen clung to the 'old' divisions and he spent his life resisting the forces making for change by insisting on treating the former marcher lordship of Cemais, of which he was a native and its lord, as a distinct entity with rights and privileges to be defended in the face of upstart officials representing the power and authority of the county.

Born probably at Haroldston in November 1528 and brought up within hailing distance of the town, Perrot's youthful connection with 'Haverford', as it was popularly referred to in medieval times, has been widely remarked upon, to explain his later attachment.[34]

However, there is little to suggest that his local 'patriotism' ran as deep as Owen's or that he shared the latter's love of county. In truth, it is difficult to credit Perrot with any Welsh, let alone Pembrokeshire, sentiment. He was frequently described by his contemporaries as an 'Englishman', a legacy perhaps of his upbringing in this most Anglicized part of Cambria. It is instructive to note that in his will of July 1566 Hugh Harries states that his properties were to be found in 'the town and county of Haverfordwest . . . in the county of Pembroke' and 'elsewhere in England'![35] Clearly, those born either side of the linguistic divide had a different sense of what it meant to be Welsh and living in Wales. Perrot seems to have been cut of a different cloth from that of his county compatriots. He appears more urbane in demeanour and cosmopolitan in outlook, factors which enabled him to transcend his environment and the circumstances of his upbringing. Indeed, without wishing to diminish his ties with the town when young, it must be remembered that he spent part of his formative years away at school in St David's and when he did return 'home' it was as likely to have included Llanegwad and Abermarlais as much as Haroldston. This was due to that fact that two months short of his third birthday in September 1531, he tragically lost to illness his father, Thomas Perrot, esquire, and, not yet four, his mother, the Gloucestershire-born and quintessentially English Mary Berkeley, re-married taking to husband the Carmarthenshire-born magnate Sir Thomas Jones.[36] Thus, Perrot was brought up in the household of his Welsh-speaking and bard-loving step-father with whom he seems to have formed a close relationship. Nevertheless, in 1546 at the age of 18 he left Haroldston for the household of Sir William Paulet, Lord St John, later the Marquess of Winchester and Lord High Treasurer of England, where he remained for much of the next five years learning the art of court etiquette and other 'gentlemanly' pursuits.

Ironically, Perrot's regard for Haverfordwest may have owed as much to his step-father's influence as to any sentimental attachment formed in childhood. Dividing his time between the Court and his estates in Carmarthenshire and Pembrokeshire, Perrot's step-father increasingly came to regard Haroldston as his chief residence and it is here, with his young and growing family, that he can be found for much of the 1530s and early 1540s. It is to his credit that for nigh on

17 years Sir Thomas Jones managed well his stepson's considerable landed inheritance. He did so with much more than his accustomed efficiency and skill: he did so sensitively, being careful to maintain traditional Perrot connections and associations whilst cultivating others anew. Masters of Haroldston since 1442, the Perrot family came increasingly to play a greater role in the affairs of the town.[37] Invested with a single messuage located in the town's extra-mural quarter, the hill of St Thomas the Martyr, in September 1432, the family quickly capitalized on their good, if modest, fortune to become not only property owners of considerable standing but members of the borough's burghal élite.[38] This stood them in good stead when, in 1479, the lord of Haverford, a predecessor of whom had been responsible for establishing the borough in the twelfth century, granted a charter of incorporation to the burgesses whereby the newly-designated 'county of the town of Haverfordwest' was to have the right of self-government.[39] Unsurprisingly, the most prominent and powerful of the townsfolk ensured that they, and they alone, would enjoy the privileges conferred by charter and through locally elected officers and a self-perpetuating ruling council, the Corporation proceeded to run the town's affairs. The Perrots, it seems, were among them, and were sufficiently well placed in this close, co-optive oligarchy to have one of their number, Sir William Perrot, appointed sheriff in April 1496, an appointment confirmed by Letters Patent of the Crown.[40]

The almost symbiotic nature of the relationship that developed between those who dwelt in the town of Haverfordwest and those who lived in the mansion house of Haroldston not only continued but was strenghthened under Perrot's step-father's stewardship. He was admitted a member of the town's burghal élite and served for at least seven years, *c*.1539-46, on the common council.[41] When the Acts of Union threatened to sweep all before them and dispose, as they had done to George Owen's beloved Cemais, of Haverfordwest's unique status, it is to him that historians turn to credit its survival and continued existence. Doubtless his strong connections at Court where he was successively Groom of the Chamber (1513) and Gentleman Usher (1532), together with the fact that since its enfranchisement in the Acts of Union, he had represented Pembrokeshire in Parliament, worked in his and the town's favour.[42] In fact, Sir Thomas Jones's legacy to the town was every bit as significant, perhaps more so, as that of his stepson, for in securing its enfranchisement as a Parliamentary seat, he elevated Haverfordwest to a position of political importance it enjoyed until it was effectively disenfranchised in 1885. Sir John Perrot reaped the benefits of his stepfather's largesse and the goodwill thus created may well have been a factor in the Corporation's decision in 1554, to exempt Haroldston (and Prendergast) from an ordinance forbidding 'foreigners', henceforth, from enjoying the privileges of burghal membership.[43] Logic and geography must also have played their part in the decision-making process for of all the major county seats, Haroldston and Prendergast lay closest to the town, their estates bordering that of the county borough. The Corporation was evidently earnest in its desire to prevent those 'not inhabiting nor dwelling within the town' from being admitted a member of the borough's charmed circle since if 'any mayor do contrary to this act he shall be deposed of his mayoralty and another put in his room and also be disgraded of his burgess-ship'.[44]

It was a significant concession and one which served to strengthen the umbilical nature of the relationship between Haverfordwest and Haroldston. On a more sinister level, the ordinance also ensured that, at a stroke, the greater gentry of Pembrokeshire were to be prevented, or at the very least hindered, from participating directly in the government and administration of the town and nor were they fully to benefit from the economic privileges enjoyed by the few that did. Thus, Perrot's rivals, principal among them at this early date Roger Barlow of Slebech, were denied a base of operations, leaving the field open to the master of Haroldston. One suspects that Perrot may have had a hand in influencing proceedings behind the scenes, for it is known that of the six members of the ruling common council responsible for seeing the ordinance through, the mayor, Hugh Harris, was well disposed towards him as was the sergeant, John Penry, 'kerver', who was a tenant of his. Indeed, that there may have been some opposition is suggested by the fact that in the town's records it is said that the ordinance was made by 'Hugh Harriez, mayor . . . with the assent of all his brethren or the most part of them'.[45] No doubt Perrot's rivals had their champions on the council but for the moment they were all but silenced as he swept to power.

Significantly, the other beneficiary of the town's largesse, Thomas Catherne of Prendergast, was not yet an enemy of Perrot. Their relationship foundered the following year when the former denounced the latter for harbouring Protestant heretics at his 'Harondayles home'.[46] The charge caused Perrot some difficulty with the pro-Catholic Crown which saw fit to imprison him for a month in the Fleet Prison in London.

The period of the Marian persecution (1555-8) proved difficult for Perrot and his commitment to the Protestant cause in the face of overwhelming government pressure to conform convinced him it was time to quit Pembrokeshire and he did so in 1557. He saw out much of the rest of Mary's reign abroad serving in the war against France and distinguishing himself at the siege of St Quentin. On his return, he proved as vigorous as ever, his star was firmly in the ascendant and he took advantage of his higher profile at the court of Queen Elizabeth to press ahead with his plans to tighten his grip on Haverfordwest. In 1559 he secured the unglamourous but lucrative post of gaoler of Haverfordwest gaol which was located in the inner ward of the dilapidated castle.[47] Doubtless, Perrot did not perform in person the task of incarcerating the hapless victims of the town's often swift and rough justice, this was done through a deputy, but he is likely to have taken advantage of his position to extract what remuneration he could from the exploitation of his prisoners. This was customary and not in any way regarded as disreputable: the post was unpaid and it relied on the vigour and discretion of the postholder to discharge his function efficiently. There was no obligation on the part of either the town authorities or the gaoler to keep the prisoners alive and, irrespective of their social distinction, the incarcerated were expected to maintain themselves. It is interesting to note that in 1567 there existed above the gaol a shop which may have been intended to serve the needs of the prisoners.[48] Ready cash was the currency of life in Elizabethan prisons and those without means, friends, relatives or sympathy were condemned to a life of ineffable misery and degradation. Bearing in mind Perrot's own experience of prison life – he was committed to the Fleet and Marshalsea no less than four times between 1554 and 1559, serving a total of three months and three days – one wonders if he had or displayed any sympathy for those in his care.

Perrot had his sights set on securing the post of mayor, 'the height of civic ambition', and in 1560 he achieved his aim. Unlike the gaolership, this was an office of responsibility which was often onerous in the demands it made upon the incumbent's time and purse. As mayor, Perrot was expected also to act as the town's coroner, escheator, justice of the peace and clerk of the market and admiral of the port, for which he received a paltry allowance of 6s. 8d. towards his Christmas festivities and two of the most lucrative fines levied during his year's term in office.⁴⁹ The mayor was expected to preside over all meetings and courts, the latter of which consisted of two ordinary courts held regularly every fortnight and a third, the Pie-Powder Court, which met on special occasions to regulate such matters as the activites of 'foreigners' and fairs.⁵⁰ For the next ten years he dominated, though not entirely subdued, the town and his attempt to run its affairs earned for him the undying enmity of some of the borough's most powerful families. Among those who were bitterly opposed to him during this time was Rhys Morgan of Slade, formerly Anastaslade, in the parish of St Martin, a merchant, burgess and member of the common council, who took every opportunity to cause Perrot maximum discomfiture. The records of the Court of Star Chamber show that in 1568 Morgan, then a JP, had enlisted the support of the mayor of Haverfordwest, George Pynde, and the sheriff of Pembrokeshire, Francis Laugharne, in his clash with Perrot, who in turn alleged corruption on their part.⁵¹ The power struggle was won by Perrot, who ousted Pynde to become mayor of the town a second time in 1570. Morgan and Perrot clashed again, in 1571 and 1572, but in view of the latter's absence in Ireland, it was a clash by proxy involving his servants.⁵²

On his return from Ireland, Perrot wrote to the Queen's chief minister, William Cecil, Lord Burghley, 'that he was determined to lead a countryman's life and stay out of debt'.⁵³ His decision to settle down in his native county and establish more firmly his roots had implications for his neighbours who faced the prospect of dealing with him in person. Not surprisingly, Perrot turned again to managing his affairs in Haverfordwest, determined, it seems, to establish once and for all his undisputed supremacy in the town. In 1575 and again in 1576, he secured consecutive terms as mayor, an uncommon occurence, if not unknown. During this time he turned also to dealing with his opponents. Among those of the burgesses to fall foul of Perrot was Thomas Folland who was said to have been 'utterly ruined and reduced to beggary' by being dragged through the courts.[54] In a litigious age, Perrot proved more adept than most in employing lawsuits as a device to browbeat or ruin his enemies. Opponents of slender means like Folland were no match for Perrot but nor, it seems, were wealthier men like his old adversary Rhys Morgan, of whom it has been estimated that he lost upwards of £500 in his conflict with Sir John.[55] By the end of the decade Morgan was in no position to offer Perrot a contest. He was a spent force, his place being taken by the younger, if largely ineffectual, Alban Stepney of Prendergast. Reluctant as ever to loosen his grip on the reins of power, Perrot ensured that he was followed as mayor by one well disposed towards him. Consequently, Jenkin Davids's election was engineered: he became mayor not once but twice in consecutive terms in 1577 and 1578. By 1580 Perrot must have felt reasonably secure and, perhaps by way of an olive branch to those whom he had been pressing hard, or more likely, as a means of publicly stamping his authority on the town and its burgesses, he made his donation. To a man of Perrot's standing, breeding and way of thinking, it was inconceivable that someone other than himself should hold sway in Haverfordwest: this was his county, this was his town and they were his people. To control the premier borough in the county was a matter of pride, and honour, but to be seen to be in control was of paramount importance.

Perrot was never again to hold the mayoralty but that he retained his powerbase within the town is amply illustrated by the fact that in 1586 his eldest son and heir, Sir Thomas, was elected to the position.[56] Indeed, of the 13 mayors elected in the 15 years after Perrot's mayoralty (1576-1591), all but three can be closely connected either with him or his son. In his father's absence, again in Ireland, Sir Thomas worked to maintain the family's influence in the town, a task made easier by his admission to membership of the common council some time before 1581. This, combined with his father's election to represent the town in Parliament in 1588, suggests that their control of Haverfordwest was complete. Nor was their dominance of the town resented by all: the borough's accounts reveal that in September 1580 (the very month that witnessed his donation) the council, 'with the consent of the brethren', allowed £1 9s. 3d. to be spent on 'Sir John Perrot's diet for his welcome home from London at Mr. Voile's house'.[57] Needless to say, Morgan Voyle, elected mayor in 1585, was a close friend of Perrot for whom his father John Voyle (thrice mayor in 1567, 1571 and 1574) frequently deputized when his patron served his second term in office in 1570. Sir Thomas too had made an impression on his fellow townsman who presented him with a gallon of wine in 1585 (at 1s. 4d. it was hardly a good vintage!) and, three years later, with a hogshead of claret costing the donors the princely sum of £4.[58]

On the other hand, prominent men like Alban Stepney of Prendergast continued to oppose Perrot, father and son. He is another alleged to have lost a small fortune of around £400 in the process.[59] Stepney, though, was not alone, for in electing him twice their MP in 1584 and 1586, the voters were sending a clear signal to the then Lord-Deputy of Ireland that all may not have been well. To what extent this can be seen as a reaction against Perrot, support for, or fear of, Stepney or simply apathy on the part of the hundred or so voters, cannot now be ascertained. Much has been made of the fractious and debilitating effects of faction in the town's political life and though there was a discernible anti-Perrot faction during the 1560s and 1570s, the 1580s may have witnessed a softening of attitudes on both sides, or else a realization on the part of Perrot's enemies that his supremacy in the town was, for the forseeable future, a *fait accompli*. This may account for the apparently perplexing behaviour of the burgesses in electing Sir Thomas their mayor and Stepney their MP all in the space of a few weeks in the autumn of 1586.[60] Unless this was a result of some titanic struggle, and we have no evidence of this, then it suggests that a deal had been struck between the two for Perrot was also returned to the same parliament but as representative for Cardiganshire.[61] In fact, the elasticity of such political and social relationships is shown in an instance in 1589 when both Sir Thomas Perrot and Alban Stepney pleaded in favour of the very much pro-Perrot and aged ex-mayor, Jenkin Davids, who had been arrested for illegal purchases of salt.[62]

There were many among the townsmen who regarded Sir John as a friend and patron and who saw in him the means to promote and protect their town. Even George Owen was honest enough to admit that he was as much 'friended' as 'feared of the gentlemen and freeholders' of the county.[63] According to Owen, John Wogan of Boulston and Thomas Revell, townsmen both but only the latter a member of the burghal élite, were to be counted 'two dear friends of Sir John Perrot'.[64] It is this side of Perrot, the thoughful even kindly individual capable of acts of apparent selfless munificence, and the very antithesis of his 'hard man' image, that may be represented in his grant to the town. That there was this 'other' side to him is suggested both by his action in a case of fraud in 1589 and as testified by one who knew him well and wrote of him in the early 1620s, his son Sir James. According to the records of the borough for March 1589, Thomas Tucker of Sealyham had covertly appropriated some acres of land on Burton Hill which formed part of Perrot's bequest to the town.[65] Unknown to the Corporation, Tucker had 'ploughed and sown' part of the land and had continued to do so for at least three years. Accordingly, 'Sir John Perrot sent for both parties; he thought Tucker's right was to none effect, willed him to take end with the town without law and desired the town to deal friendly with him and forgive rents he owed. Both parties agreed . . .'[66] Unfortunately, Perrot's bounty was rewarded with a suit at law by Tucker and others who attempted to claim legal title to the land but the case was thrown out of court and the plaintiffs ordered to desist from further action.[67] To his son, this was typical of the man for though 'he was by nature very choleric, and could not brooke any crosses, or dissemble the least injuries', yet was he 'resolute and valiant' and 'when he was pleased, or willing to show kindness, he then had as amiable a countenance as any man'.[68] If one takes this and other evidence into account, it is clear that Perrot was more than the sum total of his enemies' judgements upon him: he was as multi-dimensional and complex an individual as one would expect to find in any man. In short, his character and personality defy simple definition.

Nor must it be thought that Perrot alone suffered in this respect. The reputation of that, apparently, equally philanthropic man, Sir Thomas Canon (d. 1638) has been damned at the hands of those of his contemporaries who would do him harm. Accused of being a 'turbulent person' given to violence and `intimidation, Canon's behaviour was reported to be excessively oppressive, especially against those whom he sought to deny their legal rights and liberties in pursuit of profit or some political advantage or other.[69] No doubt there is truth in this but people like Canon and Perrot must be judged by the value systems of the sixteenth and no other century. They were men of their time who lived according to the rules set down in their society, which rules they admittedly bent and twisted. Unless they defended themselves with vigour their enemies would hardly be likely to spare either of them. Perrot has had, and still continues to have, his champions, but it is the views of his enemies that continue to hold sway. Certainly, he was no saint but neither was he as much a sinner as has been suggested by his contemporaries, most notably George Owen, Thomas Wyrriot, scion of Orielton and Griffith White of Henllan. In fact, Wyrriot, in part, may provide us with an understanding not only of Perrot's benefaction but also of its timing.

Bitterly opposed to Perrot and an enemy of many years' standing, Wyrriot, described as 'a headie man', was no mere burgess of tenuous means; he came of an old-established and distinguished county family which could trace its roots back further than even the Perrots.[70] Moreover, he was a Justice of the Peace, had served at Court and counted some among the Privy Council as either friend or patron. In the early months of 1580 Wyrriot's near year-long attempt to force Perrot into court to answer charges of fraud, malpractice and general misconduct bore fruit. In spite of his protestations that he had no case to answer and that this was a concerted campaign to ruin him by a malicious malcontent, the Privy Council nonetheless ordered Perrot to attend the next meeting of the Court of Great Sessions in Haverfordwest. According to his natural son, Sir James, his father was at the time dangerously ill suffering from the sweating sickness, a particularly virulent strain of which had claimed the lives of many across the country, but though in 'peril of his life' he attended.[71] Perrot was forced to sit through a case consisting of some seventy separate charges 'and the witnesses . . . were about that number', a considerable strain even for someone fit, healthy and in the prime of life. The case took some days to conclude but was eventually thrown out and the acquitted, no doubt grateful for the judgement of his peers, the jury of townsmen, left the court and returned home where 'lying sick then at his castle of Carew' he slowly recovered. Nevertheless, 'Wyrriot continuing his malice, or rather his madness in this', refused to let the matter rest and his persistence earned for him a rebuke from the Queen herself and an order that he pay Perrot damages to the tune of £1,000. Wyrriot's refusal to pay was followed by an order for his arrest, imprisonment and seizure of his assets. According to a contemporary, Wyrriot was

> committed to prison in Haverfordwest, and there he did remain in durance, being so wilfully bent, that he would never confess his fault, or crave favour at Sir John Perrot's hande, which if he would have done, he might have been released; but Sir John Perrot perceiving his obstinacy, suffered him to be a punisher of himself, and to pay for that in body which otherwise he could not satisfy; having fought to take away the good name and to blemish the reputation of a man of his worth.[72]

Perrot recovered and his health returned, but the experience may have left a lasting impression on a man now nearing his fifty-second birthday. Moreover, it was not long since he had prepared to face death aboard ship the previous autumn (1579), when he and his son Sir Thomas thought all was lost after the vessel 'struck ground on the Kentish Knocks' and 'stood in great peril to be cast away . . . betwixt the danger of the place and the violence of the weather'. It is perhaps in terms of this experience, his recent sickness and the unnerving, almost psychotic, behaviour of Wyrriot in pursuit of him, that we might view his donation to the town. Perrot's benefaction may have been motivated by the very real prospect of death and as a good son of the Church he wished to settle his account. Certainly, the timing and nature of his endowment fits the pattern one might expect from a sick, vulnerable individual plagued by conscience and a desire to make amends and what better way to do this than by donating former church lands which he had himself 'filched' from others! Three years later in 1583, he drew up his first known will the contents of which suggest that Haverfordwest may never have been far from the forefront of his mind. That he was a man given to thoughts of mortality and accountability is evidenced in his last extant will and testament written in May 1592:

> God I ask forgiveness for all my sins, which are infinite. Trusting only to be saved by the bitter passion, death and blood-shedding of my saviour Jesus Christ, and not by any of my works. For I confess, that I

am an unprofitable servant, committing my soul to the hands of the omnipotent God of heaven and earth. I do forgive all men, and desire to be forgiven of all men, leaving all revenge for the great wrongs I have sustained to God' justice and judgement.[73]

Of course, we cannot dismiss the possibility that the donation was the result of a deal struck in the face of Wyrriot's court action against him. It was a jury of townsmen who found in his favour and it was the town's sheriff, John Harries, who arrested the malcontent and committed him to the care of the gaoler, another townsman, none other than Sir John Perrot who duly imprisoned him in the borough's gaol. In addition, it must not be forgotten that Perrot's donation was hardly 'freely given' since he asked for something in return. According to the document he requested that, henceforth, he and his heirs were to enjoy the privileges normally reserved for the mayor and other senior serving officers in respect of the quantity, quality and price of wine, salt and any other merchandise coming into the town. Also, he requested

> that I and my heirs living and dwelling at Haroldston . . . shall be burgesses and of the council of the same town if we will. And that we shall have the nomination of one burgess . . . in any year in which such burgess may be living and dwelling in the same town and in which he shall take such oaths as the other burgesses of the same town are wont to take.[74]

The requests, or more properly, demands, for that is what they were, were unprecedented and of considerable importance for they would elevate the Perrots above all other burgesses and enable them to enjoy at will, privileges denied their fellow burgesses except during their year long terms of office. In some respects, Perrot was making more concrete the ordinance of 1554 which was effective only as long as the mayor deemed it prudent.

The generosity of his endowment cannot be denied but the mantle of philanthropic benevolence rests uneasily on the shoulders of a man memorably described by the Pembrokeshire historian James Phillips as 'unclean of lip and life, unscrupulous in his greed, ungovernable in his passions, cruel in his resentment'.[75] While admitting that Perrot was 'loved as much as he was hated' and though approving of his charitable donation, the overwhelming picture that emerges of the man in the pages of Phillips's *History of Pembrokeshire* is more villain than rogue. Shaped and governed to some extent by his Christian ethics and influenced more than he might care to admit by his Nonconformist background and vocation, Phillips could not help but regard Perrot as anything less than flawed, and deeply flawed at that. It is an uncompromising view of Perrot that cannot be laid entirely at Revd Phillips's door for though he has done much to colour our attitude towards Perrot, his was but one in a long line of similar descriptions and opinions which over the years have solidified into a bogus picture of the man. Arrogant, avaricious, litigious, hot-tempered and, at times, utterly unscrupulous, Perrot was all these things and more, but to charge and label him a royal bastard, pirate, traitor and a seducer of maidens is to exceed the bounds of historical propriety. Sir John Perrot belongs to that exclusive band around whom legends grow and even with the benefits of hindsight, it is not easy to distinguish the authentic canon from later accretions. One thing is certain: legends do not surround nonentities.

R. K. TURVEY

HAVERFORDWEST AND THE CIVIL WAR

The history of the Civil War in Pembrokeshire is complex and, in the case of Haverfordwest, particularly so, as the town changed hands on no less than five occasions.

When the King raised his standard at Nottingham on 23 August 1642, the three Members of Parliament in the county were divided. John Wogan of Wiston, the member for the county of Pembroke, was energetically for Parliament; Sir Hugh Owen of Orielton, the member for Pembroke Borough, was nominally for that party, but he also had an estate in Anglesey where Royalist influences were dominant,[1] while Sir John Stepney, the member for Haverfordwest Borough, was an ardent Royalist

The gentry of the shire, by and large, were royalist in sympathy but they maintained a cautious neutrality.[2] Families that had an association with the Devereux Earls of Essex declared their opposition to the King, as did those who had served under Essex in the Low Countries, including Rowland Laugharne of St Brides, Walter Cuney of Welston, Rice Powell and Sir John Meyrick of Fleet. Those who were Puritan in outlook, like Griffith White of Henllan, and the merchants of the towns of Pembroke, Tenby and Haverfordwest, who had close trading contacts with their Puritan counterparts in Bristol, also supported Parliament. The situation was further complicated by the fear of a Popish plot, of which Parliament had issued a warning on 13 January 1643. A month later, John Poyer, mayor of Pembroke, and John Davids, mayor of Haverforwest, arrested a Roman Catholic priest and ships' officers who were thought to be connected with the Marquess of Ormonde's army in Ireland. Poyer also drew the attention of Sir Hugh Owen to the defenceless state of Milford Haven against an invasion, but no action was taken.[3] It was feared that the Haven would be used as a landing place by Royalist sympathisers from Ireland where, it was believed, the King had intrigued with the Roman Catholics in the rebellion of 1641. On 5 March 1642, the Houses of Parliament drew up a Militia Ordnance nominating Lords Lieutenant who would command the militia in the shires according to instructions from the King 'as signified by Parliament'. The Earl of Northumberland, who had no knowledge of the locality, was appointed Lord Lieutenant of the county of Pembroke and of the town and county of Haverfordwest, with orders to carry out the decrees of Parliament. The King then issued Commissions of Array, nominating people to train the militia. In July, Parliament established a Committee of Safety to raise an army, with Robert Devereux, Earl of Essex, as Captain-General, charged with the defence of the realm. Commissioners were nominated to activate the Militia Ordnance and Parliament issued instructions to the three Members of Parliament and to 13 landed gentlemen to assemble the trained bands of the county and to prevent the levying of forces under the King's Commission of Array.[4] Sir John Stepney and Sir Richard Philipps of Picton Castle, were the only commissioners resident in the vicinity of Haverfordwest. The dispute as to whether the King or Parliament should control the militia was one of the factors that led the nation into civil war.

On 2 November 1642 the Pembrokeshire gentry were summoned to Carmarthen to meet the Marquess of Hertford, the Royalist commander in south Wales, who was on a recruiting drive raising Royalist forces, but the response was not encouraging. Among those who obeyed the summons were Roger Lort of Stackpole, who had been commissioned to raise a regiment for the King, and his brother Sampson Lort, of East Moor, and John Eliot of Earwere, but John Wogan, Sir Hugh Owen, and Sir Richard Philipps, excused themselves.[5] While it has been contended that the leading townsmen of Haverfordwest were inclined to support the King's party and were able to prevent the Parliamentarians from taking a decisive step, as they had done at Tenby and Pembroke, a letter, also dated 2 November 1642, written by Sir Hugh Owen, John Wogan and others, to the Earl of Stamford, who held Hereford, stated that the town, like Pembroke and Tenby, had been garrisoned for Parliament by the local trained bands, but John Wogan warned Stamford that they would only be able to defend themselves 'for some short time'.[6] The town would not have been able to defend itself against attack as the castle was in a state of disrepair and the town walls were in a ruinous condition. The Royalists' attempts to carry out repairs to the castle towards the end of 1643, and the expense of 'the making and strengthening of bulwarks, walls, gates and turnpikes' were to be the source of complaint by the citizens for years to come.

On 20 January 1643 Wogan, suspecting that Richard Vaughan, Earl of Carbery, who had been appointed to command the King's forces in south-west Wales, was preparing to attack the town, appealed to the mayor of Bristol for supplies and a force of 300-400 men, and sent a copy of the letter to Parliament, but no action was taken. On 19 April, John White, the member for Southwark, read a letter of warning to the House, probably written by his brother, Griffith White of Henllan, expressing fear that the Royalists might fortify Milford Haven, and the House decided that a guard-ship should be retained in the Haven, that Sir John Stepney should be disabled from sitting in Parliament, and that Carbery should be impeached.[7]

Any Parliamentary hold on the town could not have been very effective, however, as Carbery came on a visit towards the end of March and was greeted with a ringing of bells and entertained with wine and a hogshead of beer for the troops by the mayor and common council. When there was a threat to bring Royalist troops to occupy the town, the mayor informed Colonel Rowland Laugharne, the local Parliamentary leader, and on 6 June Laugharne visited the town and was entertained by the mayor.[8]

The surrender of Bristol to Prince Rupert, on 26 July, had released Royalist ships for other duties and had captured others. The warship *Fellowship* and the frigate *Hart* were sent to Milford Haven to assist with the reduction of Tenby and Pembroke. The Parliamentary ship *Swallow* entered the Haven in pursuit and *Fellowship* ran aground. *Hart* escaped up the Cleddau and ran ashore below Boulston. Two sailors killed on *Hart* were the first casualties of the war in Pembrokeshire.[9] The mayor of Haverfordwest entertained the captain of the ship and contributed towards repatriating the ship's company.[10]

Carbery took no action in west Wales until Bristol had been captured. The Royalist Association of Cardiganshire, Carmarthenshire and Pembrokeshire, which had been formed when the gentry were summoned to Carmarthen the previous November, felt sufficiently strong to challenge the Parliamentary forces and, on 29 July 1643, the King issued a 'Proclamation of His Majesty's Grace, Favour and Pardon to his Subjects the Inhabitants of the Tounes of Pembroke and Tenby in the County of Pembroke and of the Toune and County of Haverfordwest in the Domynion of Wales'.[11] On 18 August, the members of the Association were summoned again to Carmarthen to meet the Earl of Carbery and to swear allegiance to the King and to raise 'a considerable sum of money for his Majesty'. The declaration of loyalty was signed by 24 gentlemen among whom, for the first time, was Sir Richard Philipps.[12]

Richard Bateman, the mayor of Haverfordwest, was summoned by Carbery to meet him at Tenby on 5 September and, a day or two later, Carbery arrived in the town, again to the ringing of bells, and he received a civic welcome during which a quantity of sack was drunk in his honour. On 8 September the Royalist Captain Hugh Butler entered the town, with his company and, on 30 October, Sir Francis Lloyd arrived, to the sound of church bells, with troops from Carmarthen to garrison the town. The mayor and common council signed a declaration of loyalty to the King, and 'all the gentry . . . and all the trained bands came unto him [Carbery] to manifest their loyalty to his sacred Majesty.'[13] Carbery appointed his uncle, Major General Sir Henry Vaughan of Derwydd, to command the Royalist forces in Pembrokeshire, and Sir Francis Lloyd in command of the horse. Sir John Stepney was made Governor of Haverfordwest and was welcomed with a peal of bells and entertained at a banquet. The town had to meet the expenses of the occupation.

On 3 February 1644 Rowland Laugharne, now supported by several ships that had arrived in Milford Haven under Captain Richard Swanley, began to advance against the Royalists by taking Stackpole and Trefloyne, and capturing the fort the Royalists were erecting at Pill. Laugharne landed near Barnlake Pill on 23 February and cut off the road to Haverfordwest, leaving 20 musketeers on Steynton Church tower. Sir Francis Lloyd came out of Haverfordwest with 60 horse and foot, but retreated without making contact with the enemy. Sir Henry Vaughan assembled his troops, of about 450 men, and having made a show of an attack, fled the town, with Lloyd and Stepney, taking Sir Hugh Owen with them, to Carmarthen, believing that Laugharne and his troops were approaching the town. The story goes that the approaching 'enemy' was, in fact, a herd of black cattle rushing homeward in the dusk from their grazing. Laugharne rode into Haverfordwest on 25 February and placed a garrison in the town. Roch Castle surrendered two days later and the small garrisons that Carbery had placed at Picton, Boulston, Wiston, Haroldston and elsewhere, dispersed quietly.

The Parliamentary forces were convened 'to a muster at Colby Moor' on 11 April 1644, prior to Rowland Laugharne's successful advance on Carmarthen, and the Royalist garrison had to withdraw to Lord Carbery's castle at Newcastle Emlyn.[14]

Carbery resigned his command and his place was taken by Colonel Charles Gerard, an experienced and efficient professional soldier who took all before him. Having recovered Cardiff, he moved westward and captured Carmarthen and Cardigan and, by 7 July, he had taken Roch Castle, with some 300 head of cattle and 1,500 sheep which Laugharne had collected there to supply the Parliamentary forces. Laugharne fell back on Haverfordwest where the garrison withstood a blockade until the town fell on 22 July. Gerard then received orders to return to England, following the King's defeat at Marston Moor, leaving the Royalist cause again without experienced leadership. Towards the end of August, Rowland Laugharne's brother, Thomas, rashly approached Haverfordwest with a troop of horse, but he, and many of his men, were captured by the Royalists.

Gerard's ruthlessness, and his excessive sequestration of property, and the conduct of his troops, drawn partly from the Marquess of Ormonde's army in Ireland, together with the heavy contributions demanded of the local populace for their maintenance, weakened people's faith in the Royalist cause and made its supporters seek neutrality, or even retaliation. The Royalist forces were withdrawn from Haverfordwest some time in September.

On 12 April 1645 Laugharne laid siege to the royal garrison at Newcastle Emlyn but he was taken by surprise 'upon the 27th of April, the Lord's day, about six o'clock in the morning.' He claimed that Gerard fell upon him and his men and drove them back towards Haverfordwest,[15] which the Parliamentarians made no attempt to defend, the affrighted Parliamentarian rebels, it was reported, not staying to take anything along with them. But left behind all their cannon (which are four pieces of ordnance), whereof two very fair brass guns, all their arms (betwixt five and six hundred), all their ammunition and victual, with two colours of horse, and four of foot. [16]

Laugharne complained that Gerard and his men not only 'seized upon much of our ammunition and arms' but that they also did

imprison and plunder, and abuse the well-affected townsmen, range everywhere about the country, pillage and destroy that which should be present and future livelihood of our army, and have given us a sure testimony that they will leave nothing undone that mischief and violence can invent against a distressed county.[17]

Gerard had no sooner occupied the town than he moved against Picton Castle which, after an hour's assault, yielded about midnight on the 28th. Sir Richard Philipps was not at home but his son, Erasmus, and his two sisters, together with £500 and twelve trunks of silver plate, 150 arms and powder, were taken.[18] The story that the baby Erasmus was snatched out of a window by a Royalist officer has been traced to Samuel Butler's *Hudibras*, which mentions a Puritan being 'dragged through a window by his ears' by a Cavalier general.[19]

On 29 July Laugharne, believing that the Royalist garrison at Haverfordwest had it in mind to burn the surrounding corn land, assembled a force of 550 foot and 200 horse and dragoons, and two small guns, in Canaston Wood where he was joined by 250 seamen landed downstream by the frigate *Warwick*. The Royalists, under Major General John Stradling and Colonel Egerton, were unaware of this happening as their scouts in that vicinity had been killed or captured and on Friday, 1 August, they set out from Haverfordwest with a force of 450 horse, a 1,000 foot and four field guns. Battle was joined at six o'clock that evening on Colby Moor but Laugharne, with 150 musketeers and two troops, charged with great effect and, after an hour, the Royalists were utterly routed, suffering 150 killed and 700 taken prisoner and the loss of most of their armour and provisions. Stradling and Egerton rode under cover of darkness to Carmarthen. Laugharne entered Haverfordwest the next day and 'fired the outer gate and scaled the walls, gained the castle, took

[120] prisoners . . . and nearly 20 [officers] . . . one piece of ordnance
. . . and some pillage to the soldiers besides provision.'[20] Laugharne's
losses were given as two killed and 60 wounded. The King's cause
had come to an inglorious end in west Wales.

On 13 September Laugharne, by now commander-in-chief of the
Parliamentary forces in the whole of west Wales and Glamorgan,
wrote to the Speaker of the House of Commons stating that his
victory was complete and 28 September was declared a Day of
Thanksgiving in London 'for the reducing of the county of
Pembroke'. The Speaker sent Laugharne a special letter of thanks
and granted him 'and his heirs for ever', the estate of Slebech,
sequestered from John Barlow, but in October 1648 it was taken from
him and settled 'for ever' on the officers of the brigade of Colonel
Thomas Horton, the Parliamentary commander. It was recovered by
the Barlows after the Restoration.[21]

The reaction of some of the townspeople to the conditions in
which they foind themselves was demonstrated when the
Commissioners of Excise sat in Haverfordwest on 7 September 1646
and 'there came to the town hall a company of the poorest sort of
women of this town and there made a mutiny and forced the
commissioners thence to their lodgings.' The mayor, Roger Beavans,
and several aldermen, accompanied the Commissioners the next day
but the same thing happened and, 'for safeguard of the
commissioners' lives', the mayoral party 'repaired with them to their
lodging with an intent to see them safe out of town' but the women
followed them there and 'would have forced on them in their
chamber in such manner as for the space of six hours' they could not
be pacified.[22]

The heavy incidence of taxation, and contributions raised towards
payment of the Parliamentary forces continued to be a matter of
concern after the war was over and led to disaffection. Colonel John
Poyer, the governor of Pembroke, petitioned the House of Lords for
compensation but, instead, he was accused of failing to account for
certain moneys and he refused to appear before the Committee of
Accounts. He opposed the policy of disbandment of supernumerary
army units and would not hand over Pembroke Castle to the
Parliamentarian Colonel Fleming, who had been sent to take over the
castle from him, or to appear before General Sir Thomas Fairfax,

commander-in-chief of all the Parliamentary forces. Thus began the second Civil War.

Laugharne was suspect and was placed under arrest at Windsor, but he was soon back in south Wales though no longer the Parliamentary commander. Two companies of his men, supported by some of Rice Powell's men, marched towards Pembroke to join Poyer and attacked Fleming from the rear as he was being driven out of town. Fairfax sent Colonel Thomas Horton to proceed to Wales and Poyer and Powell went out to meet him and were joined by Laugharne at Carmarthen. They were heavily defeated at the battle of St Fagan's, where Horton was assisted by Captain Thomas Wogan of Wiston, the Member of Parliament for Cardigan and the future regicide. Meantime, Oliver Cromwell, under orders from Fairfax, marched from Windsor into Wales and received the surrender of Tenby. Powell was taken prisoner and his estates, together with those those of Poyer and Laugharne were sequestered. Cromwell appeared before Pembroke on 24 May and laid siege to the castle and pounded its walls with heavy guns before it submitted in the afternoon of 10 July, and Laugharne and Poyer surrendered.

Haverfordwest had stayed clear of the conflict and the mayor and common council gave an assurance to Cromwell that theirs was an open town, with no garrison.[23] Quantities of lead, were stripped from St Mary's Church and the armour house to be made into ball shot. Provisions, including eleven hogsheads and 50 barrels of beer, were also sent down river to the Roundhead camp at Carew to supply the leaguer of 6,000 Parliamentary troops outside Pembroke that had to survive on little more than bread and water, while a cask of cider and a quantity of sugar, were sent to Cromwell. The sick and wounded were housed and fed in the town and shrouds were provided for those who had fallen during the siege.[24]

On the day after the surrender of Pembroke, the following letter was sent to the mayor and aldermen of Haverfordwest, signed by the brothers Roger, Sampson and John Lort, and Thomas Barlow, who had been appointed by Cromwell to consider which places should not be retained as fortresses, with an additional note of warning from the Lord Protector:

Wee being authorized by Parliament to viewe and consider what garrisons and places of strength are fit to be demolishd, and we finding that the Castle of Haverford is not tenable for ye service of the State, and yet that it may be used by illaffected persons to the prejudice of the peace of these parts. These are to authorize and require you to summon in the hundred of Rouse [Rhos] and ye inhabitants of the towne and County of Haverfordwest and that they forthwith demolish the workes, walls, and towers of the said Castle, soe as that the said Castle may not be possesst by the enemy to the endaungering of the peace of these parts.

Given under our hands this 12th of July 1648.

To the Maior and Aldermen of Haverfordwest.

We expect an accompt of your proceedings with effect in this business by Saturday, being the 15th of July instant.

Roger Lort

Sam Lort

John Lort

Tho. Barlow

If a speedy course bee not taken to fulfill the commands of this warrant, I shalbee necessitated to consider of settinge a guarrison.

O. Cromwell. [25]

The mayor, John Prynne, and seven of the councillors, replied in the following terms:

Hon Sir,

We received an order from your honour and committee for the demolishing of the Castle of Haverfordwest, according to which we have this day set some workmen about it, but we find the work so difficult to be brought about without powder to blow it up by, that it will exhaust a huge sum of money, and will not in a long time be effected. Wherefore we become suitors of your honour that there may be a competent quantity of powder be spared out of the ships, for the speedy effecting of the work, and the county paying for same. And we likewise desire that your honour and the committee be pleased that the whole County may join with us in the work, and that an order may be considered for the levying of a competent sum of money on the several hundreds of the county for the paying for the powder and defraying the rest of the charge. Thus being overbold, to be troublesome to your Honour, desiring to know your Honour's resolves, we rest your Honour's humble servants.[26]

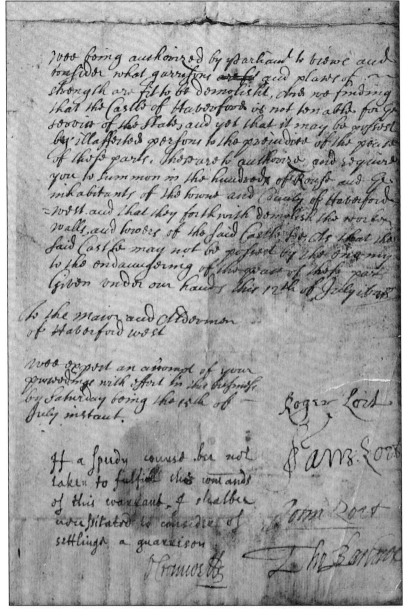

Fig. 47 Oliver Cromwell's letter to the Mayor and Aldermen of Haverfordwest commanding the demolition of the castle.

(*Pembrokeshire County Library collection*).

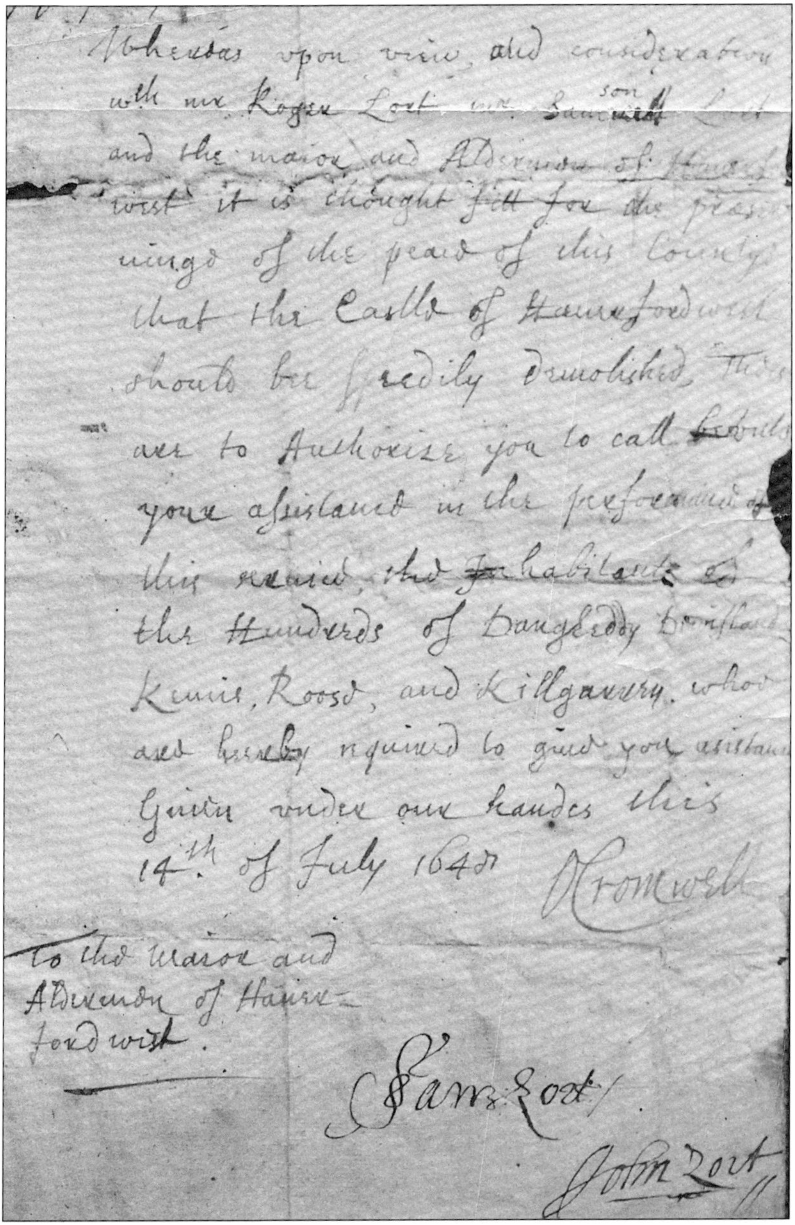

Fig. 48 Letter from Cromwell to the Mayor and Aldermen authorising them to summon the assistance of the surrounding hundreds to assist in the demolition of the castle. *(Pembrokeshire County Library collection).*

Cromwell, in his reply written the next day, agreed that the surrounding hundreds should contribute towards the cost with a levy:

> Whereas upon view, and consideration with Mr Roger Lort, Mr Samson Lort and the maior and Aldermen of Haverfordwest it is thought fitt for the preserving of the peace of this Countye that the Castle of Haverfordwest should bee speedily demolished. These are to authorise you to call unto your assistance in the performance of this service, the inhabitants of the Hundreds of Daugleddy, Dewisland, Kemis, Roose and Kilgerran, who are heerby required to give you asistance.
>
> Given under our handes this 14th of July 1648
>
> O. Cromwell.
>
> To the Maior and Aldermen of Haverfordwest
>
> Sam. Lort
> John Lort[27]

A rate of £20. 4s. 10d. (£20.24) was imposed on the town's inhabitants towards the demolition of the castle, and warrants were delivered to the high constables of the hundreds of Cemais, Cilgerran, Dewisland and Rhos to appoint men to levy the sums totalling £110, being their portions of the £130 levied towards demolishing the castle. The charge for the demolition was accounted to only £40,[28] which may indicate that the work was not carried out beyond a gesture and that the balance was diverted into the depleted borough treasury.

Cromwell was anxious to get away from Pembroke as soon as he could as the Scots, under the Duke of Hamilton, had crossed the border into England on 8 July. He had to make a forced march northward, during which his soldiers complained of having to march barefoot and without pay,[29] yet he succeeded in crushing the Scots army at Preston. His route from Pembroke is believed to have been through Haverfordwest as the borough accounts indicate that the council paid two shillings for a peal of bells and six shillings for a gallon of sack 'for Cromwell coming to town' on 16 July. He is said to have been entertained by the Prust family at their house at the bottom of Barn Street, opposite St Martin's Church, and local legend maintains that he was taken every morning by young Bobby Prust, his host's son, to Queen's Ditch, 'that he might have his morning draught of the delicious spring water.'[30] He could not have stayed long, however, as he passed through Carmarthen on 18 July.

The mayor, Thomas Davids, and the common council complained that the town had been over-assessed under the Act of Assessment of 1649 and, in April 1652, the Mayor and his son-in-law, Thomas Cozens, stayed in London to prepare a petition to Parliament seeking relief. A remembrance on behalf of the town instructed Cozens on the procedure. He was 'to have the petition fair drawn and presented to the Parliament and deliver the letter to Cromwell and Mr Speaker' and he was 'to acquaint friends with the town's condition and desire their assistance for the town's relief and a speedy answer to the petition,' among whom were Colonel Thomas Pride and Colonel William Goffe, 'being born in the town and were at the siege of Pembroke.'[31] Pride is claimed also to have been born at Ashcott, near Glastonbury.[32]

Goffe, or Gough, a regicide, was the son of Stephen Goffe, the Puritanical rector of Stanmer in Sussex, who was a lecturer, that is, a preacher supported by voluntary contributions, at St Mary's Church, Haverfordwest, in 1620. He was a religious enthusiast who arranged prayer meetings and believed that the New Model army had a divine mission to perform, and at a prayer meeting held at Windsor he called on 'Charles Stuart, that man of blood, to an account for that blood he had shed'.[33] He was later Major General and, after the restoration, a reward was offered for his arrest but he escaped to America where he died in 1679.

Thomas Pride and his musketeers occupied the House of Commons in 1648 and his exclusion and arrest of about 140 members of the Long Parliament, who were opposed to the King's trial, became known as Pride's Purge. The Rump Parliament persuaded him, on 9 January 1649, to limit his action to the Purge and it passed an ordinance erecting a court to try the King, which resulted in his execution and the declaration of the Commonwealth. He became one of 'the new gentry' and acquired Nonsuch, and he was sheriff of Surrey in 1655. He was knighted by the Protector, who performed the ceremony using a faggot stick instead of a sword. He died in 1658. The Restoration Parliament voted that he should be attainted and that his body be exhumed and hung up in its coffin at Tyburn, as had been done with Cromwell, but he managed to escape the indignity.[34]

Pride's Purge presented Haverfordwest with a problem when it came to elect a Member of Parliament after the Civil War. Sir Robert Needham, a kinsman of the Owens of Orielton, had been elected to represent the town in 1645 on the recommendation of Rowland Laugharne and sat until he was expelled by Pride. When Parliament was recalled he reassumed his seat but when he offered himself for re-election, the mayor, Henry Jones, and the councilmen informed him that 'the commonalty who are the electors are so extremely averse to a stranger that . . . nothing will satisfy them but the choosing of a native of the country to be their representative.'[35] Rowland Laugharne, who would have escaped with banishment had he not, following Pride's Purge, been condemned to death and then was saved by lot and released, made it known that he would be prepared to stand but he did not find favour with corporation or 'the commonalty' and he withdrew his candidature in favour of William Philipps of Haythog, who was elected,

For some years after the end of the war, Haverfordwest remained impoverished on account of the military occupation and heavy taxation, and the townspeople had hardly recovered from the frequent degradation they had suffered by the constant change between Royalist and Parliamentiarian seizure and the plunder and pillage of the surrounding countryside by the soldiery of both sides, when they had to face a new ordeal with the onset of the bubonic plague.

DILLWYN MILES

HAVERFORDWEST AND THE PLAGUE

On the eve of the first Civil War, Haverfordwest was probably the third-largest town in Wales, yielding place only to Carmarthen and Brecon. According to one source, it had a population of just over 2,000 in 1577, and the returns of the so-called 'bishops' census' of 1563 suggest that there were 215 houses in the three parishes of St Mary, St Martin and St Thomas, but even the town authorities themselves were not sure of the precise number of inhabitants. One document in the borough archives, which may probably be assigned to the year 1652, claimed that there were 'not above 200 houses' in Haverfordwest, whilst in writing to a number of Pembrokeshire JPs on the 18th of February that year, the mayor and a group of leading townsmen asserted that about 3,000 people lived in the town.[1] The evidence concerning the size of the town is thus inconclusive, but it is clear that Haverfordwest was the principal town of Pembrokeshire. At the beginning of the century George Owen had written that, 'being seated in the midst of the shire and most convenient for trade', Haverfordwest was 'greatly frequented of the country people, and therefore it is the greatest and the plentifulest market of the shire and is kept once every week on the Saturday . . . This market of Haverfordwest,' he added, 'is thought to be one of the greatest and plentifulest markets . . . within the Marches of Wales, especially for the plenty and goodness of victual, as namely for beef, mutton, pork, bacon, veal, goose, capon, kid, lamb, cony, turkey and all sorts of wildfowl in their season, . . . and for fish it passeth all others in Wales, without any comparison both for plenty and variety.'[2] Four fairs were held during the year, and the town had a sizeable group of prosperous merchants who traded for the most part with Bristol and the Irish ports. The most important industry in the town was the production of heavy woollen friezes, which were frequently used in the making of winter coats, and a wide range of leather goods, whilst the fact that the town was the economic and administrative centre of the shire meant that it supported a wide range of crafts and services.

With the outbreak of war, the prosperity of Haverfordwest came to an end. Its trade was greatly curtailed and it was soon occupied by Royalist troops, but on 25 February 1644 the garrison retreated ignominiously in the face of a Parliamentarian strike across Milford Haven from Pembroke, leaving behind them a hundred new red coats, supplies of food, and ten pieces of ordnance from a vessel named *Providence*.[3] However, the town had not seen the last of the King's men. In the following August it was occupied briefly by the licentious forces of the formidable Royalist commander, Sir Charles Gerard who, after retiring for a while, again took the town at the end of April 1645, his troops holding Haverfordwest until the day following the Parliamentary victory at Colby Moor on 1 August 1645. During these two periods of occupation, Gerard allowed his men to plunder the town, seized many inhabitants, forcing their friends and relatives to ransom them, and maintained his forces there on free quarter.[4]

Little further harm seems to have been sustained by Haverfordwest during the second Civil War, although Royalist troops occupied it once more during the spring of 1648, but the townsmen had to contribute towards the support of Cromwell's army during the long siege of Pembroke, maintain his sick and wounded soldiers, and pay for the demolition of Haverfordwest Castle.[5] In the summer of 1649 the Parliamentarian army intended for the reduction of Ireland was given free quarters in the town at an estimated cost of some £500, and this further impoverished the borough. Parliament's main source of income at this time was the 'monthly assessment', a tax which varied with the needs of the authorities in London and which made it necessary for the town's inhabitants to pay just over £10.2s.6d. (£10.12p) per month between March 1647 and March 1649, and £15.2s.1d. (£15.10p) monthly during the following three months.[6] Then, at the very time when Haverfordwest was faced with the heavy charge at quartering the Parliamentarian troops intended for Ireland, its monthly assessment wa raised to £45.[7] By now the plight of the town was so parlous that even Cromwell was impressed enough to support the corporation's petition to Parliament for a reduction of its crippling tax burden. Even so, the tax was soon raised to £60 per month. Some inhabitants fled from the town because they were being ruined by the assessment, and so, not surprisingly, the town proved incapable of paying in full and by the midsummer of 1653 its arrears totalled £1,260.[8]

At this juncture, an even more appalling problem was to face the mayor and common council, for the town was stricken by an outbreak of bubonic plague which resulted in the deaths of many citizens. The epidemic seems to have begun in the Irish port of Galway, being carried there, it was said, by a Spanish ship in January 1650. The mildness of that winter probably facilitated its spread in Ireland, and it was soon rampant in Limerick, Waterford and Dublin where, in the following September, 1,100 people died during the course of a single week. Dublin had close mercantile connections with Bristol, and the plague broke out there during the summer of 1650 and persisted in the city throughout the following year. In mid-May 1651 the plague reached south-west Wales, an outbreak which lasted several months occurring in Carmarthen and, according to James Phillips, it reached Haverfordwest about the beginning of October being carried there, according to popular tradition, by sailors from an infected vessel lying in Milford Haven, who visited the town's Saturday market.[9] Some support is lent to this account of its provenance by the fact that there were plague victims in the spring of 1652 at Great Pill, Newton, Waterson and Honeyborough, a group of small settlements lying a mile or two apart from each other and close to the Haven, but there is no evidence in the Haverfordwest corporation records that the plague reached the town before February 1652.[10]

The first local reference to it comes from a letter dated the 18th of that month in which the mayor, Thomas Davids, and a group of leading townsmen, informed the JPs of Pembrokeshire that one person was then ill of the plague and that three or four houses were under surveillance.[11] In another letter, of the 25th, the mayor notified two Pembrokeshire JPs that 'four died last week' and that he knew of no one who was sick, but it is clear that the infection had not been contained.[12] In early April, Davids left for London, ostensibly to press the town's case for a diminution of its tax burden (though he himself was uncomfortably aware that some believed that his main concern was with fleeing from the plague), and from that point onwards much of our information about the spread of the disease comes from letters written to him by his senior colleagues on the common council. On 26 April they wrote that seventeen people had died since his departure, that sixty others were locked up in the 'Castle Town' of St Martin's parish, and that the sickness was spreading.[13] Thereafter, with each succeeding letter, the news got worse. Early in May his colleagues informed the mayor that the plague had spread and that eleven people had died since their last letter to him, and another letter, written on 24 May, broke the news that it had spread to St Thomas's parish and to Ford (Hayscastle) and some other places in Dewisland.[14]

As soon as the JPs became aware of the seriousness of the situation, they threw a *cordon sanitaire* round the town. On 23 February, Bufton Ormond, one of the high constables of Dungleddy, ordered the petty constables of Prendergast, which adjoined the town on its northern side, to prevent movement into and from Haverfordwest, to shut up in their houses any who broke the blockade, and send him weekly reports of their actions.[15] When one of the Prendergast constables informed the mayor of these measures, he immediately wrote to two of the Pembrokeshire justices urging them to supply the town with food, pointing out that, although four people had died in the previous week, no one was sick within the town.[16] Evidently the JPs were convinced at this juncture that there was no serious danger of a widespread epidemic, for at their fortnightly meeting at Canaston, on 4 March, they granted permission for 'the country people' to attend Haverfordwest's weekly market once more. At the same time, they required the petty constables of each parish in Dungleddy already affected by plague, namely, Boulston, Prendergast and Rudbaxton, to submit the names of 'sufficient' men from whom overseers of the watch might be appointed in order to ensure that infected houses were kept under observation and their occupants isolated.[17]

To the consternation of the authorities, it became apparent during the course of the next month that the measures taken by the Haverfordwest common council had failed to check the plague, so once more the cordon around the town was drawn tight and all contacts between the town and its hinterland subjected to stringent controls. Arrangements were also made for the country folk to sell wool at Steynton and Llawhaden instead of at Haverfordwest and the town's May Fair to be transferred to Llawhaden.[18] Alarmed at this further threat to the town's economy, the Haverfordwest authorities rejoined by proclaiming that the fair would be held on the west side of Furzy Park, near Palmerston Farm, just within the borough boundary, but the ploy failed because only a few people from Roose risked attending it.[19] Yet, despite much apprehension on the part of the Haverfordwest councillors, and suspicion that they were being abandoned to their fate, the county JPs were clearly responsive to the plight of the town and, by mid May, arrangements were in hand to levy a tax on the various hundreds of the shire in order to purchase foodstuffs and other necessaries for its succour. Over £48 was collected from the shire between 18 May and 24 June, and in July the tax was raised to £80 monthly.[20] The need for aid was stressed in a letter from the Haverfordwest magistrates to the county JPs in which it was claimed that no fewer than 990 of the poorer citizens needed relief.[21] Assistance for the town was also organised on a voluntary basis. Within the rural parishes, the petty constables were urged to go from house to house soliciting contributions of money, corn, butter, cheese and other provisions to meet the needs of the town, and to keep lists of those making gifts, of those willing to contribute on a monthly basis, and of those able to help but refusing to do so. In addition, the high constables were instructed to appoint 'some able honest man' in each division of the shire to collect the provisons and arrange their transportation to Portfield, or some other place near Haverfordwest, where they might be collected by the borough authorities.[22]

As the seriousness of the epidemic became apparent, the latter took steps to check its spread, to provide medical attention for patients, to arrange for the provisioning of the town, and to organize the distribution of relief for the needy, and in particular for the growing number of orphans. As the plague was regarded as a divine visitation, the townsfolk were enjoined to 'walk more closely with God hereafter, to avoid the occasion of all sins, especially swearing, Sabbath-breaking, lying, drunkenness, lasciviousness, malice, envy, uncharitableness, which is rife in children as men,' and to pray both at the hearth and in church 'the God will withdraw his present judgement for this town, who will not deny to hear any repentant sinner.'[23] At first, the houses of plague victims were locked up and

kept under supervision by watchmen, but when the outbreak got out
of hand infected persons were removed to the pesthouse, a building
in St Martin's parish rented from Alderman William Williams.
Another building was rented from him for the use of the 'tarcoats',
the men who cared for the sick and buried the dead: probably there
were just two of them, for their joint weekly wage was only 15s,
(75p).[24] As the number of sick increased, the pesthouse became
crowded and so in late May or early June, another house, in Cokey
Street (now City Road) was acquired in which convalescents were
installed, and 'Mr Bateman's stable' was repaired and pressed into
action as a 'cleansing house'.[25] Medical attention was provided by
two barber-surgeons, Benjamin Price and James Sonnegon, who
stood to their tasks manfully and courageously, though, unfortunately,
there was some professional rivalry between them.[26] The resources at
their disposal seem pitifully inadequate to the modern eye. From a
bill submitted to the council by Price in 1653 we can get a clear
notion of the medicines he sent to the pesthouse between April 1652
and January 1653, mainly mithridate and diascordium, cordial water,
syrup of violets, lemons, roses and coltsfoot, conserve of roses,
plaister, salve, oil of camomile and oil of lilies, pills of rufus, oil of
mace, green ginger, *unguentum Egyptiacum*, spermaceti, *aurum vite*,
sack, burnt sack, and salad oil.[27] In an attempt to disinfect the public
buildings of the town, such as the churches and the town hall, they
were lime-washed and tar and pitch were burnt in them. People who
were not ill but who had been in contact with the sick were ordered
to carry white rods in the streets and all public places so that others
might avoid them. According to popular tradition, victims of the
plague were buried in shrouds by the tarcoats in a field on the north
side of City Road, known as the Mayor's Field, while those who
recovered, it seems, expected to be back at work within a fortnight of
being discharged from the 'convalescence home'.[28]

Throughout the visitation, the problem of supplying the town with
food exercised its governors greatly. Their difficulties were all the
greater because the town had already been 'beggared by the
assessment' and because those of the leading merchants and
tradesmen who were still resident in the borough were unable to sell
goods because of the town's isolation.[29] After it was shut up, the
Puritan minister of St Thomas's, Stephen Love, hired a horse and

toured the countryside exhorting people to supply provisions to his fellow-townsmen, and when the mayor, Thomas Davids, returned from London he used his house at Roblinston, Camrose, as a base from which to urge the high constables of the various hundreds to send money to the town.[30] Some of this money was paid directly to poor families, such as those of Francis Muggleston, Henry Relly, Mark Moore, James Meyler and John Morton, and much of the rest was used to buy provisions for the sick in the pesthouse and the 'convalescence home', to pay the barber surgeons and tarcoats, to disinfect public buildings and to bury those who died of the plague.

Despite the attempts to seal off the town, many of the inhabitants managed to flee into the countryside during the early stages of the epidemic. Already by 10 March the local Commissioners of the Assessment reported to the Committee of Parliament that most of the wealthiest townsmen had fled, and in late April the common council wrote to the mayor that 'the people go daily out of the town: there will be none left to maintain the poor.'[31] For most it was a case of *sauve qui peut*. By this time, the mayor himself was in London, and there he received the news, early in May, that 'the most part of the inhabitants are gone out of town and locked up their doors. There is but a few left in town, and the poor in the pesthouse do increase daily.'[32] One of the few members of the town's governing élite to stay behind was William Bowen, who described to the mayor on 24 May how, 'as for as the government of the town, I do what possible in me lies. I can give no assistance at all, for they are all gone out of town. John Edowe, being one of the high constables, is gone, and Mr William Davies, whom you appointed treasurer for the poor to receive the weekly rates, is gone presently after your departure. Were it not for William Jones and James Griffiths we should have nothing done here . . . As for the collectors and treasurers, I cannot speak with them, for they are all out of town.'[33] When Thomas Davids returned from London he found that very few magistrates or town officials remained in Haverfordwest, and that for the most part only the 'poorer sort of people' were left.

Clearly it was these who bore the brunt of the plague. There is no way of establishing the total number of deaths during the epidemic, but it is possible to chart its course in broad terms. In the last week of May, there were 31 patients in the pesthouse and the Cokey Road convalescence home; by 16 June, 49; then 54 on 21 July, and 72 on 18 August. In September the numbers began to fall – to 70 on the first, and 36 on the 29th. Thereafter the numbers of sick dwindled, until 24 November, where there was one convalescent patient left in the pesthouse.[34] During the epidemic, some families were entirely wiped out, such as those of the pound-keeper, William Williams, Walter Parrett of Bridge Street and John Bailiff of Quay Street. Abandoned though they were by many of their social betters, the poor were not entirely deserted. Both of the town's barber-surgeons performed sterling service, as did a 'strange woman' who nursed the sick with selfless devotion. Although she was greatly suspected and even abused by some, the mayor felt that she should be given encouragement, 'for I am sure that Providence guided her hither, and that she under God hath been an instrument of much good'.[35]

Coming as it did in the wake of civil war devastation and a period of crippling post-war taxation, the epidemic proved a traumatic interlude in the history of Haverfordwest. Yet, though many died of the plague, the admittedly imperfect demographic evidence suggests that the population of the town recovered quickly, and it seems clear that the effect of the 1652 plague were neither as long-lasting nor as wide-ranging as those of the Black Death, which resulted in many tenements lying vacant for well over a century. Even before the plague hit the town in 1652, trade had been seriously disrupted and many of the richest burgesses had been plundered and taxed to the point where their working capital was seriously reduced: this in turn had affected their capacity to provide jobs for the lower orders of society and to maintain corporate services. Moreover, the townfolk now had to meet a new charge, that of bringing up and maintaining a generation of orphans. The impoverishment of the town was at length recognized by Parliament, with the result that in November 1653 the tax due from the town was cut to £25 a month and its arrears cancelled but, even so, Haverfordwest remained for some years 'brought low by the burden of the great tax and sickness' and its recovery during the late Stuart period was markedly less spectacular than that of its sister borough of Pembroke which, in Queen Anne's reign, was to be described as 'the largest and richest, and at this time, the most flourishing town of all south Wales'.

JOHN HOWELLS

THE POLITICAL SCENE AT HAVERFORDWEST
1660-1918

The traveller John Ray recorded in his diary, in 1662, that Haverfordwest was 'the largest and best town that I have seen in Wales; where is an old Castle, and near the river an old religious house they call the Priory; within less than a mile of the town is a fair house Prendergast Place, the dwelling of Sir John Stepney. South of the town by Merlin's Brook is a mill. This is a town and county governed by a mayor, aldermen, sheriff and it elects a burgess for the Parliament.'[1]

Between 1547, when its first known Member of Parliament was returned, and 1660, Haverfordwest had sent 17 members to Westminster; between 1660 and 1832 (the Reform Act), it returned 21 more, and between 1832, when Narberth and Fishguard were joined to the constituency, and 1885, two members who had sat before 1832 and three new members. From 1885 to 1918 Haverfordwest formed part of the Pembroke Boroughs constituency, which sent six members to Westminster until the boroughs were merged in one county constituency for Pembrokeshire.

THE ELECTIONS.

When the Cromwellian protectorate gave way to a restored monarchy under Charles II in 1660, the corporation and freemen of Haverfordwest proved difficult to please. They would not have their Rump member, Sir Robert Needham; they were reluctant to have James Phillips of Tregibby, near Cardigan, who had manipulated the corporation for the past decade; they neither wanted a 'stranger' for their member nor a controversial local gentleman like Rowland Laugharne of St Bride's, who had changed sides in the Civil War and now backed Needham. So they settled for a compromise figure, acceptable both to the Royalist revivalists, such as Sir John Stepney, and to James Phillips, whom he called cousin. He was William Philipps of Haythog, a local squire who had suffered for his Royalism. James Phillips fell back on a seat for Cardigan. William Philipps was opposed, on behalf of the unreconstructed Commonwealth remnant, by Sampson Lort of Eastmoor, who was not a burgess and who championed the town's dissenters. The mayor, acting as returning officer, simply refused to poll Lort's adherents, alleged by Lort to be in the majority, in a petition to the Convention Parliament that ensued, which received a counter-petition to Lort's, abusing him, from the corporation. The election was voided in June 1660, but William Philipps was again returned in August, when Rowland Laugharne would not oppose him, and the corporation, backed by Sir Erasmus Philipps of Picton, foiled an attempt by Lort to outflank them by foisting Sir Frederick Cornwallis, treasurer of the royal household, on the town.[2] In the election for the Cavalier Parliament a year later, the local candidate was Isaac Lloyd, a Carmarthenshire lawyer who was based on Kilgetty after marrying the squire's widow there, herself born Wogan of Wiston. Lloyd was opposed by a courtier, Sir William Moreton, chief justice of the Carmarthen circuit, and an embarrassed returning officer made a double return, obliging the Commons to choose between them. In consequence, Lloyd took the seat, but on Moreton's petition the House objected to some of Lloyd's voters as non-ratepayers. The same allegation was made about some of Moreton's and the election was voided, though tardily: it was not until 1663 that Moreton gained the seat.[3] On his appointment as judge of the King's Bench in 1666, he was replaced with another circuit judge, Sir Frederick Hyde, related to Lord Chancellor Clarendon, and sergeant-at-law to the Queen. Isaac Lloyd did not oppose him, probably placated by restoration to the town magistracy, of which he had been deprived in 1662. Hyde's opponent was Sir Hugh Owen, who sat for Haverfordwest by some agreement with Sir John Stepney in the Short Parliament of 1640 whereby Stepney sat for Pembroke Boroughs: that was the only parliament to admit an Owen of Orielton as a member for Haverfordwest. This time Owen was backed by intruding 'foreigners' who 'terrified' the electors 'with force and armes', as the town council recalled when it ordered 20 armed constables to attend the mayoral election of October 1667 at 'the new Council House'. It was on 20 May previous that the Council had been required formally to renounce the Solemn League and Covenant imposed by Parliament in 1643 in favour of the oath of supremacy. Owen failed, though the House's election committee ruled in favour of his petition against the return, because of this being overruled by the House as a whole.[4] On Hyde's death in 1677 Sir Herbert Perrot of Haroldston, a champion of local dissenters, and a burgess of the town since 1668, defeated the lawyer William Wogan of Llanstinan, who twice petitioned in vain against the return.[5]

The end of the Cavalier Parliament in 1679 produced some turbulence in elections, henceforward to be triennial, country-wide. William Wogan defeated another lawyer Thomas Owen of Cwmeog, Nevern, in the February election, while Owen, who had petitioned,[6] defeated Wogan in the September one, by which time Wogan was hostile to the Court. Wogan's petition was never heard.[7] Owen lost the seat to Thomas Haward of Fletherhill, Rudbaxton, a friend of the Court and son-in-law of Sir Erasmus Philipps of Picton, in the 1681 election by 58 votes to 211. William Wogan, who sat for the county in that Parliament, was again returned for Haverfordwest on the accession of James II in 1685. His resistance to the King's plans to remodel borough charters conjured up a potential Jacobite opponent for him in William Barlow of Slebech, then the member for the county, but the Glorious Revolution, which he conditionally accepted, brought him the chief justiceship of south Wales, with a knighthood, and he held the seat until 1701, when he unsuccessfully contested the county.[8] His successor, William Wheeler, chosen at both the elections of 1701, was an unusual instance of a member sprung from the town, where two of his brothers lived, his mother being a sister of Richard Howells, merchant of Haverfordwest, London and Barbados. Wheeler inherited his uncle's Caribbean estate in the year of his election, and later returned to Barbados, where he had previously spent several years until 1700, as a member of the island's assembly, of which he ultimately became Speaker. The Tory squire John Laugharne of St Bride's, who replaced Wheeler in 1702, and was sheriff of Haverfordwest in 1705, met with no opposition until his death, on the night of his sixth election in 1715.

In the by-election ensuing, John Barlow of Lawrenny, a reliable supporter of the newly-established Hanoverian dynasty, was defeated, 222 votes to 181, by his distant kinsman Sir George Barlow, 2nd Baronet, of Slebech, but he gained the seat on petition two months later, having contested the validity of 79 votes cast for Sir George.[9] The latter was a nephew of the rank Jacobite, William Barlow, first president of the Society of the Sea Serjeants until his death in 1726, who had first tried to get in for Pembroke Boroughs. John Barlow died in 1718, and was replaced unopposed by Sir John Philipps, 4th Baronet, the 'Good Sir John', of Picton Castle, who later presented the town with its Old Bridge.[10]

The Picton Castle ascendancy over the corporation of Haverfordwest was established at a time when septennial elections to Parliament were enacted. It was not unchallenged. When Sir John retired in 1722 with failing eyesight, he already had a potential opponent in Francis Edwardes of Haylett, who now replaced him unopposed, but died in 1725, leaving a young son, William.[11] The gap was filled by Sir John Philipps's heir, Erasmus, hitherto restrained by his peace-loving father, but recently become a burgess of Haverfordwest and councilman. Although the Picton Castle family was generally expected to be pro-Hanoverian, not least from a family link with Sir Robert Walpole, then prime minister, Erasmus developed into a critic of the government, and felt obliged to explain himself to the premier.

He met with a challenge from the ultra-Hanoverian Wyrriot Owen, nephew of Sir Arthur Owen of Orielton, in the 1734 election, beating him by 215 to 153, and surviving a petition that was shelved.[12] Another nephew of Sir Arthur's, Hugh Barlow of Lawrenny, son of John, and brother-in-law of Wyrriot Owen, was defeated by Sir Erasmus Philipps in 1741, when the poll was 247 to 207. Two petitions against the return were withdrawn in 1743.[13] Sir Erasmus was drowned that year, and Hugh Barlow withdrew in favour of his kinsman, George Barlow of Slebech, though the latter, a burgess since 1740, was a Tory, if not a crypto-Jacobite.[14]

In 1747 Barlow made way for William Edwardes of Johnston Hall, heir of Francis Edwardes. Like Barlow he was a Sea Serjeant; and having been made a burgess on the Picton Castle interest in 1737, he was clearly acceptable to Sir John Philipps, 6th Baronet, brother and heir to Eramus, and a prominent Sea Serjeant. Unlike Sir John, however, Edwardes did not sail close to the wind in politics; he was, in practice, entirely loyal to the establishment, which rewarded him, in 1776, with an Irish peerage as Lord Kensington, which did not disqualify him from sitting in the Commons at Westminster. He was returned unopposed until his death in 1801, except for an interval, 1784-6, when he was rather rudely, as he thought, nudged out to provide a temporary seat for Sir John Philipps's heir, Richard, a burgess since 1762, and created an Irish peer, as Lord Milford, at the same time as Edwardes.[15] The latter resumed the seat when Milford became county member. William, 2nd Baron Kensington, succeeded to his father's seat, as he had been led to expect, but there had been others interested during his minority, such as William Knox of Llanstinan, and Sir William Hamilton,[16] and Lord Milford had gone so far as to offer the seat to a nominee to be chosen by Premier William Pitt in 1797.[17] Kensington was a maverick politician, and his tenure was uneasy. In 1812 he was challenged, after a three-year campaign, by Nathaniel Phillips of Slebech, representing the Orange (Orielton) interest against his own Blue, but he survived it by 220 votes to 98. By 1818 he was living in Italy, and William Henry Scourfield of Robeston Hall and Moat replaced him by an arrangement agreed by Lords Cawdor and Milford, for the Blues to cover all three Pembrokeshire constituencies. This arrangement dashed alike the hopes of Joseph Foster Barham of Trecwn, who aspired to the Blue candidature, and of Colonel John James of Pantsaeson who represented the Orange interest.[18] Scourfield was a political fence sitter, but essentially conservative and well disposed to the government of the day. In 1826, rather than face a contest, he withdrew in favour of Richard Bulkeley Philipps Grant, who assumed the surname and arms of Philipps, heir to Picton Castle on the death of Lord Milford in 1823, and a supporter of the Whigs, then in opposition.

Under the Reform Act of 1832 Haverfordwest became a boroughs rather than a borough seat, in the fashion that was prevalent in Wales generally before 1832. Narberth and Fishguard were the contributory boroughs, both far less populous: Milford was first drafted, but reallocated. Henceforward the voters had to be registered by the town clerk, and there were over 700. When the Whig ministry faltered in

1835, Philipps was under threat from Jonathan Haworth Peel of Cotts, a kinsman but not a political adherent of Sir Robert Peel, the Conservative leader. Faced with a contest, he withdrew, and Peel, a newcomer, was easily beaten, (241 to 125) by William Henry Scourfield, by now avowedly a Tory, who had become popular after launching hunt balls at Haverfordwest.[19] In 1837, Philipps, resenting Scourfield's politics, and fearful of Peel standing again and effacing his interest, returned to the fray, and defeated Scourfield by 247 to 165.[20] In 1847 Philipps, a baronet since 1828, retired on being elevated to the peerage as Baron Milford. His Whig successor, John Evans QC, was a native, son of the minister of Albany chapel.[21] The Conservative victory in 1852 spelt defeat for him by 297 votes to 203.[22] The victor was John Henry Philipps of Williamston, a crusty squire, regarded in 1847 as a likely opponent for Evans. A nephew of the late William Henry Scourfield, he succeeded to his estate and name in 1862. He held the seat until 1868, despite a strong challenge, in 1857, from William Rees, Haverfordwest Baptist and solicitor, for the Liberals. The poll was 258 to 256. Rees gave up his candidature in 1859.[23] In 1865, Scourfield was opposed by the Honourable William Edwardes, heir to the 3rd Baron Kensington, a Liberal, whom he defeated, 314 to 222.[24] Edwardes, whose father was Lord Lieutenant, was successful in 1868, when Scourfield took the county seat, against the Tory Samuel Pitman, 638 to 497. The increase in the electorate reflected the second Reform Act of 1867. This had tightened party organisation, and Edwardes was preferred to two competitors on the Liberal interest, William Walters, banker of Haverfordwest and William Owen of Withybush, architect, both proprietors of the local *Telegraph* newspaper, by the county Liberal Association. Captain Pitman was a friend of Revd James Alexander Philipps of Picton.[25] In 1872 Edwardes became 4th Baron, and a year later sought re-election on appointment as groom-in-waiting to Queen Victoria. He was then opposed for the Tories by Colonel Xavier Peel of Cottesmore, who 'telegraphed from the Continent his determination to stand'[26] This by-election was the first time the Secret Ballot Act of 1872 came into operation in Pembrokeshire, though no poll books appear to have survived for the preceding elections to 1868 for Haverfordwest. Crowds waited for the result in the streets, and cheered Kensington's victory by 609 to 558. In 1874, when he was returned unopposed, by then an unusual event anywhere in the country, Edwardes had to submit to re-election on a technicality, the returning officer having refused to accept another nomination without the receipt of £40 security.[27] In 1880, Kensington defeated the Tory Edward Denman Thornburgh Cropper, son of Edward Cropper, owner of the Rosebush slate quarry and financier of the Maenclochog railway by 686 to 522. Cropper was preferred to George Leader Owen of Withybush, who disliked not being unanimously chosen, and feared an expense of over £2,000.[28]

Kensington retained the seat until 1885, being re-elected in May that year after being made Comptroller of the Household. At the ensuing dissolution, under the third Reform Act, the borough ceased to be a separate constituency and was made a subsidiary to Pembroke. The only alternative would have been to include Haverfordwest in the county which, as William Davies, the county member, pointed out, would have deprived over 200 electors of plural votes.[29]

Davies, a solicitor formerly in partnership with William Rees in Haverfordwest, had contested the county as a Liberal in a by-election of 1876, and was successful in 1880, but for which he would probably have nudged Kensington out of the town seat at some point. From 1885 to 1918 the members representing Haverfordwest were primarily motivated by the concerns of Pembroke dockyard, and candidates were adopted by either party according to their ability to promote them. Thus Sir Charles Philipps of Picton failed to obtain the Tory candidature in 1892. Owen Cosby Philipps obtained the seat as a Liberal, 1906-10, but otherwise only the two Allens, Henry George (1885-6) and Charles Francis Egerton (1892-5), were of Pembrokeshire origin. The others are named in the appendix.

In 1918 Pembrokeshire became a unitary county constituency. Haverfordwest had been the scene of county elections from Tudor times and, apart from being showy occasions, these became exciting ones when there was a contest, as until 1832 all the electors polled in Haverfordwest. Their transport and treating to refreshments provided profits for carriers, innkeepers, vintners, printers and ribbon-makers. The largesse disposed of by candidates reached its climax in 1831 when Sir John Owen of Orielton defeated his Whig opponent Colonel Robert Greville twice, his first election having been voided on petition. The first election had lasted the maximum 15 days. Back in 1727 when John Campbell of Stackpole defeated Sir Arthur Owen, and 915 polled, Erasmus Philipps reported 'this affair cost Mr Campbell (who gave a great deal of wine) not less than £600, and Sir Arthur Owen who brought wine with him from home between 3 and 400 pounds'.[30] Of a county by-election in 1736, Campbell wrote to his son 'It was very unpleasant at Haverfordwest, being so very hot. I could not trust my ankle without my boots to walk in those uneven streets. So I dressed in a house just by the shire hall, and after I was elected they carried me (according to custom) in an armed chair to the inn where I dined'.[31] The Castle Inn had been created a generation earlier by the Barlows for election purposes. In 1741 Campbell contrived to have the county election switched to Pembroke to his own advantage, following a similar move by Sir Arthur Owen in 1715. The venue was the high sheriff's choice, and in 1770 Hugh Owen again secured Pembroke to frustrate an opponent. His son Hugh repeated the experiment in 1807, only to be defeated by Lord Milford. Subsequent elections were all held at Haverfordwest. In 1826 when Sir John Owen was unopposed, the election pageant involved 250 gentlemen on horseback preceding his carriage into the town, watched by 'at least 2,000 persons' at the top of Merlins Hill.[32] After 1832, when other polling stations were created at Pembroke, Tenby, Narberth, Mathry, Fishguard and Newport, only the poll declaration gave Haverfordwest pride of place. Election excitement was reduced when polling was curbed to one day only in 1853, but somewhat enhanced by the introduction of the secret ballot in 1872. Election campaigns became more extensive, but Haverfordwest was still the scene of political meetings. Until 1860 when the *County Guardian* was launched at Solva, it was Haverfordwest that produced the two Pembrokeshire newspapers, the *Herald* (1844) and its Liberal opponent, the *Telegraph* (1854). In 1908 suffragettes appeared in the county by-election;[33] women first got the vote in 1918. Radio and television coverage was subsequently to diffuse local excitement at elections, and the crowds in the streets, such as appeared in Haverfordwest in 1886, were a thing of the past.

THE ELECTORS

In the Tudor era, apart from the 24 councillors, the freemen (burgesses) of the borough had been entitled to vote, if duly qualified. Since 1554 the freemen, whether by birth, apprenticeship, or election, had to be resident. Qualifications outlined in the charter of 20 February 7 James I (1610) were spelt out in the corporation by-laws of 1628.[34] Yet the corporation paid little attention to the stipulation that a majority not only of themselves but also of the freemen and 'commons' was necessary to elect freemen.[34] Since 1571 the maximum number of freemen had been about 100. This was still the case in 1660. Contests had taken place from time to time in the interval, but from 1660 to 1681 they were a regular feature of Haverfordwest elections. On 4 April 1662 the Commons decided that the right of election was in the mayor, burgesses and inhabitants paying scot and lot (rates).[35] This followed the polling of unrated inhabitants on behalf of Isaac Lloyd. It is, however, the first mention of mere inhabitants being entitled to vote, apart from the return for 1656, when their participation in John Upton's election is mentioned. In the only other surviving return for the 1640-60 period, that of Hugh Owen on 7 March 1640, only the burgesses are named as electors.[36] The decision of 1662, implemented in 1663, raised the electorate to some 200.

Petitions against the validity of the returns from defeated candidates recurred in 1666, 1677 and 1679 (twice), but it was not until 1715, when the first contest since 1681 occurred, that a parliamentary decision affecting the franchise was made, on 4 July. This stipulated that the freeholders, as well as the freemen, were entitled to vote, thus not only underlining Haverfordwest's county status, but confirming the influence of the surrounding gentry, undoubted since Elizabethan times, when they began to monopolize the representation of the town. By the eighteenth century they were the most prominent and attentive members of the corporation. The 1715 decision also specified that inhabitants paying the rates should not be recipients of alms. In his petition against the return John Barlow had questioned the validity of 79 votes for Sir George Barlow: 34 were not burgesses, another 20 received alms, 15 did not pay rates, 8 were 'foreign' and two were minors (under 21).

Burgesses could be made on only three days in a year, and several cases could be proved of clandestine creations, or of not being sworn until the eve of the election. The corporation was also cautioned by the House's resolution not to make burgesses without consent of the 'commonalty'.[37]

In 1734 and 1741, Sir Arthur Owen of Orielton put up two of his nephews in turn against Erasmus Philipps of Picton. In 1734, 368 votes were cast and in 1741, 454: a rising electorate (403 had voted in 1715, but we have seen that 79 of these were discountable). Wyrriot Owen's petition of 1735 turned on the partiality shown by the Haverfordwest sheriff as returning officer, but it was not heard out.[38] Hugh Barlow's petition of 14 December 1741 alleged that unqualified votes were admitted contrary to the decision of 1715, and he was backed by an electors' petition to the same effect, but their case was abandoned in 1743.[39]

The 1741 contest was the last until 1812. William Edwardes, the Member from 1747, was a Sea Serjeant, backed by another, Sir John Philipps. On 16 July 1760 no less than 28 Sea Serjeants were created freemen by the corporation of whom they 'deserved well and particularly for that they have been so good as frequently to hold their annual meetings within this town'.[40] Such gatherings of the gentry were good for trade, and the Serjeants certainly met there in 1760 and 1762, though by then Sir John Philipps, who presented 200 guineas to the town on 4 December 1761 for the repair of the town hall, was rallying to the new king, George III. The Hanoverian establishment had seen to it that the number of town magistrates was increased by 45 between 1745 and 1761; there had been only ten in 1701.[41] The corporation was suspicious of coercion, however, and on 4 April 1751 resolved that the government should withdraw a troop of dragoons sent to prevent 'riots', since there had been none for 'many years', and the inhabitants resented bearing the cost.[42]

The alliance between Picton Castle and the Edwardeses, Lords Kensington, withstood any challenge until 1812, when Nathaniel Phillips of Slebech opposed them at the instigation of Sir John Owen of Orielton. There were 318 voters over eight days: the electorate was estimated at 400. Phillips claimed to be proving that Haverfordwest was 'by no means a close borough'.[43] His problem was soon revealed: the freemen at large could not nominate candidates for freeman status, but had to choose from corporation nominees decided by the mayor and the 24 capital burgesses in common council. The council also chose its officers, such as the town clerk and bailiffs, amounting to some 15 in all; administered local charities, so as to influence about 50 voters; and by their individual patronage of corporation tenants and shopkeepers, might influence another 50, and possibly as many, too, by kinship. Although Phillips campaigned for three years before the election, he could therefore make little headway when his opponents, the Blues, stood firm against him. In March 1810, six council vacancies were filled by them against Phillips's nominees. In October, the Blues filled another such vacancy and created 33 freemen in their interest, the mayor ignoring 24 Orange nominees. In October 1811 another Blue was chosen against his Orange opponent. It took an action in the King's Bench to secure the freedom of one Orange nominee in February 1812, and this turned on the by-law requiring a month's notice for obtaining the freedom. After the Orange defeat of 1812, when only 98 out of 318 votes were cast for them, there was no further contest until 1835, though the Orange party fully intended at first to try again, and the Blues secured large numbers of new freemen between 1813 and 1818 to reinforce their superiority, despite the later claim by the municipal reform commissioners that few were created in this period; that would only be true after 1818.[44] The Orange party withdrew their candidate in 1818 despite vociferous support for him in Haverfordwest, in consequence of a truce arranged by party leaders on both sides. It would seem that the election of the latest batch of new freemen played fast and loose with the residence rules: by 1832, of 303 freemen, only 142 were resident, and another 56 lived within seven miles of the town, which was to be an acceptable limit in future. The Reform Act that year enfranchised 260 freeholders (whose property qualification was raised from £2 to £10) and ratepayers (given the vote for their lives only); 134 freemen, 59 of whom were also ratepayers; and 260 householders (male householders paying £10 a year rent obtaining the vote). With 71 householder votes from Narberth and Fishguard, now contributory boroughs, an electorate of 723 emerged.[45] The Boundaries Act of 1833 added Prendergast, as well as Cartlett, to the constituency; Prendergast had petitioned Parliament to this effect on 29 March

1831.[46] The registration of voters thereafter made petitions against the return much rarer, though there were more frequent contests, and by 1852 there were two poll booths in the town at elections.[47]

For a generation after 1832, there was only moderate enthusiasm about exercising the vote at elections: the percentage of the electorate voting was 68 in 1835, 58.4 in 1837, 73.3 in 1852 and 69.5 in 1857, when William Rees for the Liberals prided himself on refusing to pay for a vote which would have staved off defeat in a close contest. From 1865 onward, the percentage voting was consistently over 73, but the competitive spirit of voters had been enhanced by the addition of lodgers paying £10 a year rent to the electorate under the second Reform Act of 1867.[48] The petition which required Lord Kensington to seek re-election in 1874 was based merely on a technical error by the returning officer, and neither occasion involved a poll.

When, in 1885, Haverfordwest was subsumed in the Pembroke Boroughs constituency under the Redistribution Act, the move was opposed by Viscount Emlyn in the Commons on the grounds that Pembroke Boroughs already had 25,000 inhabitants without Haverfordwest, and three-fifths of them constituted a dockyard interest, which must prevail. The government spokesman, Sir Charles Dilke, quashed this by saying that the only alternative was to merge the town in the county constituency. Lord Kensington swallowed his own removal from the House, welcoming the electoral mix proposed: he had presented a petition from Haverfordwest in favour. The county member William Davies claimed that Pembroke Dock also favoured it, and rebuked a critic who supposed that the new constituency, which was 'English' would be radicalized by the incorporation of 'Welsh' Haverfordwest; as a native of the town he could vouch for its Englishness. Emlyn failed in this, and in his bid to detach Narberth and Fishguard from the merger, which produced an electorate of 5,500.[49] In 1918, Pembrokeshire was reduced to one constituency. The property qualification for voting was abolished, and women over 30 were given the vote in parliamentary elections. This was extended to women over 21 in 1928.

The Members of Parliament

Payment of members' expenses was a dead letter by 1660. In the case of Haverfordwest, they were waived formally by members returned in 1640 and 1645. Property qualifications had been necessary in order to become a Member of Parliament for two centuries until 1911, when payment was reintroduced. All but two of the 24 members returned for the constituency from 1660 to 1885 were natives of the county, or closely associated with it. It was only in the Cavalier Parliament that two 'carpetbaggers', courtiers in fact, were returned. These two were eminent lawyers, and the same profession was followed by other members, such as Isaac Lloyd, Sir Herbert Perrot, Sir William Wogan and Thomas Owen in the later seventeenth century, and John Evans in the 19th. All the others, including these lawyers, were landed proprietors, William Wheeler being also a Caribbean planter. The Pembrokeshire estates that supported them were Haythog, Kilgetty, Haroldston, Llanstinan, Cwmeog, Fletherhill, St Bride's, Slebech, Lawrenny, Picton Castle, Haylett, Johnston Hall, Robeston West and Moat, Clareston and West Williamston.

By far the longest tenure of the seat was that of William Edwardes, 1st Baron Kensington, who sat for 52 years, not quite continuously, but always unopposed. Sir Richard Bulkeley Philipps sat for 19 years, and no other member for more than 17 years, the term achieved by Sir William Wogan, Sir Erasmus Philipps, and the 2nd and 4th Barons Kensington. Long tenures were encouraged in the eighteenth century by the Septennial Act. Several sat at some time for other constituencies as well as Haverfordwest: Sir William Moreton, Sir Herbert Perrot and Thomas Owen for English ones; Sir William Wogan and John Henry Philipps for Pembrokeshire; Sir George Barlow for Cardigan, after being defeated at Pembroke, and Sir John Philipps for Pembroke. John Evans failed at Cardigan in 1855 and the 4th Baron Kensington at Hornsey in 1885.

Evidence on the early education of the members is scanty in most cases, though we know that public schools such as Westminster (Sir John Philipps, Sir Richard Bulkeley Philipps), Harrow (John Henry Philipps) and Eton (4th Baron Kensington) educated some of them. The 2nd Baron Kensington was educated by Revd John Tasker Nash in Haverfordwest before proceeding to a private school near Watford: private or tutorial schooling on this pattern probably applies to other members. John Evans was educated at Geneva and Glasgow University, as befitted the son of a nonconformist manse. Oxford was the university attended by William Philipps, Sir Herbert Perrot, Sir Erasmus Philipps, Sir Richard Philipps (1st Lord Milford), William Henry Scourfield and John Henry Philipps. Cambridge was the *alma mater* of Sir William Moreton (who switched from Oxford) and Sir John Philipps. The latter, and his son Erasmus, also entered Lincolns Inn, but neither was called to the bar. A military career was no prerequisite, though several of the members served as militia officers: only William Philipps, who fought in the Civil War as a royalist major, and the 4th Baron Kensington, lieutenant colonel in the Coldstream Guards, had a regular military career for a time. One famous soldier, Sir Thomas Picton, born in Haverfordwest, was mentioned as a possible candidate for the town in the 1812 election, but nothing came of this; he came in for Pembroke a year later.

Several of the members were office holders. Moreton, Hyde and Wogan were royal serjeants-at-law and chief justices on the south Wales circuit, and John Evans a QC on it. Perrot was a gentleman pensioner of the Crown; the 2nd Baron Kensington was a lord of the Admiralty 1806-7; the 4th Baron was a lord-in-waiting to Queen Victoria, a Privy Councillor, Comptroller of the Household, and Captain of the Yeomen of the Guard. Most of the offices held were, however, local in significance. Haverfordwest had its own Lords Lieutenant from 1761 to 1931, and Lord Milford was one from 1770 to 1823, and also, from 1786, Lord Lieutenant of Pembrokeshire. The last office was also held by the 4th Baron Kensington. John Henry Philipps was Lord Lieutenant of Haverfordwest from 1857, and also chairman of Quarter Sessions, and he was created a baronet by Disraeli shortly before his death in 1876.

Politically, the members after 1660 were seldom of major importance, or men of learning and distinction, like Sir Thomas Canon and Sir James Perrot in the early seventeenth century. There were few orators among them. William Philipps spoke once; Isaac Lloyd, like Philipps, was named for half a dozen Commons committees, Sir William Moreton to a dozen, Sir Frederick Hyde to ten. The last two were obvious supporters of the Stuart establishment.

On the other hand Sir Herbert Perrot, who had sided with Parliament in the Interregnum and patronized the town dissenters, was deemed 'worthy' by Lord Shaftesbury, leader of the Country party. The latter also regarded William Wogan as 'honest', though he voted against the exclusion of the King's brother, James, from the throne. He spoke on legal questions and was active in committee. During James II's reign he joined the opposition, but he voted against the proposition that the throne was vacant when James fled the country in 1688. He was won over to the Glorious Revolution, despite his Tory leanings, and he signed the Association loyal to William III in 1696. He drafted several parliamentary bills. Thomas Owen, approved by the dissenters, was one of the Whigs who (out of Parliament) supported James II's policy of imposing religious toleration, but he did not change his political allegiance. His London activities had probably been a factor in his defeat at Haverfordwest in 1681, and in 1701 he came in for an English borough. Thomas Haward was a Court party man whose only gesture in Parliament seems to have been to oppose the exclusion of James as future king. He was killed in a duel, and his Pembrokeshire estate passed to his sister, Mrs Mary Tasker, who endowed a charity school for both sexes in Haverfordwest.

William Wheeler, whose father's family were Irish refugees, had a local commercial background on his mother's side. His brother John provided the town with a new market hall. His mother's brother endowed him with plantations in Barbados, and he represented the planters' interests while in Parliament. He was on leave from Barbados when he was elected for Haverfordwest and later he returned there. John Laugharne, whose father had been a Jacobite, was an unobtrusive Tory, while his successor, Sir George Barlow, was a Jacobite. John Barlow, who unseated Sir George, was a Whig who supported the Septennial Bill in 1717. His replacement, Sir John Philipps, was also a government supporter as the member for Haverfordwest, but he was better known for his activities outside Parliament as a champion of moral reform, of the Society for the Promotion of Christian Knowledge, which set up a school in Prendergast, and of persecuted Protestants on the continent. Francis Edwardes sat briefly as a Tory. Sir Erasmus Philipps, whose mother was an East India merchant's daughter, published two pamphlets on the national debt and commerce before entering Parliament. He was expected to act with the Whigs, but despite a family link with prime minister Walpole, he voted with the opposition, and felt obliged to write to Walpole in 1734 to deny factious opposition and to insist that he was a loyal subject of the Hanoverian dynasty. He resigned his council place in Haverfordwest from Italy in 1739 and was drowned in the Avon at Bath after some pigs frightened his horse, which threw him into the river. His successor, George Barlow, was a Tory and a Sea Serjeant. William Edwardes, also a Sea Serjeant, was regarded as a Tory until Whiggized by friendship with Henry Fox, who purchased Edwardes's London mansion, Holland House. Edwardes never opposed the government of the day, and was silent about it; in 1776 he obtained an Irish peerage, as Lord Kensington, though wishing for a British one. No indignity hurt him more than being pushed out of his seat by Lord Milford, a fellow Irish peer, in 1784 so that Milford could occupy it till the county seat became vacant in 1786. Kensington was too old to play a part in the stirring moments of Haverfordwest in the 1790s, when the dearth of bread brought Hook colliers to the town, as well as French prisoners from Fishguard and two local men falsely accused of collaboration with the enemy, and Irish refugees. By 1800 there were disorderly incidents, and a subscription was raised by the alarmed gentry to buy corn for the needy. Lord Milford, pining for an earldom, had also wrong-footed himself by drifting into passive opposition to the government, and was ill-adapted to leading the county against the threat of a French invasion, though by 1803 he was sufficiently provoked to call a meeting in Haverfordwest to make defence preparations. The Loyal Haverfordwest Volunteers had mustered in 1797, as had the Fencible Fusiliers. The Loyal Prendergast Independent Company was subsequently formed. The 2nd Baron Kensington was able to make up for his father's infirmity and commanded the Pembrokeshire Volunteers, who were reviewed on Portfield Racecourse in 1805 and 1813. Kensington was a keen politician, too, but volatile; after supporting Lord Grenville in opposition, he took office with him in the coalition ministry of 1806-7, then joined the Whigs in opposition. He wearied of this and flirted with George Canning in 1813, hoping it would restore him to the Admiralty Board. This got him nowhere and, in 1818, by then living in Italy, he lost his seat for Haverfordwest, a victim of the electoral compromise imposed by the party leaders in Pembrokeshire. He fulminated against them from abroad, but eventually returned as an advocate of parliamentary reform, while his heir sat for an English pocket borough. His replacement, William Henry Scourfield, despite his Blue (Whig) credentials, drifted into Toryism unobtrusively, and was nudged out by the avowedly Whiggish heir to Picton Castle, Richard Bulkeley Philipps, who supported local and parliamentary reform, though he was to draw the line at Catholic civic rights. He blanched in the face of a contest in 1835, and was much provoked to see Scourfield returned: he insisted on ousting him in 1837, but spent long spells abroad, missing the destruction of Prendergast and Haroldston tollgates by Rebecca rioters in 1843, and willingly surrendering his seat for the repose of a British peerage in 1847. His successor John Evans, a self-styled Liberal, was one of the town's most articulate members in his one parliament: he advocated wholesale legal reform and freedom of conscience. The contrast with his successor, John Henry Philipps, is piquant. The latter, a squirearchical Tory humorist with a penchant for satirical verse, overegged his maiden speech in favour of agricultural protection, but gradually settled into the skills of a gadfly in debate. The spread of the railways was his bugbear, and reduction of the national debt a favourite theme. He enjoyed committee work, and was a promoter of the Haverfordwest Infirmary (1859) and the United Counties Asylum in Carmarthen (1866). The 4th Baron Kensington, a restrained Liberal, nevertheless spoke in favour of abolishing the purchase of military commissions and of the secret ballot. He also proposed a ban on the use of public houses for election purposes. Subsequently he became a party whip and an official and spokesman for the royal household. After 1885, when Haverfordwest played second string to Pembroke, dockyard issues monopolized the members' speeches.[50]

PETITIONS TO PARLIAMENT

Apart from petitions presented by defeated candidates, detailed previously, and occasionally accompanied by petitions from the corporation or some of the electors, there were other petitions to Parliament on non-electoral issues. References to these appear in the corporation records. They usually lay behind legislation affecting the town. In the early nineteenth century, however, petitioning Parliament reached a crescendo, and members of parliament were kept busy presenting and, in some cases, supporting these manifestations of their constituents' opinions, whether from the county or diocese (as when the Anglican clergy opposed Catholic relief in 1813), which usually followed a meeting at Haverfordwest, or from the town. In 1829, Earl Cawdor was shouted down when he supported Catholic relief at a Guildhall meeting in Haverfordwest. The town's Presbyterians had petitioned against it, acting through the county member, until they eventually won over the town member. He, Sir Richard Philipps, also presented petitions against the abolition of the Welsh judicature, on 9 March and 6 May 1830, in vain. The advent of reform in 1832 only slightly abated the spate of petitions, which continued for a decade or so afterwards. Those from Haverfordwest usually reflected the concerns of the Nonconformist community, emancipated by the abolition of the Test Act in 1828, which meant that they could become *bona fide* councillors for the first time since the 1660s. Thus, in 1843 they petitioned against the award to Anglican clergy of the educational supervision of children in mines and factories, in pursuit of an equal opportunities policy.[51]

LEGISLATION

Distinct legislation from Westminster affecting Haverfordwest is hard to find until the eighteenth century, as so much regional legislation was hitherto based on larger districts, such as counties. As a county, Haverfordwest was often included in its own right in these, for example in the appointment of land tax commissioners from 1695 to 1832. Legislation concerning roads, which became frequent in the eighteenth century, was treated as a county matter as late as 1772. The radius of roads from Haverfordwest often needed repair. Those to Fishguard and St David's were involved in 1791 and 1812; the Merlin's Bridge to Pembroke Ferry road in 1788, 1790, 1808 and 1830; the Steynton to Merlin's Bridge and Merlin's Bridge to Cartlett Bridge roads in 1808, following a petition to Parliament on 12 May, and again in 1829. In consequence of an Act of 1851, the South Wales Railway Company constructed a railway which reached Haverfordwest in 1853.

By an Act of 1779, sponsored on petition not by the town member but by the other two Pembrokeshire members, a new gaol was erected for the county in Haverfordwest. In 1822, a further Act converted this gaol into one for Pembrokeshire and Haverfordwest, the town gaol being set aside for use as a lunatic asylum. The Act of 1836 to pave, light and improve Haverfordwest, Prendergast, Cartlett and Uzmaston ushered in gas lighting. It had been preceded in 1834 by an Act to supply the town with water and to erect a new bridge over the river, legislation which had to be amended three years later.

Portfield Common was enclosed by an Act of 1837. An Act of 1868 to improve the town water supply also stipulated the provision of a recreation ground and provided for the recovery of the market dues by the corporation (they had been granted to the mayor in 1730). From 1876 onwards Acts generally authorized Local Government Board orders affecting Haverfordwest.[52]

MUNICIPAL POLITICS

The reform of local government under the Municipal Corporations Act of 1835, which recognized three municipal boroughs in Pembrokeshire, Haverfordwest, Pembroke and Tenby, did much to reduce the influence of the self-perpetuating oligarchies of councillors for life operating in small boroughs like Haverfordwest. The town had 593 houses and 2,280 inhabitants in 1801; the population in 1831 was 4,300; in 1841, 4,965, rising later in the century to nearly 6,000. From 1835, the mayor still being elected annually, like the other corporation officers, there were to be four aldermen, elected triennially and eligible for re-election, and 12 councillors, four of whom were to be chosen by the registered electors every November for the wards into which the town was divided. Corporation control of the town charities was simultaneously exposed and regulated by the Charity Commissioners. Not at once, however, were these Whig reforms digested. The party basis of patronal management by the Philippses of Picton and the Edwardeses had to be overcome in the interests of municipal endeavour. There were municipal improvers in the town at this time, such as William Owen of Withybush, and town architecture was modernized with a new shire hall and bridge, clearance of the shambles about St Mary's and the tenement encroachments on Castle Square, and the addition of handsome urban terraces. But there was a counterbalancing tendency by the more conservative gentry to assert the 'county town' aspect of Haverfordwest, by establishing a pack of foxhounds by William Henry Scourfield in 1828, accompanied by annual hunt balls. In 1844 the county agricultural association was revived in the town, and a show ground constructed in 1847. The shrievalty of Haverfordwest remained an honorific position reserved for the substantial and eminent. The mayoralty was another matter. The gentry were still inclined in 1849 to be snobbish about the election of 'tradesmen' as mayors, though as the circle of merchants, professional men and men of independent means who had supplied the office in the 'genteel' eighteenth century declined in influence, retailers, some grown wealthy, skilled artisans and manufacturers could no longer be ruled out. Eventually the mayor and council could be regarded as representing the business community.

William Philipps (*c.*1615-*c.*1689) of Haythog	1660-1661
Isaac Lloyd (*c.*1628-75) of Kilgetty	1661-1663
Sir William Moreton (*c.*1605-72) of Winchcombe	1663-1665
Sir Frederick Hyde (1614-77) of Teddington	1666-1677
Sir Herbert Perrot (*c.*1617-83) of Haroldston	1677-1679
Sir William Wogan (*c.*1638-1708) of Llanstinan	1679, 1685-1701
Thomas Owen (*c.*1637-1708) of Cwmeog	1679-1681
Thomas Haward (*c.*1655-82) of Fletherhill	1681-1682
William Wheeler (died 1708) of Barbados	1701-1702
John Laugharne (died 1715) of St Brides	1702-1715
Sir George Barlow, 2nd Bart. (died 1726) of Slebech	1715
John Barlow (died 1718) of Lawrenny	1715-1718
Sir John Philipps, 4th Bart. (*c.*1666-1737) of Picton	1718-1722
Francis Edwardes (died 1725) of Haylett	1722-1725
Sir Erasmus Philipps, 5th Bart. (*c.*1701-43) of Picton	1726-1743
George Barlow (1717-56) of Slebech	1743-1747
William Edwardes, Lord Kensington (*c*1716-1801) 1747-84,	1786-1801
Sir Richard Philipps, Lord Milford (*c.*1741-1823) of Picton	1784-1786
William Edwardes, Lord Kensington (1776-1852)	1801-1818
William Henry Scourfield (1776-1843)	1818-26, 1835-37
Sir Richard Bulkeley Philipps (1801-57)	1826-1835, 1837-1847
John Evans (1796-1864) of Clareston and Foley House	1847-1852
John Henry Philipps (later Scourfield, Bart.) (1808-76)	1852-1868
William Edwardes, Lord Kensington (1835-96)	1868-1885

MPs for Pembroke Boroughs (including Haverfordwest) 1885-1918

Henry George Allen (1815-1906) of Paskeston	1885-1886
Admiral Richard Charles Mayne (1835-92)	1886-1892
Charles Francis Egerton Allen (1847-1927) of Tenby	1892-1895
John Wimburn Laurie (1835-1912) of London	1895-1906
Sir Owen Cosby Philipps (1863-1937), later Lord Kylsant	1906-1910
Hon. Christian Henry Charles Guest (1874-1957)	1910-1918

ROLAND THORNE

THE FREEMEN OF HAVERFORDWEST

'The origin of the system of freemen is not known with any certainty. It is known to have existed in Anglo-Saxon times, but its roots seem to go back into the Ancient British and Roman systems as well . . . The burgesses (later called freemen) of boroughs were those inhabitants of the towns who were of free status and were permitted and obliged to bear arms for the defence of their towns, being also in most cases owners or tenants of dwellings in the town.'[1] They enjoyed the exclusive right of trading in the borough and were exempt from tolls and dues. They alone were eligible for municipal office, and they alone had the franchise for parliamentary elections. These privileges were conferred by charters granted by the king or a feudal lord with a view to encouraging settlement and promoting trade and industry in a borough, as well as increasing its military strength. The charters incorporated them as corporate bodies, consisting of a mayor and other officers, and common councillors elected from among the freemen of the borough, which enhanced the status and power of the freemen and enabled them to gain control of the borough.

The earliest reference to a charter relating to Haverfordwest is found in letters explanatory under the seal of Adam Houghton, Bishop of St David's (1361-77) in which he declared that he had 'discovered in the archives of the church of St David's' a certain old writing, purporting that Henry II 'had made grants of a certain nature to the towns and inhabitants of Pembroke and Haverford'.[2] The charter making these grants was dated 17 March 1168 and, in the case of Pembroke at least, it confirmed the 'liberties, immunities and free customs' granted by his grandfather, Henry I. The earliest charter of which there is record was granted by King John, on 17 November 1207 which confirmed Robert, son of Richard fitzTancred, in the lordship of Haverfordwest and granted him a market and a fair on the Feast of St Philip and St James.[3] Robert, however, was deprived of his inheritance by the King when he returned from Ireland in 1210 and, three years later, the lordship was sold to William Marshal, Earl of Pembroke, and became part of the earldom.

William Marshal, before his death in 1219, granted the town a charter which decreed that 'a man, whatever his status may be, who dwells there [in the town] for a year and a day without being challenged shall be free'.[4] The charter was confirmed by his eldest son, William Marshal the Younger, at Chepstow on 8 September 1219, when it was further decreed that 'no merchant be in our land who is not resident in our borough, and ships coming with merchandise in to Milford go not elsewhere in our land to sell their goods unless at Pembroke and Haverford.' In a later charter he granted to 'our beloved and faithful burgesses of Haverford . . . a merchant guild for the convenience of them and their town' and decreed that they should be free of mill tolls and tolls for erecting stalls at markets and fairs. Gilbert Marshal, the third son, after he succeeded his brother as Earl of Pembroke in 1234, confirmed the burgesses' freedom from payment of toll, pontage or passage.[5]

TRADE GUILDS

The monopoly of trade by the burgesses was consolidated by the establishment of guilds, grants for the incorporation of which were made by the mayor and common council. In 1499 the guild of cordwainers and shoemakers petitioned the mayor and corporation for ordinances for the protection and government of their craft within the borough. The extent of protection provided by such an ordinance is indicated in a deed of incorporation of the glover and whittawers[6] granted by the mayor, Sir John Perrot, in 1560, to John Webb and others, in which it was laid down that they should 'choose their master and wardens on 25 March yearly' and that no person other than glovers or whittawers shall occupy, or set up, that occupation without licence of the master and wardens, and that no other person shall buy any sheep skins.[7] A deed of incorporation of the guild of feltmakers, hatmakers and haberdashers in 1613 enacted that 'the company shall assemble in Feltmakers' Hall on 8 July annually to appoint two masters and two wardens' and that 'no foreigner or stranger, notwithstanding he has been brought up in the trade in any other town, shall set up the trade here unless he be resiant and also have a testimonial as to his apprenticeship and good name and pays £20 for his freedom within twelve days and bestows a breakfast on the company, except he marry a widow or a daughter of a freeman of the company and then he shall be admitted on payment of £10 and a dinner.' It warned that 'freemen who make insufficient or unlawful wares shall forfeit 6s. 8d.' (33p) and that 'quarrels among the brotherhood shall be first examined before the masters and wardens.'[8] The guilds were, therefore, self-governing bodies and it was only when they could not agree among themselves that they resorted to the discipline of the mayor and common council.

The Royal Commission on Municipal Corporations of 1835 reported that 'there were anciently guilds of trades' in the borough but that 'many of these companies have long ceased to exist; some of them still extant in form, but have dwindled into jovial clubs, and retain no trace of their original constitution. The last and only recent attempt on the part of the guilds to exercise their ancient privileges was made by the guild of cordwainers, in the case of one Davis', who had carried on the trade of a shoemaker without the consent of the guild. The wardens, having distrained his goods as a penalty, were sued by Davis in an action of trespass. The defendants justified the trespass under by-laws made by the corporation of Haverfordwest 'founded on a custom to exclude foreigners from trading in the borough'. The jury found that there was no such custom and the report states that:

> this verdict has put an end to the pretensions of the cordwainers guild, and there is no probability that such questions will be raised hereafter by any other company. In practice, the internal trade of the borough, (with the exception of the liability of the non-burgesses to pay toll) is unrestricted.[9]

The grants to the guilds of tailors, saddlers, glovers, feltmakers, cordwainers and shoemakers, carpenters, blacksmiths and gunsmiths are extant.[10]

The charters granted to the borough of the town and county of Haverfordwest, as in many other English and Welsh boroughs, were based on the privileged liberties granted to the burgesses of Breteuil-sur-Iton, in Eure, which William fitzOsbern gave to the town of Hereford.[11] Robert de Durward, bailiff of Hereford, in about 1282, sent instructions on 'the customs of Hereford' to the burgesses of Haverfordwest at their request and in return for a payment of £5, and it is likely that the earlier charters granted to the town, and certainly those of the Marshals, were influenced by the Breteuil liberties. It is noted that Roger de Montgomery, Earl of Shrewsbury, had based the charters of Shrewsbury on the Breteuil customs before he and his son, Arnulf, occupied Pembroke.[12]

The town was incorporated by a charter, dated 30 April 1479, granted by Edward, Prince of Wales and Lord of Haverford, and as he was only nine years of age at the time, he granted it 'of the mandate of the Lord his father and by the advice of the Lords of the Council together with the assent of his mother, the Queen'. The charter decreed that the town should have a mayor, sheriff and two bailiffs and conferred upon it the status of a county as 'the county of the town of Haverford', and this status was confirmed by the Act of Union of 1543. The constitution of the corporation, established by the charter of 1479 was renewed and clarified in a charter granted by James I in 1610 which granted the town another two fairs.

In 1500 the Crown granted the fee-farm of the town to the mayor and corporation at an annual rental of £26 12s. 4d. (£26.62) and as the government of the town was henceforth in the hands of the corporation, the town became 'free of the shackles of feudal overlordship'.[13] In 1536, after the lordship of Haverfordwest was abolished under the Act of Union, William Barlow, Bishop of St David's wrote to Thomas Cromwell urging that 'the shire town be Haverford West, in the midst of the shire (whither men may at all seasons repair) and not as hitherto Pembroke, which is not only remote, but also inconvenient.'[14]

THE COMMON COUNCIL

Under the charter of 1479 the mayor nominated the 24 common councilmen, or capital burgesses, but they were later elected by the burgesses at a general meeting and held office for life subject to a motion by the mayor and council 'for ill-government, ill behaviour, or any other reasonable cause'. The mayor and common councilmen in common council formed the governing body of the corporation that ordered and managed its general affairs, distributed the funds and superintended the charities.

On the first hundred court after the feast of St Michael, the mayor and councilmen returned 'three of their body to the burgesses' from whom the burgesses elected one to be mayor. The mayor, during his year of office, was the chief magistrate, and he was coroner, escheator, clerk of the market, deputy lieutenant and admiral of the port. He had a salary of £30 and was entitled to the fishery of the river from the borough boundary at Higgon's Well to the Priory Mill, and received a couple of fowls from each of the corporation tenants, and 200 apples out of every shipload arriving at the quay, and he also received 'the mayor's kechyn', a brawn, at Christmas. The sheriff was elected on the same day in a similar manner except that the nominations could be from the councilmen or from the burgesses at large. He was allowed £10 to pay for a breakfast on Whit Monday when the boundaries of the borough were perambulated, and he received the same number of apples out of every shipload as the mayor. Two bailiffs were elected on the same day, and two serjeants-at-mace. The town clerk was appointed for life, and the chamber reeve and the town crier were appointed 'during pleasure' by the mayor and council from among the burgesses. At one time there were high and petty constables, water bailiffs, a bell man, and a beadle dressed in a gown of grey friese, and there was a company of waits, arrayed in liveries of grey friese faced with green Levant taffeta and trimmed with green mockado, who provided entertainment for the townspeople during the latter part of the sixteenth century.

The office of admiral of the port indicated the importance of Haverfordwest as one of the head ports for Customs collections between 1375 and 1400.[15] In Elizabethan times the great bulk of the town's maritime trade was with Bristol which established a close tie between the merchants of the two ports.

From early times the freemen were referred to as burgesses and in the report of the Royal Commission of 1835 'freeman' and 'burgess' are used synonymously. The report describes the qualification for the admission of freemen:

> The Freedom of the borough is acquired, 1st. by birth; 2d. by servitude; and 3d. by election.
>> 1st. The burgesses by birth are all the sons of burgesses, whether born before or after their father's admission.

2d. The burgesses by servitude are persons who have served an apprenticeship of seven years to one or more burgesses in succession within the borough.

3d. The burgesses by election, styled *ex gratia* burgesses, are persons elected to be such by the body of burgesses.

The report states that there were 292 burgesses of whom 141 were resident and 151 non-resident. The figure given for 1424 was 360 burgesses, but this may be an exaggerated figure.[16]

The councilmen were tradesmen and burgesses 'of the better sort' and, in 1540, they comprised nine mercers, three corvisors, a tailor, a tanner, a sherman, a frieser, a glover, six gentlemen, and an esquire, in the person of (later Sir) Thomas Jones of Haroldston.

By right of its county status, with an assize and quarter sessions, Haverfordwest was granted the right to have a Custos Rotulorum in 1545 and, in 1761, its own Lord Lieutenant. The first Lord Lieutenant and Custos Rotulorum was Sir John Philipps, Bart., of Picton Castle, and it remained in the Philipps family. When Sir Charles Philipps died in 1924, Lord Kylsant was appointed in his place, despite the fact that the right to appoint a Lord Lieutenant had been withdrawn by the Territorial Army and Militia Act of 1921. Lord Kylsant resigned in 1931. Sir Charles's son, Sir Henry Philipps, was then appointed Custos Rotulorum, but within a short time the office was merged in that of the county of Pembroke.

Under the terms of the Act of Union, Haverfordwest was allowed to return a burgess as member of parliament. Richard Howell, merchant and a member of the council who had been mayor in 1541, was the first to represent the town and county at Westminster and he was succeeded by Richard Taylor, mercer and councilman in 1553. Thereafter, the merchant freemen had to give way to the burgesses 'of better sort', such as Thomas ab Owen of Pentre Ifan (1558), Alban Stepney (1572), Sir John Perrot (1588), Sir James Perrot (1597), Sir Thomas Canon (1625), William Philipps of Picton (1660), Sir Herbert Perrot (1677), Sir William Wogan (1685), Sir John Philipps, Bart. (1718), Sir Erasmus Philipps, Bart. (1741), Lord Milford (1784), and Lord Kensington (1786).

The gentry burgesses also managed to obtain seats on the common council. Under an ordinance of 1554, the squires of Prendergast and

Haroldston were eligible to be burgesses of Haverfordwest but others of the squirearchy were made burgesses and were elected to the council. Burgesses who were not permanently resident were known as burgesses *de vento* (of the wind) as their interests were elsewhere but it served them to have a stake in the town. There is no figure for the number of such burgesses at Haverfordwest in 1324 but they numbered 30 per cent of the total number at Cardigan and Carmarthen, whereas Tenby had less than 10 per cent.[17] Their failure to attend meetings, however, led to complaint and in 1660 it was reported that 'the affairs of this Town are very often and much retarded for want of a full number of common council to meet and advise for the public weal thereof and that chiefly occasioned by the election of so many country gentlemen whose affairs elsewhere hinder them from meetings here.' The common council therefore decided that only professional people whose business kept them in the town should be elected, and in 1719 it was further resolved that the number of country gentlemen serving on the council should be limited to five, but in the following year the order was repealed as it was considered to be prejudicial to the town. The common council in 1831 included Earl Cawdor, Lord Kensington, Sir Richard Philipps, Bart., MP (later Lord Milford), Sir William Philipps, Bart., The Hon. William Edwardes (later Lord Kensington and Lord Lieutenant of the county of Pembroke), Nathaniel Phillips of Slebech, William Henry Scourfield of Robeston Hall, Robert Innes Ackland of Boulston, George Lort Phillips of Ashdale, James Higgon of Scolton and his son, John, George Roch of Butter Hill and his son, George, all of whom, together with five others, are shown as having no profession or trade, together with James Thomas and Thomas Martin, clergymen, George Harries and John Lloyd Morgan, physicians, and William Evans and James Phillips, attorneys, the latter being the town clerk. Ten of the members were 'substantially resident,' five were wholly non-resident', and ten lived within distances of the borough of up to 16 miles. The Royal Commission observed that

> the offices and management of the Corporation are exclusively confined to members of the prevailing political party. The Lord Lieutenant (who is a member of the common-council), the county magistrates and the common-councilmen, are all members of that party, with the exception of one of the latter body. That member,

however, was attached to the prevailing party at the time of his election. The election of partisans upon vacancies on the common-council is secured by the influence of that body over the burgesses. The number of burgesses within the parliamentary limits is about 200. Of these the members of the common-council and their relatives, with the county magistrates, form a body of 42. The rest consist for the most part of persons of inferior rank, of whom many are in the enjoyment of charities in the gift of the common-council, and many more are easily influenced by the promise or hope of like preferment. Adding to this class the corporation tenants, and the burgesses in the employment of the common-council, it appears that that body is enabled to command a constant majority amongst the burgesses . . . The common-councilmen therefore, though nominally elected by the burgesses, are in fact appointed by the common-council itself; and this body, in whom the government of the corporation is vested, is, when stripped of appearance, a self-elected irresponsible body.[18]

The report also revealed that in addition to those connected with, or dependent upon the council, of the 192 burgesses voting, there were 58 who had 'been made burgesses *ex gratia* by the Corporation, for the purpose of voting with them' and two who had 'been put in Office by the influence of individual common-councilmen.'

As the franchise for parliamentary elections was limited to the freemen, much depended on the ability to create additional freemen in time for the elections. Following the death of John Laugharne on the night of his election in 1715, Sir George Barlow of Slebech defeated the Whig, John Barlow of Lawrenny, but John Barlow petitioned, claiming that burgesses had been clandestinely admitted on days other than the three days allowed for the purpose, and he unseated Sir George and took his place. When there had been no contest since 1741 and, in 1812, Lord Kensington was opposed by Nathaniel Phillips of Slebech, who had formed an Orange party within the corporation, there was a great argument over the admission of burgesses which was referred to the King's Bench. The numbers of voting freemen had been augmented when Edward, son of Sir Erasmus Philipps of Picton, married Elizabeth, the daughter and heiress of John Canon of Kilgetty and united the Picton and Kilgetty estates, and the freemen of Kilgetty, known as 'the Black Hundred', became freemen of Haverfordwest and turned the scale in favour of the Philippses in many a parliamentary and municipal contest.[19]

The demands for greater democracy brought about the Municipal Corporation Act of 1835 which threw the freemen's rights of trading open to all and prohibited the admission of freemen by gift or purchase, but it provided that their rights of admission otherwise and their rights of property or to participate in charities should be unaffected. The freemen had lost their power and privileges, but their institution, their property and funds remained.

The manipulating of the freemen appears to have continued at Haverfordwest, however. In the parliamentary election of 1852 the sitting member, John Evans, QC, whose son, George Essex Evans became 'the national poet of Australia', complained that he had lost to John Henry Philipps (who later assumed the name of Scourfield) of Williamston because of the control that Philipps exerted over the freemen. Evans had received a majority of votes in the contributory boroughs of Fishguard and Narberth, but at Haverfordwest the freemen had been pressurized to vote for Philipps. A commentator noted that many of the freemen resided long distances from the town and, 'needless to say that those freemen who came home to poll had a week's "good time", and not at their own expense.'[20]

The manner in which the freemen jealously guarded their privileges is illustrated in the 'acts made in the town and county of Haverfordwest by Hugh Harries, mayor . . . with the assent of all his brethren, or the most part of them', on 20 October 1554. There were 27 such acts and among them those which ordained that:

> No stranger or foreigner shall buy any manner of wares or merchandise withinthe town unless he do so from a burgess.
>
> No foreigner, that is non-resident, shall be made a burgess, but the houses Haroldston and Prendergast are excepted at the will and pleasure of the mayor and his brethren.
>
> Common-councilmen failing to obey a summons of the mayor to appear upon an hour or a day's warning shall pay a fine of 3s. 4d. (17p). The sheriff, bailiffs, serjeants and town clerk shall give their attendance upon the mayor going to market, church and court and other places and home to his house and especially upon holidays, court days and market days, upon the pain of fine of 3s. (15p), without lawful excuse.

Every burgess having dunghills, miskins or gutters upon his front shall make them clean and every man shall pave his front.

No man shall keep any cattle on Portfield common unless he be a burgess, and no sheep or goats shall pasture the common; no furze hewed or fern hacked.[21]

PORTFIELD COMMON.

The burgesses had originally been given right of common without stint for all commonable cattle at all times of the year on the common land at Portfield, – a name derived from the Old English *port*, meaning a town, and *feld*, unenclosed or common land. The restriction of the acts of 1554 were necessary because the common had been 'overcharged by the cattle of foreigners and inhabitants not being burgesses, by reason whereof the cattle of the burgesses had been famished', and as it was felt that the burgesses themselves had been overgrazing, it was further ordered that 'no burgess shall keep on the commons above 4 heads of his own cattle.' Sheep and goats, belonging to all and sundry, had previously been allowed to graze the common but they had devoured the pasture and the furze and had destroyed 'the most part of the hedges of the closes of the burgesses' and, therefore, they were forbidden. In 1639 again, there were 'great complaints made by the poorer burgesses that the commons called Portfield are surcharged by the rich burgesses who bring their whole stock to depasture there', and the common council decreed that 'no burgess shall set to pasture on the commons more than four head of cattle and forty sheep and six head of swine, the swine to be ringed and yoked' and instructed that 'the order shall be openly read the next Sabbath day after morning prayer in the several churches of the town by the minister of each parish.'[22]

The common council noted, on 2 August 1727, that 'whereas certain gentlemen are determined for the good of this Corporation to have a horse race on the Common of the Town and County called Portfield', sufficient ground should be allotted for that purpose and the expense to be defrayed by the Corporation. An account of the Pembrokeshire Hunt Races held on the racecourse in 1822 revealed that the races were held on Tuesday, Thursday and Saturday during the last week of October and were followed each evening by a ball at the Assembly Rooms to which the ladies of quality were conveyed in their sedan chairs, and an ordinary, that is, a public meal, at a fixed price that was provided for the commonalty alternately at the Castle Inn and the Mariners Inn at each of which one of the race stewards would preside.[23]

The Royal Commission complained, in 1833, that 'in its present state the common is unproductive to the great majority of the burgesses, who have no cattle to depasture', and stated that 'the land is very good and, if inclosed, would yield a considerable income.' It was stated that 'an individual had offered, some years since, to take the common at a rent of £500 a year, and inclose it at his own expense', but the council and the burgesses had not been able to agree upon terms, some feeling that the proceeds should be applied to public purposes, and others that it should be divided among the burgesses.[24]

In 1838, an Act of Parliament for the enclosure of Portfield Common reached the statute books. The commissioner appointed to divide, allot and enclose the common and waste lands and to carry the Portfield Inclosure Act into execution, was John Wilson, barrister-at-law, the recorder of Carmarthen. The common, it was stated, contained 'by estimation six hundred acres or thereabouts which were extraparochial and not included within any manor or lordship, and the Freemen of the said Borough [of Haverfordwest] were or claimed to be entitled to the pasturage of, and the right to stock, the said common pastures, and to other rights of common in and upon the said common and waste lands and that the said Freemen had for a long period of time depastured their horses, cattle and sheep thereon'. In order to meet the cost incurred in administering the Act, the commissioner was authorized to sell as much of the land as may be expedient and he disposed of 47 lots, most of them small plots and none over five acres, except for an area of ten acres at Caradoc's Well and a parcel of 42 acres lying to the east of Temperness farm, amounting in all to 127 acres. Eighteen acres were allotted for carriage roads and four acres for private roads, and small areas as public watering places for animals and other purposes. An area of land measuring 42 acres lying between Snowdrop Lane and the Racecourse, and a parcel of 35 acres running south of Portfield Gate were allotted to the mayor, aldermen and burgesses, who were 'entitled to the soil and freehold of the said commons and waste lands called Portfield' by way of 'recompense, compensation and satisfaction . . . for and in lieu of their rights or claim to the soil of the said lands, and also, for and in lieu of all other their rights and interests in, over, or under the said lands or any part thereof.' The mayor, aldermen and burgesses were also allotted parcels of land for the extraction of stone and gravel, and also sand-pits and clay-pits, for use in the building and maintaining public carriage roads across the common.[25]

The mayor, aldermen and burgesses were allotted

> so much and such parts of the said Common and waste lands as include the present Race Course and the area within the Course and containing by admeasurement 85 acres 2 roods and 5 perches or thereabouts . . . to be for a place of recreation and exercise for the neighbouring population at their free will and pleasure . . . to be holden by and vested in the said Mayor Aldermen and Burgesses for the purposes aforesaid for ever hereafter, and to be depastured by sheep but by sheep only at all times of the year, except such times as public Races shall be held upon the said race Course.[26]

The Haverfordwest Borough Act of 1868 constituted a committee of management for the racecourse comprising the mayor, four members of the Borough Council, and five representatives of the Freemen's Trustees, with power to enclose and to improve the land so as to make it more available for public enjoyment. The commissioner allotted and awarded 'unto the Trustees for the Freemen of the Borough and County of the Town of Haverfordwest for the benefit of the Freemen of the said Borough and their successors for ever all the residue and remainder of the said land,' containing 251 acres and 16 perches.[27] The estate is managed by the Trustees, comprising nine of the freemen who are elected every three years by the body of freemen. The income from the estate is distributed annually in equal shares to the freemen by the Trustees.

THE GILD OF FREEMEN.

The Local Government Bill published in 1971 made no reference to the rights of freemen and it was only after representations had been made by the Freemen of England (later the Freemen of England and Wales) that the Minister to the Department of the Environment agreed to insert clause 248 stating that 'nothing in this Act shall affect any person's status, or the rights of any person to be admitted as a freeman,' but as borough councils had been abolished, it decreed that the roll of freemen would henceforth be kept by the proper officer of the relevant district council. The Act, for once, distinguished between freemen and burgesses, whose rights and privileges were preserved in clause 246. The Local Goverment Act of 1994 preserved the status of burgesses and freemen in the same manner as the 1972 Act and directed that the admission of freemen should be by the chairman of the county council and that the roll of freemen should be kept by the proper officer of the council.

The Act of 1972, which took effect from 1 April 1974, abolished the Haverfordwest Borough Council and transferred the responsibility for keeping the Freemen's Roll and the admission of Freemen to the Preseli District Council. It was felt, however, that measures should be taken to safeguard the position of the freemen and, at the instigation of Colonel J.H.V. Higgon, OBE, a special freemen's dinner was held on 29 November 1971, attended by about a hundred freemen, together with visiting freemen from London, York, Birmingham and Slough, at which the idea of forming a Gild of Freemen of Haverfordwest was formulated. The Gild was established in November 1973 and it has a badge, designed by the Wales Herald of Arms Extraordinary, later the Gild's archivist, depicting the lymphad, a one-masted galley, that appears on the town's common seal, the sail bearing the Prince of Wales's plumes with reference to the charter granted in 1479.

In 1974 the Gild decided to appoint burgesses for life from 'persons of repute who have rendered outstanding service to the town'. There are 260 Freemen (1998), of whom 82 are resident and 178 non-resident, many of them living abroad, and 38 Burgesses. The chairman of the admitting local authority is made a Burgess for year of office only. The affairs of the Gild are managed by a Court of Wardens, comprising freemen and burgesses, the members of which wear scarlet gowns bearing the Gild badge. The Gild has adopted St Martin's Church, the town's oldest church, as its spiritual headquarters.

DILLWYN MILES

THE HAVERFORDWEST CHARITIES

A concern for the less fortunate members of society became apparent with the rise of the Tudor gentry and, from the sixteenth century onward landowners, wealthy merchants and prosperous tradesmen gave or bequeathed money or property for the spiritual, intellectual and material needs of the poorer members of the community. Bequests were often handed in trust to the mayor and corporation, or to church wardens, or to overseers of the poor, to be applied to charitable uses, frequently in accordance with the wishes of the benefactor.

The town and county of Haverfordwest was uncommonly well endowed in this respect. The full number of its benefactors is not known, as many of the bequests have been lost, or otherwise disappeared, but there are records extant of close on 40 charities.

The earliest, and most bountiful, charity was Perrot's Charity. By indenture dated 20 September 1580, under the hand and seal of Sir John Perrot, knight, of Haroldston, 'in consideration of the love which he bore towards the burgesses of the town and county of Haverfordwest,' and as the mayor, sheriff, bailiffs and burgesses had agreed that he and his heirs should be able to purchase as much wine, salt or any other merchandise coming in to the port on the same terms as the mayor and burgesses, and likewise the victuals coming in to the market, and that he and his heirs should be burgesses and members of the common council and, furthermore, that they should have the right to nominate a burgess each year, he would give and grant to Maurice Canon, mayor, and seven common councilmen, and their heirs, certain messuages, lands, tenements, burgages and hereditaments within and without the town, 'all which premises with their appurtenances had been purchased by Sir John Perrot from Queen Elizabeth'. The rents and profits arising from the premises were to be disposed 'to the improvement of the town and for the repair of the streets, bridges, walls, conduits of water, and other decays of the said town; also for the rebuilding of a new quay in the said town, and for all other good works which should be necessary or convenient for the improvement of the said town.'

The properties as listed in the deed, were 'lately found to be lands concealed and afterwards obtained by me from the hands of our Lady the Queen as by letters patent of our Lady the Queen bearing date the 22nd day of September in the 17th year of her reign,' namely 1575, and comprised the following (description of the premises given in a corporation book in 1720 are given in brackets and further notes in square brackets):

1. Messuage or tenement (now a farm of 60 acres) [North Camrose Farm] in the parish of Camrose.
2. Tenement (farm of 105 acres) at Wolfsdale.
3. Messuage (storehouse) in Ship Street next to Old Three Crowns.
4. Tenement (two houses) on the north side of High Street.
5. Tenement (house) on the south side of High Street [part Shire Hall].
6. Tenement (house and garden) in Barn Street [Little Vildas].
7. Tenement (stables) in Dark Street.
8. Tenement (house and garden) in Dark Street.
9. Two tenements (two houses) in St Mary Street [Old Post Office].
10. Three tenements (house) in St Mary Street [Old Council Chamber].
11. Tenement (house in Pillory Street) on the south side of St Mary's Church.
12. Tenement (Blue Boar public house, in Dew Street).
13. Tenement (house and yard) in Market Street.
14. Two tenements (two houses and a garden) in Market Street.
15. Tenement ((house and yard) on the east side of Market Street.
16. Burgage (four houses) on the south side of Goat Street.
17. Tenement (Meeting-house on the Green) [Albany Chapel].
18. Tenement (houses) in Hill Street [Albion Terrace].
19. Tenement in the upper end and west side of Dew Street [Old Show Yard].
20. Tenement (house and garden) in Dew Street.
21. Tenement (three houses called Rat Island) in the middle of Dew Street.
22. Tenement (two houses and a garden) in Dew Street.
23. Tenement (two houses and gardens) in Dew Street.
24. Tenement (two houses and a garden) in Dew Street.

25. Tenement (house and garden) in Dew Street.
26. Tenement (two houses and gardens) in Dew Street.
27. Tenement (house and garden) in Dew Street.
28. Two closes (with six or seven cottages, bounded on the north by Shoalshook brook) near Cartlett.
29. Two tenements (house and garden) in Bridge Street.
30. Garden (two-acre meadow) near Jury Cross in the parish of St Martin.
31. Tenement (two houses near the Bridge) in the parish of St Martin [Fishguard Arms].
32. Small parcel called Kilfiggin (Moor's nursery garden, with five cottages) near the Bridge.
33. Tenement (seven or eight houses, gardens, stables and coach houses) in Castle Town
34. Two closes in Burton Hill (three meadow pastures) in the parish of St Martin.

Much of the property has been sold and the proceeds invested in securities administered by the Perrot Trust. The Trust still holds some dwelling-houses in the town, including the twelve almshouses in Perrot's Terrace. A number of the other charities were combined by the Charity Commissioners in 1911 as 'The United Charities Trust' and these were incorporated in Vawers Trust in 1995. They included:

1581 William Walter, sheriff in 1578 and mayor in 1581, 1592 and 1597 and, according to his memorial in St Mary's Church, 'Alderman of this Towne who deceased the 18th June Anno Dom 1611.' He made his bequest during the year of his mayoralty 'for such uses as the Corporation should think fit.'

1590 Thomas Canon, mayor of the year and in 1602, 1606 an 1612, left a sum of money towards the repair of the Guildhall.

*c.*1600 Dr Dolbin left £20 to assist poor apprentices.

*c.*1600 James Deane of Oxford left £20 to provide 'loans for beginners'.

1607 William Vawer, a native of Haverfordwest, merchant and alderman of Bristol, bequeathed in his will land and premises in Haverfordwest and the rent charge of No 4 Welsh Back, Bristol, the profits of which were to provide eight pence a week to be given to 'five poor decayed men, being burgesses' aged 50 or over who were not known or reputed to be drunkards, adulterers, fornicators or persons of lewd life. They were provided with gowns of 'black lowe cotton frize' and had to attend the mayor to and from church every Sunday. The mayor had to 'appoint and procure a learned person to preach a sermon at St Mary's Church on the fourth Sunday after the feast of St James' (25 July), to pay him 5s. 8d. and to invite him and the five almsmen to dinner, for which he could charge the charity 16d. for 'the procuring dinner' and 8d. each for the almsmen's dinners. Since 1908 the 'Black Coat Charity' has been administered by Vawer's Trustees and the beneficiaries are 'poor and decayed Freemen pensioners needing support.

1613 Thomas Lloyd of Cilciffeth in the parish of Llanychaer, sheriff of the county of Pembroke in 1596 and again in 1613 when he conveyed certain lands, tenements, etc., the issues and profits thereof to be 'paid and expended in maintenance and sustentation of a sufficient and fit pedagogue within the Town and County of Haverforwest and should for ever cause a Grammar School to be kept where scholars are to be instructed in such learning and knowledge as is fitting to be taught in a Grammar School.' The pedagogue should be a 'meet, able, discreet and learned man in the Latin tongue' to keep the school for the sons of 'the poorer sort of people'. The school, at that time, adjoined St Thomas churchyard.

1639 Sir Thomas Canon, mayor of the town on five occasions and Member of Parliament for Haverfordwest, left £120 for the repair of churches and relief of the poor. His nephew, Morris Canon, refused to pay the legacy and, in 1650, the Court of Great Sessions issued a writ of sequestration against him and the sheriff of the county of Pembroke took into his hands the closes of land called Cashfield and the Temperness farm.

1646 James Haward of Gray's Inn, a member of the Haward family of Flether Hill in the parish of Rudbaxton, gave an annuity charged upon the manor of Merton and other hereditaments in the county of Surrey, yielding £20 annually for the relief of ten poor people of Haverfordwest.

1654 John Milward left property in Haverfordwest and in Bordersley in the county of Warwick, through which the Birmingham-Warwick canal later passed. The income of the charity was divided so that the master of the grammar school at Haverfordwest and the master of King Edward School, Birmingham, received a third each, and the other third was for a scholar to be sent alternately by the two schools to Brasenose College, Oxford.

1662 William Meyler, mayor in 1625 and 1635, left land adjoining Fiddlers Hall, at the top of City Road, to provide twenty shillings annually for distribution among the poor in the almshouses at Easter and

Christmas, and ten shillings to the vicar of St Mary's for instructing the said poor.

1663   Elizabeth Nicholls of East Sheen in the county of Surrey left an annuity of £6 charged upon the Boulston estate for the relief of poor aged women of honest and good repute living within the parishes of St Mary and St Thomas.

1684   Mary Tasker, late of Castle Pill in the parish of Steynton, and sister of Thomas Haward of Flether Hill, bequeathed her farm of East Dudwell in the parish of Camrose and other property and securities for the purpose of building an almshouse 'for the breeding and maintenance of poor children of both sexes between the ages of nine and thirteen', who should be apprenticed to convenient trades. In 1706, a school was built next to the almshouse for the education of the children.

1700   Richard Howell of Haverfordwest left £300 for the mayor and aldermen to purchase land, three-quarters of the profits of which to be devoted towards the maintenance of the poor of the town and the remainder to be paid to the vicar of St Mary's church towards his maintenance. He bequeathed a further £100, the income from which was to be used for the relief of the poor of the town.

1704   Martha, wife of Nicholas Holland, gave £10 'to be lent to two young glovers for three years without interest', and then to two more and so on.

1707   Thomas Roch of Butter Hill in the parish of St Ishmael's left an annual payment of £1 3s. 4d to the priests of St Mary's, St Martin's and St Thomas's towards the teaching of poor children.

1709   William Middleton, a London merchant, left the annual income of £100 to the vicar of St Mary's for preaching catechising sermons, and the income from another £100 to be applied annually to the setting out of four poor apprentices.

1715   John Laugharne of St Bride's, sheriff of the town in 1705 and Member of Parliament for fourteen years, gave £20 per annum out of the tithe of Tremain, near Cardigan, to the vicar of St Mary's for reading prayers daily and instructing children in the church catechism, with a proviso that the money should revert to his heir-at-law in the event of Popery or any other persuasion becoming the established religion.

1719   William Wheeler, Member of Parliament for the borough 1701-02, an ironmaster who rented Blackpool Forge from Sir George Barlow of Slebech, provided £10 to be distributed annually to 40 poor people of the town at the rate of half-a-crown per person.

1723   Owen Phillips gave £40 the interest of which to be given to a poor burgess, or the widow of a burgess, of good character, Protestant and able to repeat by heart the Lord's Prayer and the Ten Commandments, and 40 shillings yearly to the vicar of St Mary's to preach sermons on Ash Wednesday and Ascension Thursday.

1735 Elizabeth Llewhelin, widow of Thomas Llewhelin, mayor in 1713, left the interest of £10 for the vicar of St Mary's to preach a sermon annually on Good Friday.

1739 Mary Llewhelin, spinster, sister of the above, bequeathed £100 from the interest of which 20 shillings to be paid annually to the vicar of St Mary's and the remainder to be distributed as Robert Prust, alderman and mayor in 1723, should think fit.

1740 Sibles Paramour, widow, gave £10 the interest thereof to be used to buy bread for the poor at Christmas.

1744 Rebecca Faerton left £200 the interest of which to be given to poor widows at the discretion of Robert Prust.

1751 An anonymous donor gave £100 the interest upon which was to be applied in support of poor insolvent debtors confined in gaol within the town.

1764 William Fortune left £100 the interest on which to be distributed among the poor of the town.

1774 William Bowen, alderman, gave three houses in Dew Street and another on Tower Hill from the rents of which ten shillings was to be paid annually to the vicar of St Mary's for preaching a sermon on Low Sunday.

1802 Joseph Fortune, mayor in 1785, bequeathed the sum of £5 annually to be paid to the poor of the town.

1811 Captain Thomas Parr bequeathed £5 annually to buy bread to be given by the rector and church wardens of St Thomas to the poor of the parish at Easter.

1852 James Griffiths, mayor in 1840, left premises in High Street the revenues of which, after paying for the upkeep of his grave in St Thomas's churchyard, to be distributed by the trustees, which must include the vicar of St Martin's and the pastor of Bethesda Baptist chapel, between poor persons in the town not being aided by, or connected with, any Public or Private Institution of Charity.'

1869 James Bevan of Weston-super-mare bequeathed to the church wardens of St Martin's and the two senior deacons at Bethesda chapel the sum of £100, the annual income of which to be used to purchase bread and coal for the poor of the parish of St Martin at Christmastide.

Other charities, of an unknown date, include a bequest of £30 by Anne Bowen, the interest on £20 of which to be given annually to the poor, and the interest on the remaining £10 to be paid to the vicar of St Mary's for preaching a sermon on 30 January each year, and Dr William Flaerton and his wife, Mary, who gave the sums of one shilling and sixpence weekly to buy bread for the poor of the town, to be distributed every Wednesday in St Mary's Church, and ten shillings per annum to the vicar.

The charities were not always administered properly by the bodies of trustees. Some were lost by neglect or by injudicious investment, and others by misappropriation. In October 1831 public dissatisfaction was such that a meeting of 'many of the inhabitants was held at the Castle Inn . . . to take into consideration the propriety of instituting measures for putting into their proper channels the various charitable funds of the town which had for many years been misapplied by the Corporation.' The meeting was held under the chairmanship of Morgan Rice James, who was to be mayor in 1835. Documents were perused and the meeting came to the conclusion that there had been 'great abuses' in managing the charities, which should have yielded £664 that year, and it was resolved 'to use every legitimate measure to effect a real reformation.' It was found that there had been no payment out of the Perrot Trust for half a century. The Sir Thomas Canon charity was not applied to its proper use and the money had been diverted to the coffers of the corporation. The income from the Thomas Lloyd bequest, amounting to £144, together with £18 from the Milward bequest, had been paid to the headmaster of the grammar school for instructing only four boys. The terms of the William Walter Trust, the revenue of which was to be employed 'for such uses as the Corporation should think fit', had been generously interpreted by that body and its member 'thought fit to pocket the lot'. The part of the rents that were paid in kind, comprising eighty six hens, two capons and two turkeys, had been 'devoured by a certain perpetual Deputy', and the meeting deplored that 'instead of the poor having the benefit, this person's kitchen was substantially supplied by means of this fund'. This state of affairs was remedied and the trusts remaining charities have long since been properly managed.

DILLWYN MILES

ARMS AND INSIGNIA

On 26 June 1326, the Treasurer and Barons of the Exchequer were ordered to 'cause a seal for the rule of the castle and honour of Haverfordwest in Wales' to be made and sent to Robert de Penres, constable of the castle, 'as the King [Edward II] wills that the seal shall be newly made and appointed in the castle for preserving the liberties pertaining to the castle and honour aforesaid.'[1] An earlier reference to the seal appeared in Letters Patent dated 31 March 1315 granting rights of water in Dew Street to Walter Drinulle, chaplain. It is likely, however, that the corporation possessed a seal in the latter half of the thirteenth century

The obverse of the Common Seal of the Borough of the Town and County of Haverfordwest bears a lymphad, a single-masted galley with sails furled and yardarm lowered, a feature often employed by ports to indicate maritime importance. On the forecastle a man stands blowing a horn, and on the stern stands another hornblower. A flag flies at the masthead and a steering-oar hangs over the stern. The medieval artist has filled empty spaces with conventional designs and decorations: a star and two quatrefoils. The whole is surrounded by the legend: ✠SIGILLUM COMUNE DE HAVERFORDIA. On the reverse of the seal is a fortified gatehouse, upon the central tower of which stands a sentinel blowing a horn, and from the side towers banners fly in contrary directions. The lion rampant on the dexter and the eagle regardant on the sinister are not supporters but medieval decorations, as is the wyvern in base. The surround is inscribed: ✠O LECTOR SALVE C(O)ELI PATEANT TIBI VALVE (Hail, O reader: may the gates of heaven stand open for thee).

The obverse, surrounded by the words 'Borough of Haverfordwest' appears on the mayor's badge of office which is shaped in the form of a Celtic shield with crossed mace and fasces and decorated with four roundels that bear, respectively, a Tudor rose, a wyvern, the inscription 'Charters granted by Edward I, Edward II,

Fig. 50 Common Seal of the Borough of the Town and County of Haverfordwest, with lymphad on the obverse and fortified gate house on the reverse.
(Crown copyright: Royal Commission on the Ancient and Historical Monuments of Wales).

Edward V' and 'Henry VIII, Elizabeth and James I', and a label inscribed: CYMRU AM BYTH. The badge is suspended from the mayor's chain of office comprising a series of links in the form of the letter H, signifying Haverfordwest, held together by small rectangles linked to shields upon which are engraved the names of those who have held the office of mayor since 1887, and enamelled shields bearing the arms of the monarchs who granted charters to the town, and the reputed arms of George Leader Owen of Withybush who, with his wife Jane, widow of Sir William Maxwell of Calderwood, presented the chain to the borough in 1887 in commemoration of the Jubilee of the reign of Queen Victoria whose portrait hangs on a medallion beneath the royal arms and above the badge. The badge of the Sheriff also bears a device based on the fortified gatehouse, although the sentinel appears to wear a World War II tin helmet. The badge is inscribed LIBERA VILLA ET COMITATUS DE HAVERFORDIA (The Free Town and County of Haverford) and the town's motto. The chain has silver links inscribed with the names of those who have held the office since 1953, when it was presented to the borough by former sheriffs to commemorate the coronation of Queen Elizabeth II.

The Mayor is attended on ceremonial occasions by a sword-bearer and two mace-bearers. One mace bears the date 1630 but its partner disappeared around the middle of the last century and 'an exact copy' was made to replace it in 1865.

On the fifth of October 1966 armorial bearings were granted and assigned to the 'Mayor, Sheriff, Bailiffs and Burgesses of the Borough and County of the Town of Haverford, alias Haverfordwest', by Garter, Clarenceux, and Norroy and Ulster Kings of Arms comprising arms and crest and supporters – Barry wavy *argent* and *azure* a lymphad sail set proper and flags flying *gules* on a chief *vert* a castle triple towered between two plumes each of three ostrich feathers *argent*, and for the crest a wreath *argent* and *vert* out of the battlements of a hexagonal tower a demi-man winding a horn proper habited per pale *vert* and *argent* on his head a steel cap proper. There was a further grant of supporters, that is to say, on the dexter side a dragon *gules* the underside of the wings charged with a cross *or* thereon five cinquefoils *sable* and on the sinister side a lion *sable* about the neck a ancient crown with chain reflexed over the back. The armorial bearings were designed by Major Francis Jones, Wales Herald of Arms Extraordinary. The castle flanked by ostrich feathers on the upper part of the shield commemorate the castle and the fact that the town and lordship had been granted in 1343, by King Edward III to Edward, Prince of Wales, better known as The Black Prince and held by him and several later princes. The blue and white waves represent 'the tidal river Cleddau' and the 'trading ship under sail expresses the maritime associations of the town'. The red dragon of Wales has the golden cross of the see of St David's blazoned on its raised wings 'to commemorate the three ancient churches within the borough', and the black lion with gold collar derives from the arms of Philipps of Picton, a family long connected with the town. The sentinel sounding a bugle-horn on top of a tower, in the crest, is clad in a jerkin parti-coloured white and green, the colours worn by the Prince of Wales's Welsh troops in the French campaigns, and these colours are repeated in the crest wreath and in the mantling attached to the helm. On a scroll beneath the arms is the motto taken from the town's seal.

DILLWYN MILES

NOTES AND REFERENCES

Foreword.

1 James Phillips, *The History of Pembrokeshire*, London 1909, 28 and 55.
2 P C Bartrum, *A Welsh Classic Dictionary*, National Library of Wales 1993, 12.
3 Peniarth MSS 215.
4 Phillips, *op. cit.* 70 and 80.
5 *Ibid.* 70.
6 *Ibid.* 79.

The Origins and Topography of Medieval Haverford.
Terrence James

This paper based on an article in the *Joural of the Pembrokeshire Historical Society*, No. 4, 1990-91, 51-73, with additions. I would like to thank the editor and the society for permission to reprint it. Once again, I would like to acknowledge the Dyfed Archaeological Trust for sponsoring the original project and the Royal Commission on Ancient and Historical Monuments in Wales for permission to reproduce photographs. Much of the original historical research was based on the Haverfordwest Deeds deposited in the Pembrokeshire Record Office (PRO), and I made considerable use of B. G. Charles' typescript schedule. From it I created a computerized database and have deposited printed catalogues indexed by personal and street name in the PRO. This material should be of considerable help for medieval and family historians researching the history of the borough. Finally, I would like to thank Mr Dillwyn Miles, the editor, for his knowledgeable assistance.

1 B. G. Charles 'The Haverfordwest Records' typescript schedule of the Haverfordwest Records, a deed collection housed at the Pembrokeshire Record Office, NLW, 1960.
2 C. J. Delaney & I. N. Soulsby, 'Haverfordwest: the Archaeological Implications of Development', Urban Research Unit, UCW Cardiff, 1974, 3.1.
3 Lauran Toorians, 'Wizo Flandrensis and the Flemish Settlement in Pembrokeshire' *Cambridge Medieval Celtic Studies*, Vol 20, 1990, 110. For background to the period see I. W. Rowlands, 'The Making of the March: Aspects of the Norman Settlement in Dyfed' *Proc. of the Battle Conf. on Anglo-Norman Studies* III (ed. R. Allen Brown), 1980, and David Walker, 'The Norman Settlement in Wales', *Proc. of the Battle Conf. on Anglo-Norman Studies* (ed. R. Allen Brown), 1978.

4   R. R. Davies, *The Age of Conquest. Wales 1063-1415*, 1991, 98; *Brut y Tywysogion* (Red Book of Hergest version) ed. T. Jones, 1955.

5   Toorians, 105, 115; Davies 159.

6   H. Bugge, *Contribution to the History of Norsemen*, iii, 1900, 6; B. G. Charles, *Old Norse Relations with Wales*, 1934, 142-3.

7   B. G. Charles, *Non-Celtic Place-Names in Wales*, 1938, 79 and *The Place-names of Pembrokeshire*, 1992, ii, 643.

8   The possibility of settlement in the Iron Age is highly likely, given the number of raths in the vicinity and the defensible nature of the castle site. Roman incursions in Pembrokeshire have recently been proved based on a new road from Carmarthen established as far as Wiston. If one projects its line westwards, this would run a few miles north of Haverfordwest (Terrence James, 'A Roman Road West of Carmarthen', *Archaeology in Wales*, 30, 1990.) Chance finds from Haverfordwest recorded in the county SMR include a number of Roman coins with a tight date range between AD 253 and 268/9 as well as one of Hadrian (AD117-38) from Bridge Street. There is much later evidence (about 90 years after the town's foundation) for Norse traders at Haverford, three of whom were rated among the Ostmen of Dublin around 1200, (Charles, 1934, 160, citing *Hist. & Municipal. Docs. of Ireland*, 22, 24, 46) but this has nothing to do with the town's origins.

9   Toorians, 111.

10   J. E. Lloyd, *A History of Wales from the Earliest Times to the Edwardian Conquest*, 1911, 592.

11   Giraldus Cambrensis *Speculum Duorium, or a Mirror of Two Men* (eds.) Yves Lefervre & R. B. C. Huygens, trans. Brian Dawson (gen ed. Michael Richter) 1974.

12   Giraldus Cambrensis *The Itinerary through Wales* (trans. R. C. Hoare), revised Everyman edn. 1976, 77. cf. edn. trans. by Lewis Thorpe, Harmansworth 1978.

13   Toorians, 105, 112.

14   Giraldus, *Itinerary*, 80.

15   Toorians, 106.

16   *Speculum*, 39.

17   Richard Fenton, *A Historical Tour Through Pembrokeshire*, with additions. Brecon, 1903, 347.

18   Roger J. Rees, 'Slebech Commandery and the Knights of St John', *Arch. Camb.* (1897), 203. It is clearly difficult to date these grants since they only survive in a later confirmation of Anselm *c.*1230-31. Rees has offered the following general dates for them: Haverford burgages *c.*1145 and Coferum *c.*1160. Tancred (wrongly called Richard Tancred) is said by Davies to have died in 1130, Giraldus Cambrensis *De Invectionibus*, W. S. Davies, *Y Cymmrodor*, xxx, 1920, p. 144.

19   W. Dugdale, *Monasticum Anglicanum*, (ed. J. Cayley) 1817-30, vol. iv, 444; Green MS, Vol 12, p. 158. Bound MS collection of Francis Green papers in Haverfordwest Library Reference Section. The reference in *Annales Cambriae*,

to the building of a major new church dedicated to St Thomas in the year 1223 must be viewed with suspicion, given the fact that the three parish churches and the priory were in existence prior to Robert's removal as lord in 1210. This adds credence to Richard Suggett's suggestion (see p. 125 *infra*) that the reference may be to a rebuilding, and not to St Thomas's but St Mary's.

20   Green, F. 'Pembrokeshire Parsons', Appendix II, *West Wales Historical Records*, VI, 1916, 43-9.

21   e.g. *Speculum*, 269.

22   Terrence James, *Carmarthen: an archaeological and topographical survey*, 1980, 28-9.

23   David Crouch, *William Marshal. Court, Career and Chivalry in the Angevin Empire 1147-1219*, 1990, 98.

24   *Annales Cambr.*, Roll Ser. 80, 67-8.

25   *Cal. Patent Rolls* herinafter *CPR*, 1213, 105.

26   D. J. C. King, 'Pembroke Castle' *Arch. Camb.*, 1978, 78; Crouch, *ibid.*, 79.

27   Crouch, *ibid.*, 79, 110.

28   R. W. Bankes, 'On the Early Charters to towns in South Wales', *Arch. Camb.*, 4th series, Vol. ix, 1878, 96-99.

29   Sidney Painter, *William Marshal: Knight-errant, Baron and Regent of England*, 1933, 270.

30   A. Ballard, *British Borough Charters 1042-1216*, 1913, xxxv; A. Ballard & J. Tait, *British Borough Charters 1216-1307*, 1923, 11, 104.

31   M. Beresford, *New Towns of the Middle Ages*, 1967, 208.

32   *Ibid*, 212.

33   An analysis of the Haverfordwest deeds clearly shows a number of prominent families, like the Sturmins, Dowstows and Cokeys, frequently involved in property transactions. One of the Dowstows became a prior of Haverfordwest Priory in 1380 (Green, 1916, 48). It is an interesting possibility that in the thirteenth century the reeves of the borough (and there were always two) were not chosen from burgesses within the town, but from families who were associated with the townships outside, like the families who took (or gave) their names from settlements that still exist, e.g. Drim and Pelcam. (Both farms have surviving ringworks, although the latter is thought to be prehistoric). The probability is that the reeves were burgesses *de vento*. For a comparison on the trend of burgess familes to accumulate property see my 'Medieval Carmarthen and its Burgesses: a study of growth and burgess families in the later thirteenth century', *Carmarthenshire Antiq.* xxv, 1989, pp. 9-26.

34   Beresford, 263.

35   Lloyd, 660.

36   *Brut*, 221.

37   *CPR*, 1247-58, 8.

38   *Inq. Post Mortem.* Edward I, ii, 267, x, 163; 1281-91, 60.

39   Lloyd, ii, 735.

40   *CPR*, 1256-66, 503.

[41] *Ibid*, 348.

[42] Doubt has now been cast on King's assessment of the early date for Pembroke's walls, which he argued were the work of William Marshal (D. J. C. King & Mark Cheshire, 'The Town Walls of Pembroke', *Arch. Camb.*, 1982, 77-84). See N. D. Ludlow, 'Pembroke Castle and Town Walls' *Fortress*, No. 8, 1991, 25-30 *passim*.

[43] L. T. Smith, *The Itinerary of John Leland*, 5 vols, reprint of 1908 edition, 1964, iii, 51, 63, 65, and iv, 177.

[44] C. Plat, *The English Medieval Town*, 1976, 51.

[45] *Ibid*, pp. 50-51; D. H. L. Turner, *Town Defences in England and Wales*, 1970, pp. 13, 16, 91.

[46] See p. 00 *infra*; *CPR*, 1272-81, 54, 56.

[47] J. R. S. Phillips, *Aymer de Valence, Earl of Pembroke*, 1972 250-1; *CPR*, 1281-92, 146.

[48] *CPR*, 1281-92, p. 333; *CPR*, 1292-1301, p.576; see p. 20 above.

[49] Great caution must be exercised in relying on this type of calculation. The figure includes an unknown number of chensers and burgesses *de vento*, which would reduce the actual number of burgage plots. The figure of 390 is thus only a theoretical maximum, and may have been closer to 300 burgages.

[50] Charles, 1960, see footnote 1; see also B. G. Charles, *Calendar of the Records of the Borough of Haverfordwest 1539-1660*, 1967.

[51] Heather James, 'Topographical Notes on the Early Borough of Kidwelly' *Carms. Antiquary*, XVI, 1980, 6-17.

[52] Charles, 1960, 1, No. 951.

[53] PRO. Hav. Borough 2157.

[54] *Report on the Municipal Corporations*, 1835.

[55] M. Aston & J. Bond, *The Landscape of Towns*, 1976, 87; Plat, 40.

[56] Dugdale, 444-5.

[57] PRO. DX/289/1.

[58] J. W. Phillips & F. J. Warren, *The History of Haverfordwest*, 1914, 86.

[59] Charles, 1960, No. 843.

[60] F. Jones, *The Holy Wells of Wales*, 1960, 206.

[61] Charles, 1960, No. 781.

[62] *Ibid.*, No. 988.

[63] Jones, *Holy Wells*, 204, locates a well to Caradog about a mile south-west of the town.

[64] For a discussion on the Friary see Barbara Jones, 'The Dominican Friars of Haverfordwest: their Sites and Lands before and after the Dissolution of the Monasteries', *The Journal of the Pembrokeshire Historical Society*, 3 (1989), 77-91.

[65] R. C. Easterling, 'The Friars in Wales' *Arch. Camb.*, 1914, 338; A. Jones, 'The Property of the Welsh Friaries at the Dissolution', *Arch. Camb.*, 1936, pp. 34-7; C. F. R. Palmer, 'The Friars Preachers, or Blackfriars, of Haverfordwest', *Reliquary*, xxiv, July 1883, 11-13.

66 John Watt, *The Church in Medieval Ireland*, 1972, 62.

67 *Ibid.*, 47, 72.

68 *CPR*, 1256, 482.

69 F. G. Cowley, *The Monastic Order in South Wales 1066-1349*, 1977, 135-6.

70 Green MSS, Vol. 12, 326-7.

71 *Inquisitions Ad Quod Damnum*, List, Pt ii, 1906, 609.

72 G. Williams, *The Welsh Church from Conquest to Reformation*, 1976, 493.

73 Heather James, 'The Cult of St David in the Middle Ages', *Cult and Continuity*, essays to P. A. Rahtz, eds. M. Aston & M. O. H. Carver, Oxbow Books, 1992; reprinted with minor alterations in 'The Cult of St David in the Middle Ages', *The Journal of the Pembrokeshire Historical Society* 7 (1996-7), 5-25.

74 The last element is from Old English *lacu*, Middle English *lake*, Medieval Latin *laca*, meaning 'stream', 'stretch of river', cf. Frains Lake, The Ritec, The Laques (Laugharne), Laques Fawr (Llansteffan).

75 Green, *Pembs Parsons*, 1916, 46.

76 *Ibid.*

77 See pp. 55-78 *infra*, and 'Haverfordwest Priory Excavations' *Archaeology in Wales*, Vol. 27, 1987, 27-9.

78 The date at which parishes first come into existence is uncertain, but these three are always referred to as churches as distinct from chapels. None of them was subservient to another.

79 Both customs officials 'died through the pestilence', E. A. Lewis, 'Tabular analysis of the Extant Custom Returns for the County of Pembroke and the Lordship of Haverford 1301 to 1547', *A Contribution to the Commerical History of Wales,* (reprinted from *Y Cymmrodor*, XXIV).

80 H. Owen, *A Calendar of the Public Records relating to Pembs.* Vol. 1, Haverfordwest. Cymmr. Rec. Ser. No. 7., 1911, 135. B. G. Charles, in his *Calendar of the Records of . . . Haverfordwest*, .1 offers a figure of 127. Calculating the actual number is difficult, but there are some 105 whole and another 62 half, quarter, third and even smaller burgages listed, which I suggest equates to something over 150 dwelling units.

81 Ian Jack, *Medieval Wales* (The Sources of History: Studies in the use of Historical Evidence), 1972, 212.

82 Charles, *Calendar of the Records of . . . Haverfordwest*, 1.

83 H. Owen, 'A Survey of the Lordship of Haverfordwest in 1547', *Arch. Camb.*, 1903, 135.

Haverfordwest Castle *c.*1110-1577.   *D. J. Cathcart King*

1 Giraldus Cambrensis, *Itinerarium Cambriae*, (Rolls Series, 21.6), 85-6. For Caradog see J E Lloyd, *History of Wales*, 1911, ii, 591-3 and notes.

2 Lloyd, *op.cit.* 425, n.77.

3   In passing, it must be recalled that many of our older antiquaries mention the castle as having been founded about 1113 by 'Gilbert, Earl of Clare' (more correctly Gilbert de Clare, Earl of Pembroke), while his son Richard de Clare, appointed Richard fitzTancred as his constable. Camden is evidently the origin of these statements; in fact, he mentions neither Earl Gilbert nor the date 1113, and gives no reference to his source of information (see Gough's edition, iii, 144). Actually, Tancred and his family were proprietors, evidently tenants-in-chief, and not officials of the earls. Haverfordwest did not form part of the earldom until 1213.

4   *Rotuli de Oblatis et Finibus,* 218; *Rotuli Chartarum,* 173.

5   *Annales Cambriae* (Rolls series, 20) 67-8. Only one MS text of this chronicle deals with Robert's story.

6   The question of the purchase money shows surprising discrepancies in the rolls: *Rotuli de Oblatis et Finibus,* 499, says £1,000; *Rotuli Litterarum Clausarum,* i, 158-9, gives 500 marks (£333 6s. 8d.), while the *Pipe Rolls 16 John* (Pipe Roll Society, NS, XXXV, 51) and 2 Henry III (PRS, NS, XXXIX, 33) give the figure 1,000 marks (£666.13s.4d.) which was the amount actually paid by the earl.

7   *Brut y Tywysogyon,* Red Book of Hergest version, ed. Jones, University of Wales Press, 1955, 221; *Peniarth MS 20* version, translation, ed. Jones, UWP, 1952, 8.

8   *Calendar of Patent Rolls* (1258-66), 503.

9   Henry Owen (ed.) *A Calendar of the Public Records relating to Pembrokeshire* (Cymmrodorion Record Series, vii, part 1) 4, citing Coram Rege Roll; Mic., 1 Ed. I, no. 34, 17d.

10   *Cal. Pat. Rolls* (1272-81), 54, 56

11   *Cal. Pat. Rolls* (1281-92), 330-1.

12   Brown and Calvin in *History of the King's Works* (HMSO, 1963) ii, 670-1.

13   *Cal. Pat. Rolls* (1292-1301), 576; *Calendar of Charter Rolls,* iii, (1300-26).

14   *Cal. Pat. Rolls* (1307-13) 145, and (1371-2), but see *Calendar of Close Rolls* (1323-7), 484.

15   *Cal. Pat. Rolls* (1330-4), 225.

16   Owen, *op.cit.* 117; for the succession of the Black Prince see *Cal. Close Rolls* (1354-60), 583.

17   *Cal. Pat. Rolls* (1374-7), 22, for grant to Felton, and pardon for the Black Prince; (1385-20) for grant to Clanvowe. The deaths of these two life-tenants are indicated by Crown appointment of constable in 1381: see *Cal. Pat. Rolls* (1377-81), 627 and of custos in 1391, *Cal. Pat. Rolls* (1391-6), 15.

18   *Cal. Pat. Rolls* (1391-6), 210.

19   Monstrelet's *Chronicles,* chapter 15; *Chronique du Religieux de Saint-Denys* (ed. Bellaguet, Documents inédits sur l'histoire de la France, Paris. 1841) 111, 334.

20   *Cal. Pat. Rolls* (1446-52), 175; Crown appointment of constable, 510.

21   *Cal. Pat. Rolls* (1452-61), 340; *Rotuli Parliamentorum* v, 291, 380.

22   *Cal. Pat. Rolls* (1461-7), 119; *Rot. Parl.* vi, 10.

23 *Cal. Pat. Rolls* (1476-85), 349.

24 *Ibid.* 414.

25 *Cal. Pat. Rolls* (1485—94), 220,

26 *Calendar of Inquisition post mortem, etc.: Henry VII*, vol. iii, no. 723.

27 *Letters and papers of the reign of Henry VIII*, v, 634, no.1499. It will be observed that the grantees of Haverford were not, on the whole, very lucky.

28 Owen, *op.cit.* 27-8, 65, 120, 161-9.

29 *Cal. Pat. Rolls* (1560-3), 522

30 Printed in *Royal Commission on Ancient Monuments in Wales and Monmouthshire*: *Inventory for Pembrokeshire*, 109; also *Archaeologia Cambrensis*, 6th. Series, iii, (1903) 40-1.

31 Leach, *History of the Civil War in Pembrokeshire*, 71-3, 94, 111.

32 See documents in *Archaeologia Cambrensis*, 4th series, vii (1876) 55-8.

33 Fenton, *A Historical Tour through Pembrokeshire*, (1811), 205.

Haverfordwest Castle 1577-1964   *Michael Freeman*

A schedule of many historical references to the castle is available at the Pembrokeshire Record Office (PRO).

1 Lewis Thorpe, *Gerald of Wales: The Journey through Wales*, London 1978, 143-4.

2 B. G. Charles, *Calendar of the Records of the Borough of Haverfordwest 1539-1660*, Cardiff 1967, 73.

3 *Arch. Camb.* 1896, 193ff.

4 PRO. PQ/C/3/1.

5 PRO. D/Hig/177.

6 Francis Green, 'Haverfordwest Castle' in *The Pembroke County Guardian*, 27 Dec 1907.

7 PRO. HDX/579/2.

8 PRO. HDX/579/3.

9 H M Vaughan, 'A Synopsis of Two Tours made in Wales in 1775 and 1811' in *Y Cymmrodor XXXVIII*, 74.

10 Mrs Morgan, *A Tour to Milford Haven in the year 1791*, 199.

11 E. H. Stuart Jones, *The Last Invasion of Britain*, Cardiff 1950, 217.

12 PRO. HO/130/4.

13 T. Jones, *Acts of Parliament Concerning Wales 1714-1901*, no. 1655.

14 PRO. PQ/AG/75.

15 *Ibid.*

16 PRO. DX/101/12.

17 Ministers' Accounts 1207, no. 13.

18 Henry Owen, *A Calendar of the Public Records of Pembrokeshire*, I, London, 1911.

19 *Ibid.* 118.

20   *Ibid.* 169.
21   D. J. Cathcart King, *Castellarium Anglicanum*, New York 1983, 393.
22   PRO. PQ/C/3/1.
23   PRO. HO/130/4.
24   Morgan, *op.cit.* 199.

The Augustinian Priory   *Siân Rees*

1   I wish to acknowledge the generosity of the Guild of Freemen of Haverfordwest for donating the priory ruins to the Secretary of State for Wales in 1982, and to record my personal thanks for the Gild's continuing interest in, and support for, our work on the site. I would also like to thank Stuart Harrison and John Cole for reading and commenting on this chapter, and John Cole for the reconstruction-drawing of the priory.

2   The Buck drawing of the priory in 1745 shows the priory from the south, with sections of the precinct wall still standing to some height against the low lying marshland.

3   A W Clapham, 'Haverfordwest Priory. Report on the Excavations of June, 1922', *Arch. Camb.,* LXXVII, Seventh Series Vol II, (1922), 327-34; E. A. Rahbula, 'Further Excavations at Haverfordwest Priory', *Arch. Camb.,* LXXIX, Seventh Series Vol IV, (1924) 334-9.

4   Clapham, *op. cit.,* 329.
5   Clapham, *op. cit.,* 332.
6   Clapham, *op. cit.,* 333.
7   Clapham, *op. cit.,* 332.
8   Clapham, *op. cit.,* 329.
9   S. E. Rees, 'The Secret Garden. The Discovery of a Medieval garden at Haverfordwest Priory.' *Heritage in Wales*, Winter 1996, no 6, Cadw Welsh Historic Monuments.

11   Glanmor Williams, *The Welsh Church from Conquest to Reformation*, Cardiff 1976, 366.

11   David M. Robinson, 1980: *The Geography of Augustinian Settlement in Medieval England and Wales*, British Archaeological Reports. British Series, 80, fig. 4.

12   F. G. Cowley, *Studies in Welsh History. The Monastic Order in South Wales*, Cardiff 1977, 66.

13   *Valor Ecclesiasticus temp. Henr. VIII....* ed. J. Caley, Record Commission, 1810-34 Vol 4, 389-90.

14   Robinson, *op. cit.,* 275.
15   Williams, *op. cit.* 351-2.
16   Cowley, *op. cit.* , 101-8; 208.
17   Williams, *op. cit.* , 267.
18   *Ibid. op. cit.,* 375.

19   Glanmor Williams, *Wales and the Reformation,* Cardiff 1997, 134.
20⁰ Fenton, *A Historical Tour Through Pembrokeshire,* London, 1910, 208.

The Churches and Chapels.   *Robert Scourfield*

I wish to express my gratitude to John Owen, the county archivist; Thomas Lloyd for the use of some of his notes; Ruth Cook for typing, and Pat Evans, secretary of the Bethesda Baptist Chapel.

THE CHURCHES.
1   National Library of Wales (NLW), MS 6875F.
2   John Newman, *The Buildings of Wales: Glamorgan,* Cardiff, 1995, 662.
3   David Smith, *They Did it Their Way,* Haverfordwest, 1992, 5.
4   NLW, *op. cit.*
5   *Transactions of the Ancient Monuments Society,* Vol. 29, 1985.
6   Richard Fenton, *Historical Tour through Pembrokeshire,* London 1811, 218-19.
7   Samuel Lewis, *Topographical Dictionary of Wales,* I, London 1833.
8   Lambeth Palace Library, Incorporated Church Building Society (ICBS) file 2433.
9   *Ibid.*
10   *Pembrokeshire Herald (PH),* 9.11.1860.
11   *Ibid.* 8.2.1861.
12   *Carmarthen Journal (CJ),* 20.6.1862.
13   Smith, *op. cit.,* 6.
14   *Ibid.*
15   *PH* 29.9.1865.
16   *The Ecclesiologist* (25) 1867, 313.
17   *Haverfordwest and Milford Telegraph (H&MT),* 6.6.1866.
18   *PH,* 20.8.1869.
19   *H&MT,* 3.8.1870.
20   *St David's Archdeaconry Magazine,* December 1893.
21   *Tenby Observer (TO),* 5.6.1895.
22   *St David's Archdeaconry Magazine,* May 1895 and June 1896.
23   *H&MT,* 1.7.1903.
24   Smith, *op.cit.,* 66-7.
25   *The Welshman,* 21 February 1908.
26   Smith, *op.cit.,* 80.
27   Prue Edwards, *pers. comm.*
28   *PH* 6.12.1889.
29   *The Star,* 3.3.1797.
30   Information given by Henry Mathias to Edward Laws (1888), NLW MS 6875F.
31   Pembrokeshire Record Office (PRO), HPR/2/29.
32   NLW MS 6875F.

33   Fenton, *op. cit.* 213.

34   *CJ* 10.11.1843.

35   Lambeth Palace Library ICBS 3322.

36   *PH* 19.1.1844.

37   *Ibid.* 6.9.1844.

38   *The Ecclesiologist* (8), 1848, 253-4.

39   *PH*, 13.11.1863.

40   *H&MT*, 19.10.1859.

41   *The Welshman*, 27.4.1860 and 22.6.1860.

42   *PH*, 22.6.1860.

43   *CJ*, 7.6.1861.

44   *Building News* (Vol. 11) 1864, 569.

45   *Ibid.*

46   *CJ*, 3. 3.1876.

47   *CJ*, 16.9.1881.

48   PRO, HPR/2/41 and DX/254.

49   *The Welshman*, 20.6.1884.

50   *H&MT*, 16.6.1886; *PH* 2.7.1886

51   *H&MT*, 9.3.1887.

52   *PH*, 6.12.1889.

53   *Tenby Observer (TO)*, 5.12.1889.

54   PRO, HAM/HT/1/21.

55   *Pembrokeshire County Guardian (PCG)*, 2.2.1912.

56   *PH* 17.4.1903 and *H&MT*, 30.8.1905.

57   *H&MT*, 14.9.1905; *The Welshman*, 20.9.1907.

58   *PCG*, 2.2.1912.

59   *TO*, 5.12.1889.

60   NLW MS 6875F.

61   *PH*, 2.11.1851.

62   *Ibid.*

63   Lambeth Palace Library ICBS, 128.

64   *PH*, 28.11.1851.

65   Lambeth Palace Library ICBS 4364.

66   *PH*, 8.7.1853.

67   *CJ*, 1.6.1856.

68   *PH*, 26.12.1856.

69   *PH*, 13.2.1857 and *H&MT*, 29.4.1857.

70   *The Builder*, 3.4.1880.

71   *PH*, 19.8.1881.

72   Father J. Coffey, *Centenary of St Davids's and St Patrick's Church,* 1972, 3.

73   *H&MT*, 31.10.1855.

74   *Ibid.*, 5.4.1871.

75   Terence O'Brien, *Living Walls: Life and Times of the Parish Church of St David and St Patrick, Haverfordwest.* (unpubl.) 1998, 2.

[76] *The Welshman*, 3.5.1872.
[77] *H&MT*, 17.5.1905.
[78] Coffey, *op.cit.* 8.

THE CHAPELS.

[1] R Brinkley, 'Religion and Education' in *Pembrokeshire County History III: Early Modern Pembrokeshire 1536-1815*, Haverfordwest, 1987, 243.
[2] *Haverfordwest & Milford Telegraph (H&MT)*, 6.8.1890.
[3] *H&MT*, 22.1.1873.
[4] *Ibid.*, 6.8.1890.
[5] *Ibid.*, 2.3.1904.
[6] *Ibid.*, 8.4.1908.
[7] *Ibid.*, 6.1.1909.
[8] Pembrokeshire Record Office (PRO), DFC/8/50.
[9] *H&MT*, 2.11.1864.
[10] *Ibid.*, 2.11.1864.
[11] *Ibid.*, 17.2.1864.
[12] *Pembrokeshie Herald (PH)*, 7.6.1872.
[13] *H&MT*, 26.3.1876.
[14] *Ibid.*, 23.7.1903.
[15] *Pembrokeshire County Guardian (PCG)*, 3. 9. 1920.
[16] T. H. James, *The History of Bethesda Baptist Church, Haverfordwest*, 1980, 3-4.
[17] *Ibid.*, 4.
[18] *H&MT*, 9.10.1878; James, *op.cit.,* 5.
[19] *H&MT*, 11.3.1842.
[20] *PH*, 31.10.1856.
[21] *PH*, 11.10.1878; James, *op.cit.*, 7.
[22] *The Welshman*, 4.6.1880.
[23] James, *op.cit.*, 8 .
[24] W. J. Edwards, *These Hundred Years*, Haverfordwest 1857, 9.
[25] *H&MT*, 6.10.58.
[26] Edwards, *op.cit.,* 13.
[27] *Ibid.*
[28] *PH*, 22.6.1868.
[29] Edwards, *op.cit.,* 13-14.
[30] *Ibid.*, 14-15.
[31] *Ibid.*, *H&MT*, 29. 7. 1891.
[32] Edwards, *op.cit.*, 21-2; *PCG*, 23.4.1920.
[33] *H&MT*, 26.3.1862.
[34] James, *op.cit.*, 9.
[35] *Western Telegraph*, 17.6.1992; 24.6.1992.
[36] W L Richards, *A Well-founded Ship: History of Tabernacle Congregational Church*, Haverfordwest, 1988, 15-17.

37   *PH*, 29.11.1844

38   W. Evans and O. S. Symond, *The History of the South Pembrokeshire Calvinistic Methodist Churches*, Wrexham, 1913, 7.

39   *PH* 29.11.1844.

40   L J Meyler, *John Wesley in Pembrokeshire,* 1956, 5.

41   *Ibid.,* 7.

42   *Ibid.,* 10.

43   *Carmarthen Journal (CJ),* 17 and 24.4.1818.

44   *PH,* 22.5.1874.

45   *CJ,* 11.3.1881.

46   *H&MT,* 3.5.1911.

47   David Howell, 'Primitive Methodism in Pembrokeshire: The Chapel in a Rural Society', *The Pembrokeshire Historian,* 7 (1981), 52-60.

48   Stephen Griffith, *A History of Quakers in Pembrokeshire*, Llandysul, 1990, 11-12.

49   Howell, *op.cit.,* 14.

50   David Salmon, 'The Pembrokeshire Quakers' Monthly Meeting', *West Wales Historical Records,* XII (1927), 5-6.

51   *Ibid.,* 4.

52   Brinkley, *op.cit.,* 254.

53   *Ibid.*

54   *Western Telegraph,* 17.6.1892; 24.6.1892.

55   *PH,* 17.1.1868; 24.1.1868.

56   B. Rawlins, *The Parish Churches and Nonconformist Chapels of Wales,* Salt Lake City, 1987, 222, 351 and 555.

57   *PH,* 24.8.1877.

58   *Western Telegraph,* 17.6.1992; 24.6.92.

The Buildings in Context   *Richard Suggett*

1   I am grateful to the Commissioners and Secretary of the Royal Commission on Ancient and Historical Monuments in Wales for allowing me to draw freely on the resources of the National Monuments Record for Wales when preparing this chapter.

2   By Robert Scourfield in this volume (pp. 79-119), and in the volume on Pembrokeshire in the *Pevsner Buildings* of Wales series.

3   This volume *passim*; Ian Soulsby, *The Towns of Medieval Wales,* Chichester, 1993, 139-42.

4   W. H. Hemp, 'The Town Seal of Haverfordwest', *Archaeologia Cambrensis,* 7th. series, vol. ii (1922), 383-9, where the seal is assigned a late-thirteenth-century date; Giraldus Cambrensis, *Speculum Duorum, or A Mirror of Two Men,* ed. Michael Richter (Cardiff, 1974), 36-8; John Leland, *The Itinerary in Wales in or about the years 1536-9,* ed. Lucy Toulmin Smith, London, 1906, 63, 115-6.

5   B. G. Charles, *The Place-names of Pembrokeshire*, Aberystwyth, 1992, II, 647-8; Haverfordwest Deed 1141; N.L.W., Picton Castle Deeds 12, 107.

6   Three parallel vaults under 2,4,6 High Street, one entered from a pointed doorway in Dark Street, and another at 36 High Street, noted in the National Monuments Record by A. J. Parkinson.

7   P. H. Lawson and J. T. Smith, 'The Rows of Chester: Two Interpretations', *Chester Archaeological Society's Journal*, XLV (1958), 1-42; Margaret Wood, *The English Mediaeval House*, London, 1965, ch. 6.

8   Haverfordwest Deeds 1009 & 1072; N.L.W., Picton Castle Deeds 32.

9   Rees Davies, *The Revolt of Owain Glyn Dŵr* (Oxford, 1995), 194; J. E. Lloyd, *Owen Glendower. Owen Glyn Dŵr*, Oxford, 1931, 103; *Calendar of the Public Records Relating to Pembrokeshire*, ed. Henry Owen (*Cymmrodorion Record Series,* no. 7), I (1911), 28.

10   See pp. 11-13 above; R. I. Jack, 'Fulling-mills in Wales and the Marches before 1547', *Archaeologia Cambrensis*, CXXX (1981), 103.

11   Charles, 1992, II, 646-7; Henry Owen, 1911, 136-7.

12   B. G. Charles, *Calendar of the Records of the Borough of Haverfordwest 1539-1660* (Cardiff, 1967), p. 47; *OED*, s.v. 'balk' (sense 11). Paradise: Haverfordwest Deed 931.

13   Henry Owen, 1911, 86-97.

14   W. G. Thomas, 'The Architectural History of St Mary's Church, Tenby', *Archaeologia Cambrensis,* CXV (1966), 134-65; R. F. Walker, 'Tenby', in R. A. Griffiths (ed.), *Boroughs of Mediaeval Wales*, Cardiff, 1978, 300-2.

15   See p. 20 above..

16   *Annales Cambriae*, ed. John Williams (Rolls Series, London, 1860), 76; Roger Stalley, 'The Medieval Sculpure of Christ Church Cathedral, Dublin', *Archaeologia*, CVI (1979), 117, 121 (n. 74), draws attention to this passage and the connection between St Mary's and Wells. The Wells figures are illustrated in the Courtauld Institute's *Illustration Archive I, part 6: Wells* (London, 1978); some of the Haverford figures are illustrated in Fred J. Warren, *The History and Antiquities of S. Mary's Haverfordwest*, Letchworth, 1914.

17   As at Tenby, there is a contradiction between the number of empty burgages and the ambitious alterations to the parish church. As Walker notes ('Tenby', 313) the enlargement of Tenby parish church 'need not indicate an increase in population or in general prosperity, but perhaps only the increased wealth of a few burgesses.' See Terrence James's chapter above (pp. 31-2) for an analysis of Haverford's decayed burgages.

18   On the regional distribution of church roofs (including vaulting), see Peter Smith, *Houses of the Welsh Countryside*, London, 1988 edn., 671-91.

19   Haverfordwest Deeds 849, 1016; B. G. Charles, *George Owen of Henllys*, Aberystwyth, 1976, 120, for heraldic glass.

20   Tower building is noted in Glanmor Williams, *The Welsh Church from Conquest to Reformation*, Cardiff, 1962, 432-3.

21   Sanctus bellcote illustrated in Warren, 1914, pl. facing p. 66; Black Friars'

bells: 'Original Documents', *Archaeologia Cambrensis Supplement* (to vol I, 4th series), xli; Francis Green, 'Early Wills in West Wales', *West Wales Historical Records*, VII (1917-18), 145-52. Bulton's will may refer to the new tower, but this is doubtful.

22 Thomas Wright, *Three Chapters of Letters Relating to the Suppression of Monasteries*, London, 1843, 183-7.

23 Glanmor Williams, *Welsh Reformation Essays*, Cardiff, 1967, 11-12; 'Original Documents', vol. i, *Archaeologia Cambrensis Supplement* (1877), i.

24 Leland, *The Itinerary in Wales*, ed. Lucy Toulmin Smith, pp. 63, 115-16; John Speed, *The Theatre of Great Britain* (London, 1611-12; 1676 edn), book ii, ch. 3, p. 107; cf. George Owen, *Description of Penbrokshire*, part iii (1906), 359; Henry Owen, 'A Survey of the Lordship of Haverford in 1577', *Archaeologia Cambrensis*, 6th ser., III (1903), 46.

25 *Letters and Papers...Henry VIII*, vol. xi (London, 1888), 570; Act 34-35 Henry VIII. c. 26; *The Statutes of Wales*, ed. Ivor Bowen, London, 1908, 130-1.

26 Owen, 'A Survey of the Lordship of Haverford', p. 41.

27 See the Appendix for these buildings.

28 Richard Fenton, A *Historical Tour Through Pembrokeshire* (Brecknock, 1903 edn), 124-5; Charles, 1967, 59-60, 66; *Tours in Wales (1804-13) by Richard Fenton*, ed. John Fisher, London, 1917, 195 (for Conway).

29 Thomas Dineley, *The Account of the Official Progress of the First Duke of Beaufort through Wales, 1684*, ed. R. W. Banks (London, 1888), 275; John Lewis, *Welsh Monumental Brasses*, Cardiff, 1974, 86-7.

30 Charles, 1967, 5; Charles, 1992, II, 648.

31 NLW, Great Sessions 4/785/3/116; Charles, 1967, 76.

32 Great Sessions 4/791/5/74; 4/792/3/17; 4/791/5/55; 4/793/5/31x (illegal admission of Quakers as burgesses).

33 James Phillips, 'Haverfordwest in 1572', *Archaeologia Cambrensis*, 5th series, XXII (1896), 208.

34 W. G. Thomas, 'The Old House', *The Archaeological Journal*, CXIX (1962), 324-5; Great Sessions 25/14, m. 22 (goods of William Hutton of Tenby).

35 Owen, *The Description of Penbrokshire*, ed. Henry Owen, part iii, 352-9; NLW, Picton Castle 1610; the 'old house' in Quay Street illustrated by H. Thornhill Timmins, *Nooks and Corners of Pembrokeshire*, London, 1895, 177-8 (identified by Thomas Lloyd as Clibborn House, demolished *ca*. 1930).

36 Francis Jones, 'Some Records of a Sixteenth Century Pembrokeshire Estate', *Bulletin of the Board of Celtic Studies*, vol. xiii (1948-50), 94; Lewys Dwnn, *Heraldic Visitations of Wales*, ed. Samuel Rush Meyrick, Llandovery, 1846, I, 177; Charles, 1976, 122.

37 Michael Laithwaite, 'Totnes houses 1500-1800', in Peter Clark (ed.), *The Transformation of English Provincial Towns*, London, 1984, ch. 2; Roger H. Leech, 'The Prospect from Rugman's Row: the Row House in Late Sixteenth- and Early Seventeenth Century London', *The Archaeological Journal*, vol. 153 (1966), 201-42.

38 This vol, figs. 42 and 43; *The Archive Photographs Series: Haverfordwest*, comp. Haverfordwest Civic Society (Chalford, 1997), 11. Nos 7, 9 & 11 High Street still retain disguised timber fronts.

39 Dillwyn Miles ed., *The Description of Pembrokeshire: George Owen of Henllys*, Llandysul, 1994, 78.

40 Charles, 1967, 66, and index under 'words'.

41 Great Sessions 4/794/5/19 (out pinion); 4/793/5/37 (half roof); 4/792/2/377 & 4/793/7/43 (pair of stairs); 4/792/5/29 (mixen); 4/801/1/38 & 801/2/24 (Shitternslake).

42 Charles, 1967, 11-17; Fenton, 114.

43 Notably the finished cloth trade gave way to the less profitable export of wool and yarn and by the early seventeenth century the Bristol clothiers obtained most of their wool from the ports of Milford Haven: Charles, 1967, 29-30; *Merchants and Merchandise in Seventeenth-century Bristol*, ed. Patrick McGrath (*Bristol Record Society's Publications*, vol. xix, 1955), 142-3.

44 *The Welsh Port Books*, ed. E. A. Lewis (*Cymmrodorion Record Series* xii, London, 1927), 330.

45 Buck's View; Francis Jones, 'Some Records of a Sixteeenth Century Estate', 103-4, for references to cellars and chambers on and around the quay. The 'tower-house' taken down in Quay Street in 1983 seems to have been a house of this type (*Western Mail* 9 March 1983). A fine commercial vault survives in The Harford Cafe, Quay Street.

46 *Description of Pembrokeshire*, ed. Miles, p. 141; B. G. Charles, 'Haverfordwest Accounts, 1563-1620', *National Library of Wales Journal*, vol. ix (1955-6), 172-3, 176-8; Phillips and Warren, *History of Haverfordwest*, 89, 114; Charles, 1992, ii, 648; Charles, 1967, 176.

47 Phillips and Warren, 152-7; NLW Lucas Deeds and Documents 1502; Great Sessions 4/804/3 (presentment of peddlers and trader's petition), 4/785/1/1 & 4/785/2/54 (extortion by clerk of the market).

48 Mrs Morgan, *A Tour to Milford Haven, in the Year 1791*, London, 1795, 198-221.

49 John Howard, *The State of the Prisons* (London, 1777), 465-6; Fenton, 115; Samuel Lewis, *A Topographical Dictionary of Wales* (London, 1833), vol. i, 397.

50 The Mayor, Bailiffs & Burgesses of Pembroke v. Alexander Perry and others, Great Sessions 28/185; *First Report of the Commissioners on the Municipal Corporations of England and Wales* (London, 1835), 242-3.

51 *Report of the Commissioners on Municipal Corporation Boundaries* (London, 1837), part ii, 149; Richard Suggett, *John Nash Architect in Wales* (Aberystwyth, 1995), 44-8, 117; Mrs Morgan, 195-7; NLW MS. 16989C, f. 290 (Colt Hoare's tour, 1796).

52 *Acts of Parliament Concerning Wales 1714-1901*, ed. T. I. Jeffreys Jones (London, 1966), nos. 195, 197, 1878, 1945; Phillips & Warren, 126; Samuel Lewis, I, 399.

53 Howard Colvin, *A Biographical Dictionary of British Architects 1600-1830* (London, 1995). 718; Paul Joyner, *Artists in Wales c.1740-c.1851* (Aberystwyth, 1997), 88. (Both sources drawing on Thomas Lloyd's unpublished research.)

54 *Report of the Commission on Municipal Corporation Boundaries*, part ii, p. 150.

55 Drawings probably by Thomas Ellis (cf. Joyner, *Artists in Wales*, 33) kindly made available to the writer by Mr. Gerald Oliver of Haverfordwest.

Sir John Perrot and Haverfordwest. *R. K. Turvey*

1 The document is currently on display in the Pembrokeshire County Record Office at Haverfordwest Castle.

2 Perrot's copy of the document is not to be found among the family muniments in London and is therefore presumed to be irretrievably lost.

3 The translation used here is that first undertaken by Henry Owen in 1899.

4 G. D. James, *The History of The Charities of Haverfordwest* (Haverfordwest, 1965), 13.

5 B. G. Charles (ed.), *Calendar of the Records of the Borough of Haverfordwest 1539-1660* (Cardiff, 1967), 12.

6 G. D. James, *op. cit.*, 4.

7 George Owen, *The Description of Penbrokshire*, ed. Henry Owen (Cymmrodorion Record Series, 4 vols., London, 1892-1936), III, 359.

8 H. Owen, 'A Survey of the Lordship of Haverford in 1577', *Arch. Camb.*, Sixth Series, iii (1903), 39.

9 Dillwyn Miles (ed.) George Owen, *The Description of Pembrokeshire*, Llandysul, 1994, 141.

10 *Ibid.*

11 G.D. Owen. *Elizabethan Wales: The Social Scene* (Cardiff, 1964), 105.

12 Built by the Duke of Somerset during the late 1540s out of the ruins of the suppressed Abbey of Bridgettines, Syon was not a 'town house' in the true sense of the word for it was located some miles outside Elizabethan London (opposite Kew) but it served as Perrot's base for when he was in the capital. He was also to be found in his father's former town house located in London at Islington.

13 Matthew Griffiths, ' "Very Wealthy by Merchandise"? Urban Fortunes' in J G Jones (ed.), *Class, Community and Culture in Tudor Wales* (Cardiff, 1989), 212.

14 E. A. Lewis, *The Welsh Port Books 1550-1603* (Cymmrodorion Record Series, London, 1927), xxviii-xxxvi.

15 *Ibid.*, 79.

16 *Descrip. of Pembs.*, ed. Dillwyn Miles, *op.cit.*, 141.

17 R Flenley, *Calendar of the Register of the Council in Wales, 1569-91* (Cymmrodorion Record Series, London, 1916), 140.

18 B. G. Charles, *op.cit.*, 228; G. D. Owen, *op. cit.*, 105.

19 Public Record Office, Star Chamber, 5/R29/14. For brief details of this and all other cases from the records of the Court of the Star Chamber cited in this work, see *A Catalogue of Star Chamber Proceedings relating to Wales*, ed. I, ab O. Edwards, Cardiff, 1929, 134.

20 G. D. Squibb, *Reports of Heraldic Cases in the Court of Chivalry 1623-1732* (Harleian Society, vol. 107, London, 1956), 44-6. The eyewitness was John Canon of Haverfordwest who was giving evidence in a court case involving Sir John's kinsmen, the Perrots of Herefordshire.

21 B. G. Charles, *op. cit.*, 11.

22 G, D, Owen, *op. cit.*, 105.

23 For the most recent brief, but concise, accounts of Perrot's life and career, see P. W. Hasler (ed.), *The House of Commons, 1558-1603* (3 vols., London, 1981), II, 205-7; S.T.Bindoff (ed.), *The House of Commons, 1509-58* (3 vols., London, 1982), II, 86-8; R. K. Turvey, 'Sir John Perrot (1582-92): A Fourth Centenary Retrospective', *The Journal of the Pembrokeshire Historical Society*, No. 5 (1992-3), 15-31.

24 For fuller details, see P.W.Hasler, *op.cit.* I, 322-3; J. E. Neale, *The Elizabethan House of Commons* (London, 1949), 255-60.

25 P. W. Hasler, *op.cit.*, I, 322-3.

26 J. E. Neale, 'More Elizabethan Elections', *English Historical Review*, lxi (1946), 23-4.

27 S. T. Bindoff, *op.cit.* , I, 280-1.

28 *Calendar of Patent Rolls, 1560-3*, 445, 447.

29 PRO, Star Chamber 5/P8/32; J. Phillips, 'Glimpses of Elizabethan Pembrokeshire', *Arch. Camb.*, Fifth Series, xiv, (1897), 316.

30 This estimate is based on that made in a supplementary appendix (page 370) in Ferrar Fenton's 1903 edition of his grandfather Richard Fenton's *A Historical Tour through Pembrokeshire*, published originally in 1811. Perrot's modern biographer, P. C. C. Evans, did not see fit to question the valuation perhaps on account of the difficulty in establishing the rental incomes and property valuations connected with the premises. However, it is likely, but not certain, that the valuation should be appreciably higher and that, at the very least, we should revise our estimation of the Trust's original endowment. For P. C. C. Evans's thesis and biographical sketch on Perrot, see 'Sir John Perrot' (Unpublished University of Wales [Cardiff] M.A. thesis, 1940) and 'Sir John Perrot', *Dictionary of Welsh Biography*, 747-49.

31 G. D. James, *The Charities of Haverfordwest*, (Haverfordwest 1965), 4.

32 G. D. James, *Sir John Perrot* (Haverfordwest, 1962), 22, 24. Given the time scale involved and allowing for inflation and other economic and financial variables, it is almost impossible to translate accurately the value of the original endowment into modern terms, but the current annual income may be taken as a good indication of the true worth of Perrot's legacy. I should like to thank the current Clerk to The Trustees of the Sir John Perrot Trust, Mr. Paul Lucas, for discussing aspects of the Trust's work and for supplying information pertaining to its activities.

33   *Descrip. of Pembs.* ed. Dillwyn Miles, lvi.

34   R. K. Turvey, 'A Note on the Date of Birth of Sir John Perrot', *National Library of Wales Journal*, Vol. 30 (1994), 233-8.

35   Francis Green, 'Harries of co. Pembroke', *West Wales Historical Records*, VIII (1919-20), 106.

36   R. K. Turvey, 'Sir John Perrot, Henry VIII's Bastard? The Destruction of a Myth', *The Transactions of the Honourable Society of Cymmrodorion* (1992), 79-94.

37   *Idem.*, 'The Perrot Family and their Circle in South-West Wales during the Later Middle Ages' (Unpublished University of Wales [Swansea] Ph.D. thesis, 1988), 324, 516-20.

38   *Ibid.*, 321.

39   B. G. Charles, *op. cit.*, 1-2.

40   PRO, *Calendar of Ancient Deeds*, Series D, III, 554.

41   B. G. Charles, *op. cit.*, 19-21.

42   S. T. Bindoff, *op. cit.*, II, 451.

43   B. G. Charles, *op. cit.*, 23.

44   *Ibid.*

45   *Ibid.*

46   P. W. Hasler, *op. cit.*, II, 206.

47   Henry Owen, *A Calendar of the Public Records Relating to Pembrokeshire* (Cymmrodorion Record Series, 3 vols., London, 1911-18), I, 95. Those jailed for crimes committed outside the town were kept in 'the Cocke House being the Country gaol'. B. G. Charles, *op. cit.*, 73.

48   B. G. Charles, *op. cit.*, 180.

49   *Ibid.*, 2.

50   G. D. Owen, *op. cit.*, 102.

51   PRO, St Ch., 5/T31/26; M60/6; 6/2/T21; 9/M35.

52   PRO, St Ch., 5/M60/6; G15/25; G16/1.

53   *Calendar of State Papers: Ireland, 1574-85*, 62.

54   Glanmor Williams, *Recovery, Reorientation and Reformation Wales c.1415-1642* (Oxford/Cardiff, 1987), 351.

55   British Library, Lansdowne MS., 72 f.2.

56   P. W. Hasler, *op. cit.*, I, 322-23.

57   B. G. Charles, *op. cit.*, 185.

58   *Ibid.*, 196, 204.

59   British Museum, Lansdowne MS., 72 f.2.

60   This assumes Perrot's mayoralty ran from Michaelmas 1586-7 (the exact date of his election has yet to be ascertained). The parliamentary election was held some time between 14 September and 29 October 1586.

61   P. W. Hasler, *op. cit.*, I, 322-23. A similar deal may have been struck between Stepney and the Perrots in 1588 since Sir John Perrot secured Haverfordwest while Sir Thomas Perrot seems to have stood aside to enable Stepney to have the Cardiganshire seat.

62 B.M., Add. MSS., 12507, f.221.

63 B. G. Charles, *George Owen of Henllys* (Aberystwyth, 1973), 76.

64 *Ibid.*, 77.

65 Perrot and Tucker were kinsman, the latter being a great-grandson of Richard Tucker and Alice Perrot daughter of Sir William (Sir John's great-grandfather). See Mrs C. O. Higgon & F. Green, 'The Tuckers of Sealyham', *WWHR*, VIII (1919-20), 177-180.

66 B. G. Charles, *op. cit.*, 37.

67 *Ibid.*, 38.

68 R. Rawlinson (ed.), *The History of that most eminent statesman Sir John Perrot* (London, 1728), 18-19. The original seventeenth-century manuscript, or a contemporary copy, which Rawlinson is credited with publishing, is currently housed in the Bodleian Library, Oxford, as Wood MS., D. 33. There is sufficient evidence to attribute the authorship of this manuscript, the long accepted anonymous life of Perrot, to his son Sir James (1571-1637). A critical edition of this manuscript is currently in hand.

69 For further details of Canon's alleged oppression and malpractice, see H. A. Lloyd, *The Gentry of South-West Wales 1540-1640* (Cardiff, 1968), 160 (n.3 & 4).

70 R. Rawlinson, *op. cit.*, 118. Gerald of Wales refers to a Stephen 'Wiriet' of Pembrokeshire as early as the 1180s. Giraldus Cambrensis, *The Journey Through Wales/The Description of Wales*, ed. and trans. Lewis Thorpe (London, 1978), 151.

71 For this and subsequent quotations in the following two paragraphs, refer to R. Rawlinson, op. cit., 114-22.

72 *Ibid.*, 129.

73 *Ibid.*, 307.

74 Cited, see n. 1 & 3.

75 James Phillips, *A History of Pembrokeshire* (London, 1909), 370.

Haverfordwest and the Civil War.   *Dillwyn Miles*

1 J. F. Rees, *Studies in Welsh History*, Cardiff 1947, 152.

2 B. Howells, 'Government and Politics 1536-1642' in *Pembrokeshire County History*, III, Haverfordwest 1987, 158.

3 A. L. Leach, *The History of the Civil War (1642-1649) in Pembrokeshire*, London 1937, 26-8

4 *Ibid.* 31-2

5 Rees, *op. cit.* 85.

6 *Ibid.* 84-5.

7 Leach, *op.cit.* 49-50.

8 B. G. Charles, *Calendar of the Records of the Borough of Haverfordwest 1539-1660*, Cardiff 1967, 13

9 Leach, *op.cit* 52-4

10   Charles, *op.cit.* 13,

11   Leach, *op.cit.* 51.

12   R. Mathias, 'The First Civil War' in *Pembrokeshire County History*, Volume III, Haverfordwest, 1987, 176.

13   Leach, *op.cit.* 57.

14   Terrence James, 'Carmarthen's Civil War Defences' in *The Carmarthenshire Antiquary*, xxvii, 1991, 27.

15   Leach, *op. cit.* 105.

16   J R Phillips, *Memoirs of the Civil War in Wales*, London 1874, ii, 251.

17   *Ibid.* 249.

18   Mathias, *op.cit* 194.

19   Leach, *op. cit.* 227.

20   Phillips, *op. cit.* ii, 267.

21   *Ibid.* 113.

22   Charles, *op. cit.* 76.

23   Charles, *op. cit.* 15.

24   Leach, *op.cit.* 230.

25   Pembrokeshire Record Office (PRO) HAM/26.

26   PRO HAM/27.

27   PRO HAM/28.

28   Charles, *op. cit.* 82, 101.

29   Godfrey Davies, 'The Early Stuarts' in *The Oxford History of England*, Oxford University Press 1959, 155.

30   G. D. James, *The Town and County of Haverfordwest and its Story*, Haverfordwest 1957, 49.

31   Charles, *op. cit.* 107.

32   *Dictionary of National Biography.*

33   Davies, *op. cit.* 153-4.

34   *Dictionary of National Biography.*

35   Charles, *op. cit.* 167.

Haverfordwest and the Plague.   *John Howells*

The editor wishes to thank Professor Kenneth O. Morgan for his consent to reproduce 'Haverfordwest and the Plague 1652' which first appeared in *The Welsh History Review*, 12 (1985), 3, 411-419. Unless otherwise indicated, references are to documents in the Haverfordwest Borough Records at the County Record Office.

1   Nos. 286 and 580' B.M. Harleian MS. 595.

2   B. Howells (ed.), *Elizabethan Pembrokeshire: the Evidence of George Owen*, Haverfordwest 1973, 43.

3   A. L. Leach, *The History of the Civil War (1642-1649) in Pembrokeshire and on its Borders,* London 1937, 71.

4   No. 536.

5   Nos. 268, 532, 539 and 616.
6   Nos. 532 and 539.
7   Nos. 266(a}, 289, 303, 532, 534 and 538 (b and c).
8   No. 345.
9   James Phillips, 'The Plague at Haverfordwest, 1651-2' in *Arch. Camb.* series 5, vol. XII, no. XLVI, 1895, 81.
10   No. 580.
11   No. 286.
12   No. 287.
13   No. 293.
14   Nos. 301 (a) and 305.
15   No. 582.
16   No. 287.
17   No. 583.
18   Nos. 305 and 584 (ii).
19   No. 305.
20   No. 549.
21   No. 584(i). This number is probably an exaggeration: see No. 549.
22   No. 584(i).
23   James Phillips, 1895, *op.cit.*, 82.
24   No. 549: also James Phillips, *The History of Pembrokeshire*, London 1909, 520.
25   Nos. 306 and 549.
26   Nos. 299 and 301(a).
27   No. 574. Mithridate was an electuary and regarded as a universal antidote or preservative against infectious diseases. Diascordium was a medicine made of the dried leaves of water-germander and other herbs. For some details of contemporary treatments of the plague, see T. Lodge, *A Treatise of the Plague . . .* London, 1603.
28   James Phillips, 1909, 529.
29   Nos. 266(a) and 580.
30   Nos. 306, 310 and 549.
31   No. 293.
32   No. 305.
33   No. 301(a).
34   Nos. 548, 557 and 578.
35   No. 299.

The Political Scene 1660-1918.   *Roland Thorne*

Guidelines for much of this chapter were provided by Mary E. Jones, 'The Parliamentary Representation of Pembrokeshire, the Pembroke Boroughs and Haverfordwest 1536-1761' (MA thesis, University of Wales, Aberystwyth, 1958) and *The History of Parliament: The Commons* volumes for 1660-1690 (ed. B. D.

Henning, 1983), *1715-1754* (ed. R. R. Sedgwick, 1970), *1754-1790* (ed. Sir L. Namier and J. Brooke, 1964), and *1790-1820* (ed. R. G. Thorne, 1986).

1   John Ray's diary, 8 June 1662.
2   Pembs Record Office, Haverfordwest Borough Records 356-7, 360-370, 381, for which see also *Calendar of the Records of the Corporation of Haverfordwest* (Board of Celtic Studies, University of Wales, History and Law Series, xxiv (1967) ed. B. G. Charles, 164-172; and *Pembs Life and Letters 1572-1843*, Pembs Record Series, I (1972), 34-42..
3   *Commons Journals* (hereafter *CJ*), viii. 396, 491.
4   *Ibid.* ix. 3, 26; Haverfordwest Borough Records 2142, ff 159-161, 171, 175.
5   *CJ*, ix. 484, 518.
6   *Ibid.* ix. 570
7   *Ibid.* ix. 643
8   Haverfordwest Borough Records 415, 2128.
9   *CJ*, xviii. 138, 199.
10   Christopher Cobbe-Webbe (alias John Brown), *Haverfordwest and its story* (1882), 84.
11   NLW, Picton Castle MS 1476, Lady Philipps to her son Erasmus, 30 Oct 1721; MS 1451, Sir John to Lady Philipps, 4 Jan 1722.
12   *CJ*, xxii. 334.
13   *Ibid.* xxiv.19, 30, 73, 340, 404; NLW, Orielton MSS, parcel 10; NLW MS 1352E, John to Pryse Campbell, 12, 27, 29 Jan, 3 Feb 1743.
14   NLW MS 1352 E, John to Pryse Campbell, 14 Dec 1743.
15   NLW MS 6106 D, Lord Kensington to Sir Hugh Owen, (copy) 8 Jan 1784.
16   *HMC Var.* vi. 212; Morrison, *Nelson and Hamilton Papers,* I.189.
17   PRO, Kew, Chatham MSS, PRO 30/8/158, f 151.
18   R. D. Rees, 'The parliamentary representation of S. Wales 1790-1830' unpublished Ph.D. thesis, Reading Univ. 1962, ii. 313; Bodleian Lib, Oxford, c.431, Foster Barham MSS, Bundle 5.
19   *Carmarthen Journal,* 5-26 Dec 1834, 2 Jan 1835; *The Times,* 6 Jan 1835; NLW, Lucas MSS 3128-3130.
20   Pembs RO, D/HIG/ 276-7; D/RTP/Sir R. B. P. Philipps, box 5, 33-4, 38-9; *The Times*, 5, 12, 13 July 1837.
21   *The Times,* 10 May, 12 July, 2 Aug 1847.
22   *Ibid,* 3, 8, 9 July 1852; W. D. Phillips, *Old Haverfordwest* (1925), 23-9; NLW MSS 3010 D, Poll declaration 8 July 1852.
23   W. D. Phillips, *op. cit.* 40-41; *The Times,* 9, 16, 24, 30 Mar 1857, 18, 30 Apr 1859; T. M. Bassett, *The Welsh Baptists* (1977), 295, 300, 310; G. Douglas James, *Historical Notes of Haverfordwest* (1950), 56.
24   *The Times,* 6, 11 July 1865.
25   *Ibid,* 11 July, 16, 18, 22, 28 Sept 1868.
26   *Ibid,* 6, 7, 12, 14, 20, 25 Nov 1873.
27   *Ibid,* 5 May 1874.

28   Pembs RO, D/HIG/280-1; W D Phillips, *op. cit.* 115; NLW MSS 2983 B; 6875
      F, f 51.
29   *Hansard,* 297 975-977.
30   NLW ms 6106 D, Erasmus Philipps diary, 5 Sept 1727.
31   NLW ms 1352 E.
32   *The Times*, 28 June 1826.
33   *Ibid,* 6 July 1908.
34   Haverfordwest Borough Records 1640, 2148 ff 221, 377 dated 16 Oct 1628,
      bye-law no 14.
35   See note 3.
36   PRO, Kew, C 219/45, 1656 return; Pembs RO, HAM/19, 1640 return (copy
      dated 17 Feb 1662)
37   See note 9.
38   See note 12.
39   *CJ,* xxiv. 73, 340, 404; Haverfordwest Borough Records 2148, f 74..
40   Haverfordwest Borough Records 1645, ff 52-3; 2143, f 59b.
41   David W Howell, *Patriarchs and Parasites*, (1986), 141, 143.
42   *Ibid,* 161; Haverfordwest Borough Records 2143, ff 44, 63.
43   T. H. Oldfield, *Parliamentary Representation of Great Britain* (1815), vi.107.
44   *Parliamentary Papers (Commons)* (1831-2), (112), 530; R D Rees, *thesis cit.,* i.
      309-312; Haverfordwest Borough Records 1635-1645, 2144, f 5 *et seq.*
45   *Parliamentary Papers (Commons)* (1831-2), 41, 149; xxiii (1835), 233.
46   *CJ,* lxxxvi. (I) 457.
47   NLW MS 3010 D, Sheriff's notice 3 July 1852.
48   For the percentages see Arnold James and John E. Thomas, *Wales at
      Westminster* (1981). See also *Pembs County History, Modern Pembs 1815-1974*
      (1993), 249-50.
49   See note 29. A register of Haverfordwest voters in 1884 is in NLW 2965 A, and
      lists of freemen voters, 1882-1892 in Pembs RO, D /RTP/HAM/194-202, along
      with electoral lists for 1907-1909 (HAM/203-204).
50   This section draws on the *History of Parliament: The Commons* biographical
      sections, as described at the beginning of the footnotes.
51   The evidence for petitions is derived from the Haverfordwest Borough Records,
      the *Commons Journals,* Hansard and newspaper coverage.
52   The section on legislation derives from T. I. Jeffreys Jones (ed.), *Acts of
      Parliament concerning Wales 1714-1901* (1959).

The Freemen of Haverfordwest   *Dillwyn Miles*

1   R. Walker, 'Outline of Law relating to Freemen' in *Freemen of England*, York
     1915, 12.
2   Report of the Royal Commission on Municipal Corporations: Borough of
     Haverfordwest 1835, 233.

3   Henry Owen, (ed). *A Calendar of the Public Records relating to Pembrokeshire I: Haverford*, London, 1911, 127.

4   Maurice Beresford, *New Towns of the Middle Ages: Town Plantation in England, Wales and Gascony*, Gloucester 1967, 208.

5   Owen, *op. cit.* 131.

6   B. G. Charles, (ed). *Calendar of the Records of the Borough of Haverfordwest 1539-1660*, Cardiff 1967, 6.

7   *Ibid.* 30.

8   *Ibid.* 47-8.

9   Report of the Royal Commission, *op. cit.* 234.

10 Charles, *op. cit.* 5.

11 Beresford, *op. cit.* 199 and 332.

12 *English Historical Review* XV, 1900, 307 and 500.

13 Charles, *op. cit.* 1

14 *Calendar of Letters and Papers.* Henry VIII, xi, 570.

15 Beresford, *op. cit.* 254.

16 Report of Royal Commission, *op.cit.* 236-7.

17 *Ibid.* 255.

18 Report of the Royal Commission, *op. cit.* 237.

19 James Phillips, *The History of Pembrokeshire*, London 1909, 557.

20 W. D. Phillips, *Old Haverfordwest*, Haverfordwest 1925, 39.

21 Charles, *op. cit.* 22-9

22 *Ibid.* 72.

23 W. D. Phillips, *op. cit.* 61.

24 Report of the Royal Commission, *op. cit.* 241.

25 *Award of John Wilson, Esq., the Commissioner under The Portfield Inclosure Act*: Haverfordwest Borough Council 1961, 1-5.

26 *Ibid.* 34.

27 *Ibid.* 35.

Haverfordwest Charities   *Dillwyn Miles*

Further Report of the Commissioners for Inquiring concerning Charities, 1839.

Arms and Insignia   *Dillwyn Miles*

Close Rolls 19 Edw II; Owen, Hy. (ed.) *Calendar of Public Records relating to Haverfordwest, 44.*

INDEX